The Art of Balance in Health Policy

Japan has a healthy population compared to the rest of the world, yet the Japanese pay relatively little for medical care. This book analyzes how the health-care system works and how it came into being. Campbell and Ikegami, taking a comparative perspective, describe the politics of health care, the variety of providers, the universal health insurance system, and the fee schedule cost constraints at both the macro and micro levels. They pay special attention to issues of quality and to the difficult problems of assuring adequate high-tech medicine and long-term care. Although the authors discuss the drawbacks to Japan's stringent cost-containment policy, they also keep in mind the possible implications for reform in the United States. Egalitarian values and a concern for "balance" among constituents, the authors argue, are essential for cost containment and for access to health care.

The Art of Balance in Health Policy

Maintaining Japan's Low-Cost, Egalitarian System

JOHN CREIGHTON CAMPBELL
University of Michigan

NAOKI IKEGAMI
Keio University School of Medicine

CAMBRIDGE
UNIVERSITY PRESS

PUBLISHED BY THE PRESS SYNDICATE OF THE UNIVERSITY OF CAMBRIDGE
The Pitt Building, Trumpington Street, Cambridge CB2 1RP, United Kingdom

CAMBRIDGE UNIVERSITY PRESS
The Edinburgh Building, Cambridge CB2 2RU, United Kingdom
40 West 20th Street, New York, NY 10011-4211, USA
10 Stamford Road, Oakleigh, Melbourne 3166, Australia

© John Creighton Campbell and Naoki Ikegami 1998

First published 1998

Printed in the United States of America

Typeset in Times Roman

Library of Congress Cataloging-in-Publication Data
Campbell, John Creighton.
The art of balance in health policy : maintaining Japan's low-cost,
egalitarian system / John Creighton Campbell, Naoki Ikegami.
p.   cm.
Includes bibliographical refernces (p.   ).
ISBN 0–521–57122–7
1. Medical care – Japan – Finance.   2. Medical care – Japan – Cost
control.   I. Ikegami, Naoki, 1949–   .   II. Title.
RA410.55.J3C35   1998
362.1'0952 – dc21   97-23853
                                                          CIP

*A catalog record for this book is available from
the British Library*

ISBN 0 521 57122 7 hardback

Contents

Tables and Figures

Preface

WHY should Americans care about the Japanese health-care system? An easy question. Japan has an exceptionally healthy population, number one in the world in terms of life expectancy and infant mortality, and excellent by other less precise criteria as well. Although medical care is not the main determining factor in good health, certainly it is not irrelevant that everyone in Japan has access to medical care of decent quality at little direct cost to the consumer. Moreover, Japan achieves these good results with an exceptionally small burden on the economy: spending on medical care is only slightly more than half that of the United States, and indeed is lower than in most advanced nations.

The Japanese were not always so successful in holding down spending. Back in the 1970s, health-care costs were exploding in Japan as in America, going up at a much faster rate than inflation or economic growth. Japanese officials responded in the early 1980s with some small but significant adjustments to their system. These succeeded in constraining spending – since that time health care has continued at a level of about 7 percent of Gross Domestic Product (GDP) – without cutting back on access or significantly altering the way medical care is delivered.

American officials had tried a variety of cost-cutting devices without much effect. The cost of medical care continued to escalate in the 1980s, exceeding 14 percent of GDP in 1994, even though an increasing number of Americans lacked health insurance. In the 1990s, President Clinton tried to meet both the access and cost problems with a revolutionary reform of the entire health-care system, based on a set of academic theories that combined ''managed care'' with market competition. This attempt failed but was followed by a new attack on costs by big employers allied with big insurance/provider complexes, based on similar theories.

This attack on costs had some immediate success, though whether it will hold down the growth rate of health-care spending in the long run remains

vii

Preface

to be seen. What is obvious is the impact on the medical-care delivery system. "Managed care" works by limiting choice at the point of delivery by patients and physicians, and in the eyes of many, it is seriously threatening both quality and access in the American health-care system.

This perception of threat, the turmoil in health-care institutions, and the increasing number of practical problems that are developing as the logic of "managed care" unfolds may combine to make the next few years promising for serious health-care reform. We hope that such reforms will give equal weight to the problems of quality, access, and cost. Moreover, we hope that this time Americans will think less about academic theories and more about real-life lessons – including lessons from Japan.

This book is an account of Japanese health policy and the medical-care system from an American point of view. Our approach is rather unconventional for the health policy field. We have kept statistics and detailed descriptions of programs to a minimum, and we do not spend too much time on the specialized hypotheses raised by academic health economists.[1] Instead, we emphasize the political economy of health care in a broad sense, with particular attention to how the central institutions that account for Japan's low cost structure and other important characteristics have developed over time. We also look for underlying principles in health policy, and find that a practical emphasis on "balance" – and on egalitarian values more generally – helps account for Japanese success.

Throughout the book, most of our comparisons are with the United States since our main intended audience is readers who are interested in the American health-care system. However, we hope that our analysis will also contribute to discussions about health-care reform elsewhere, about Japan's public policy and its decision-making process, and about the development of the welfare state in modern society.

Specifically, in the first chapter we demonstrate that medical costs in Japan are indeed low and controlled, and we briefly run through some of the social and cultural factors that help explain that result before providing an overview of how the system works. Chapter 2 describes the actors, arenas, and agendas of health-care politics today. Chapter 3 shows why Japanese physicians and

1 Some such accounts are included in our companion edited volume, *Containing Health-Care Costs in Japan* (Ann Arbor: University of Michigan Press, 1996), and in Aki Yoshikawa, Jayanta Bhattacharya, and William Vogt, eds., *Health Economics of Japan: Patients, Doctors and Hospitals Under a Universal Health Care System* (Tokyo: University of Tokyo Press, 1996).

hospitals are the way they are, including why they do not cause rapid cost expansions, and outlines prototypes of the six main types of providers. Chapter 4 describes the fragmented yet egalitarian health insurance system in relation to conflict or potential conflict among social groups.

We then turn specifically to the main mechanism for cost control, the universal fee schedule. Chapter 5 takes a macro perspective to see how repeated political negotiations over fees at the national level have been an effective way to regulate total medical spending. Chapter 6 looks at how providers' behavior is structured by the fee schedule and other micro-level regulations. Chapter 7 assesses several dimensions of quality, the area in which Japanese health care is most often criticized. Finally, Chapter 8 summarizes our arguments and tries to draw some lessons for both Japan and the United States.

The initial writing responsibility for these chapters is as follows: Campbell, 1, 2, 4, 5; Ikegami, 3, 6, 7; the concluding Chapter 8 was drafted jointly. All chapters went through substantial rewriting, stimulated by meetings of two or three hours up to a couple of weeks at various spots in Japan and North America. Campbell of course took final responsibility for the English text, while Ikegami did so for the Japanese version, which has already been published by Chūō Kōron Shinsho under the title *Nihon no Iryō: Tōsei to Baransu Kankaku* (literally *Japan's Health Care: Regulating and Balancing*). Incidentally, many Japanese readers have remarked to us that it is the first time they had ever seen anything positive about the Japanese health-care system (and the book has sold some 40,000 copies).

Although we retain some small differences of opinion, nearly everything in the book is truly a joint product. Indeed, it has been quite an experience to have a Japanese physician and an American political scientist collaborating on a book.

We have followed two sets of conventions that should be noted. First, *names* – people's names are given in the Japanese order, family name first. Unfortunately, no such simple rule can determine what to call organizations and programs in English. They are often given different English titles even in official documents, and many of these titles – whether or not they are direct translations of the Japanese terms – are quite misleading. We generally pick the title that seems most accurate to us among those in common use, although in one case we adopted a usage we have not seen elsewhere. Kokumin Kenkō Hoken, the health insurance program for non-employees, is usually called "National Health Insurance," but we find that confusing and call it "Citizens' Health Insurance" or CHI, which is actually a more faithful gloss on the Japanese than the usual term.

Second, *money* – amounts given in Japanese yen are not intuitively meaningful to most readers, so it is helpful to give an equivalent in dollars, but at what exchange rate? Any choice is arbitrary in some respect. We take a simple and radical approach of converting all money figures (except when otherwise noted) at the rate of ¥180 to $1. That figure is close to the level of the "Purchasing Power Parity" (PPP) rate in the early 1990s, and by using the same conversion rate throughout, the amounts are comparable over time. The alternative would be to use either contemporary actual exchange rates (which varied between ¥360 to ¥80 to the dollar from the 1970s to the '90s) or the estimated PPP rate year by year, which varied from ¥183 to ¥292 per dollar in the period 1970–93.[2] Both methods are awkward, particularly for comparisons over time. In any case, these dollar equivalents should be seen only as an approximate indication of the size of some money amount. Any serious analysis of trends or comparisons requires careful attention to the difficult problems of adjusting for price changes and equivalents in foreign currency.

ACKNOWLEDGMENTS

Finally, we should thank many institutions and individuals. Campbell's work on this project originated with a Fulbright fellowship in 1989–90, and he is grateful to the U.S–Japan Joint Educational Commission and to the Faculty of Law at Keio University (and host Sone Yasunori) for making an initial year of study possible. The two authors first met at that time. We observed that the prospect of substantial reform in the American health-care system seemed to be growing, and we noted that few in the United States knew much about what we saw as the very relevant Japanese experience in this area. That led us to apply to the Center for Global Partnership of the Japan

2 The calculation of PPP is based on a common market-basket of goods and is generally held to be more appropriate than official exchange rates for goods that are not internationally traded (i.e., services such as health care). Calculations from the OECD, conveniently collected along with many health-care statistics for the industrialized nations in George J. Schieber, Jean-Pierre Poullier, and Leslie M. Greenwald, "U.S. Health Expenditure Performance: An International Comparison and Data Update," *Health Care Financing Review* 13:4 (Sept., 1992), pp. 1–87. More recent data is periodically published only in electronic form as *OECD Health Data*.

Foundation for support, mainly to convene two conferences on the Japanese health-care system, held in Washington, D.C., in November 1991, and at Ito City in March 1993. The participants were mainly young Japanese researchers in the health policy area plus some senior American specialists.

The conference papers have been published as *Containing Health Care Costs in Japan* under our editorship.[3] These papers were one important source of information for this book, along with Ikegami's experiences over the years and explanations that we sought and received from a number of real experts on Japanese health policy. Preeminent among these was Takagi Yasuo, once Japan's leading journalist specializing on the health-care system, then a researcher in a government-sponsored institute, now Professor of Human Life Sciences at Sendai Shirayuri Women's University. We would also like to thank Hiroi Yoshinori, Katsumata Yukiko, and Takahara Ryōji for much helpful information. Excellent research consultation and assistance were provided at various stages by Yamada Takeshi, Ikeda Shunya, Tominaga Ikuko, Cathy Peters, and especially Masuyama Mikitaka. We are grateful for penetrating comments on the entire manuscript by Joseph White and Gregory Kasza as well as two expert reviewers for Cambridge University Press. And we are certainly grateful for the patience and understanding of our wives, Ruth Campbell and Ikegami Yoko.

John Creighton Campbell
Naoki Ikegami

---

3   Ann Arbor: University of Michigan Press, 1996. This book is cited as *Containment* in the footnotes.

1

Low Health-Care Spending in Japan

IT is remarkable, in all the discussion of health-care reform in recent years, that so few Americans are aware of this very simple and vital fact: Every other industrialized nation in the world spends much less on health care than does the United States, even though each provides universal health coverage.[1] Every characteristic on the following list is true of Japan and of a clear majority of Organization for Economic Cooperation and Development (OECD) nations; none is true of the United States:

- Virtually the entire population is included in mandatory health insurance.
- Most enrollment is automatic with little choice of coverage for either consumers or insurers.
- The benefit package in all programs covers nearly all regular health care.
- Payment for health insurance is largely determined by ability to pay, through contributions as a share of income.
- Differences in burdens across social groups are reduced by such mechanisms as support from general revenue and cross-subsidization among insurance plans.
- Nearly all prices are strictly controlled by a fee schedule.
- The fee schedule is periodically renegotiated between insurers and providers.
- Spending that is not directly related to health care, such as medical

---

1 Cf. Mark A. Goldberg, Theodore R. Marmor, and Joseph White, "The Relation between Universal Health Insurance and Cost Control," *New England Journal of Medicine* 332:11 (March 16, 1995), pp. 742–744. For analyses of health-care systems in various nations, see the works of the pioneer in this field, William Glaser, such as *Health Insurance in Practice: International Variations in Financing, Benefits and Problems* (San Francisco: Jossey-Bass, 1991), and the recent book by political scientist Joseph White, *Competing Solutions: American Health Care Proposals and International Experience* (Washington, DC: Brookings, 1995).

research and administrative expenses for insurers and providers, is kept quite low.

* Total health-care spending is tracked and controlled, at least indirectly.

"Ah, but the United States is a different kind of country," comes the response. Well, France, Canada, the Netherlands, and Japan are quite different, too, in their values and their political and social arrangements. Within the common framework, such differences have in fact led to significant variation in how the health-care system of each country functions today, and indeed still more variety in the stories of how these systems developed over the years. For full understanding one has to look at a health-care system as a whole, in the context of its nations' culture and institutions.

It is in that spirit that we describe the Japanese system here. We note that it is probably the least understood major system even among health-care experts in the United States and elsewhere, partly due to language barriers and partly to an impression that the Japanese case is so different that it does not really offer many useful comparisons.[2] We hope to demonstrate that this impression is off-base and that some aspects of the Japanese experience – even beyond the features that it shares with most other industrialized nations – are particularly worthy of attention by Americans interested in health-care reform.

Japanese health care certainly has its weak points. Hospitals in Japan appear quite run down (at least to Americans), too many medicines are prescribed, patients' rights are underdeveloped, and there are fewer incentives for providing top-quality medical care compared with the American system.[3]

---

2   E.g., Theodore R. Marmor, "Japan: A Sobering Lesson," *Health Management Quarterly* 14:3 (1992), pp. 10–14, reprinted in his *Understanding Health Care Reform* (New Haven CT: Yale University Press, 1994), pp. 195–201. For some later thoughts, see his "Afterword: National Health Insurance, Cost Control, and Cross-National Lessons – Japan and the United States," in *Containing*, pp. 286–296.

3   For accounts of such problems and of how the health-care system fits into Japanese society, see such works as Daniel I. Okimoto and Aki Yoshikawa, *Japan's Health Care System: Efficiency and Effectiveness in Universal Care* (New York: Faulkner and Gray, 1993); Margaret Powell and Masahira Anesaki, *Health Care in Japan* (London: Routledge, 1990); Edward Norbeck and Margaret Lock, eds., *Health, Illness and Medical Care in Japan: Cultural and Social Dimensions* (Honolulu: University of Hawaii Press, 1987), particularly William E. Steslicke, "The Japanese State of Health: A Political-Economic Perspective," pp. 24–65; Emiko Ohnuki-Teirney, *Illness and Culture in Contemporary Japan* (Cambridge: Cambridge University Press, 1984); and John K. Iglehart, "Health Policy Report: Japan's

Bureaucratic power has led to some sleazy relationships with private business, as revealed in 1996 by two scandalous stories. One was about how close ties between government regulators and the drug industry had allowed HIV-tainted blood products to be given to hemophiliacs.[4] The other was about bribes going to high-level officials to get government subsidies for nursing-home construction.

All these are indeed serious problems, but they should not obscure the significance of what Japan has achieved. In our view, universal coverage, more freedom, less complexity, lower cost, and a healthy population are the right goals for a national health-care system. The United States has not done very well by these measures.

The substantial similarities observed across the health-care systems of all the other industrialized nations have two important implications. First, people in these other countries have managed to learn from each other – better than Americans have. Second, after a lot of trial and error in different environments, it appears that these countries have the basic principles right. Our task is to describe how these basic principles (plus some local wrinkles) operate in the Japanese health-care system.

LOW COST

We begin with the cost of health care. The United States devotes over 14 percent of its Gross Domestic Product (GDP) to medical care, and Japan about 7 percent. This gap is wider than the difference in defense spending between the two countries (5.4 percent vs. 1.5 percent in 1990 if common definitions are used). The defense spending gap has often been cited as a major advantage for Japan in the economic competition between the two countries. Resources could go into productive investment that would bring economic growth and improve the standard of living of the people rather than paying for weapons and personnel that for the most part would never be

---

Medical Care System," *The New England Journal of Medicine* 319:12 and 17 (September 22 and October 17, 1988), 807–812, 1166–72.

4 The rate of hemophiliacs infected, about 40 percent, was actually about the same as in the United States, but undoubtedly lives could have been saved with quicker action. The story had simmered for a decade but splashed over in 1996 when a Health and Welfare Minister named Kan Naoto forced public release of the old records. For an account, see Eric Feldman, "Law, Blood and Bureacracy in Japan," unpub., January 1997.

used. Of course, if that spending prevented the nation from being destroyed, it would be worth it, but the economic burden is nonetheless clear.

The point that health-care spending differences might lead to a similar economic advantage to Japan has not been widely recognized, but the case is even more compelling.[5] Investment in health care can certainly be regarded as "productive" as long as the marginal dollar spent improves the health of the population (an effect that is desirable for its own sake as well as raising labor productivity). But there is no evidence that all the extra money that the United States spends every year compared with Japan does lead to significantly better health in general, although of course some individuals – a recipient of a heart transplant, for example – will greatly benefit. It is true that Americans as a whole do get better services in some respects, such as more comfortable hospitals, but on the other hand, the substantial amounts of money saved on health care in Japan serve to improve the standard of living of its people in some way, either immediately or (to the extent the funds are invested) in the future.

Statistics can always be manipulated to make a point, and when dealing with complicated systems, one should be careful before concluding, for example, that one country's health-care expenditures are higher or lower than another's, or that a growth rate has really gone up or down. Some observers believe that Japan's apparent success in cost containment is mostly a statistical artifact, and such doubts deserve good answers.

Are Costs Low?

First, could it be that much of the gap between Japanese and American health-care expenditures is because many items that are included in the American calculations are left out in Japan's? In fact, there is considerable difference in scope between the standard measures of health expenditures published by the governments of the two countries. We therefore asked Katsumata Yukiko of the Social Development Research Institute in Tokyo to estimate these differences as closely as possible.[6] Table 1.1 displays her adjustments to the

---

5   See Robert G. Evans, "Health Care as a Threat to Health: Defence, Opulence, and the Social Environment," *Daedalus* 123:4 (Fall, 1994), 21–42.
6   See her "Comparison of Health Expenditure Estimates between Japan and the United States," in Naoki Ikegami and John Creighton Campbell, eds., *Containing Health Care Costs in Japan* (Ann Arbor: University of Michigan Press, 1996), pp. 19–32.

Table 1.1. *Health Expenditure in Japan, 1990*

	Billion yen	% GDP	% (F)
(A) National Medical-Care Expenditure	20,607.4	4.7	68.6
(B) Public grants and subsidies	3,623.8	0.8	12.1
(C) Expenditure not included in (A), (B), or (D)	3,675.4	0.8	12.2
(D) Expenditure not accounted for in health sector	1,757.2	0.4	5.8
(E) Estimated under-the-table expenditure	389.4	0.1	1.3
(F) Total = (A) + (B) + (C) + (D) + (E)	30,053.2	6.9	100.0

(A) All expenditure paid through social insurance including patients' co-payments. Official estimate made by Japan's Ministry of Health & Welfare (Kokumin Iryôhi).
(B) Grants and subsidies provided by national and local governments (i.e., subsidies to public hospitals, public health expenditure) excluding those provided through (A).
(C) Expenditure not accounted for in (A), (B), or (D) (i.e., expenditure by nonprofit organizations, extra-charge rooms, normal pregnancies). [Note that OECD's estimate is equivalent to 98.5% of (A) + (B) + (C).]
(D) OTC drugs, social service nursing homes, construction expenditure of private sector health-care facilities, R & D, etc. These categories are included in the U.S.'s health expenditure in the OECD Health Data but are normally excluded for the other countries.
(E) Estimated amount of gifts given to physicians on discharge and extra payments made by patients in geriatric hospitals (based on generous estimates from available evidence).
Source: Calculated by Katsumata Yukiko of the Social Development Research Institute from Economic Planning Agency data

most commonly used official index of health spending in Japan, called National Medical-Care Expenditure (Kokumin Iryōhi).

Although this official Japanese estimate underreports spending by about one-third under American definitions, the corrected total is still about one-half the level of health spending in the United States. The main items that need to be added (and their size in 1990 as a percentage of total health spending) are over-the-counter (OTC) pharmaceuticals, including traditional "Chinese" medicines (2.9%); nursing homes for the elderly (1.3%); fees paid for acupuncture, massage, and moxa (1.1%); and direct payments by consumers for elective dental care (0.9%). Another category that should be added, though not found in the United States, is the practice of "gifts" paid to get treated by a high-status physician or to be cared for by a good hospital for the elderly (discussed later in Chapter 4). Some observers have guessed

5

that such payments make up a substantial portion of health-care costs, but Katsumata's systematic and actually rather generous formula indicates that they would amount to no more than 1.4 percent of health-care spending in 1990.[7]

These categories together with several smaller items total 7 to 8 percent of Japanese health-care spending, or well under 1 percent of GDP.[8] Using American definitions, then, total spending on health care in Japan comes to about ¥ 30 trillion in 1990, or 6.9 percent of GDP, compared to 12.1 percent of GDP in the United States that year. Converting yen to dollars at the Purchasing Power Parity (PPP) rate used in this book (¥180 to the dollar), total health-care spending in Japan is $167 billion, compared to $666 billion in the United States. In per capita terms, each Japanese spent $1,352 and each American $2,566 on health care in 1990. [9]

It turns out that the new Katsumata estimates of Japanese health-care spending, once adjusted for definitional differences, are quite close to the estimates independently produced by OECD statisticians, who have built a consistent dataset for the purpose of cross-national and over-time comparisons. We therefore can be confident that Figure 1.1, based on OECD data, is a reasonably accurate picture of Japanese health-care spending relative to that of several countries. In fact, Japanese spending is lower than in nearly all advanced nations, although it is important to note that Japan is not as far below the OECD average as the United States is above it. This is true in terms both of percentage of GDP, which represents the share of national

---

7 The estimate was based on the following assumptions: All patients discharged from general hospitals gave gifts of ¥30,000 to their physicians, with the exception of those hospitalized in extra-charge rooms, who gave gifts of either ¥100,000 (non-university hospitals) or ¥300,000 (university hospitals). Using 1990 data on hospitalization, the total comes to ¥269.6 billion. Extra charges in geriatric hospitals were estimated as ¥119.8 billion for 1991 by Niki Ryu, *90 Nendai no Iryō to Shinryō Hoshū* (Tokyo: Keiso Shobo, 1993). Combined they amount to about 1.4 percent of total health-care spending.

8 Others have estimated that 3–4 percent of GDP should be added on for these various extra costs: e.g., Powell and Anesaki, *Health Care*, p. 119. Such larger estimates are generally not backed up by a breakdown into categories or details on the process of estimating.

9 Different exchange rates give somewhat different impressions (see the Preface). In Katsumata's article, the OECD estimated PPP rate for 1990 of ¥195.6 to the dollar was used, making Japanese per capita spending $1,239. At the market exchange rate for 1990 of $1 = ¥144.8, the total figure for Japan would be $208 billion, or $1,684 per capita – still a gap of almost $2,000 for each man, woman, and child even with the most conservative figures.

6

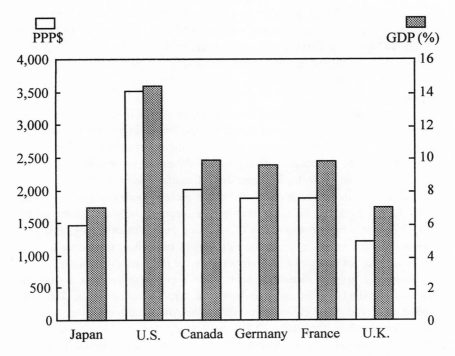

Figure 1.1 Total Health Expenditure in PPP U.S. Dollars and Ratio to GDP, 1994 [*Source*: *OECD Health Data 96* (1996)].

economic resources consumed by the health-care industry, and of health spending per capita measured in PPP.

In short, even after making all possible definitional adjustments, Japanese health-care spending clearly is very low, particularly when compared with the United States.

Were Costs Leveled Off?

We turn now to longitudinal data to examine how much spending has risen over time. Most Japanese, reacting to the annual newspaper headlines that national medical spending has reached a record high, seem to be convinced that costs are rising astronomically. That perception is quite correct in terms of total expenditures: From 1960 to 1990, Japanese spending in medical care rose from about ¥500 billion to ¥29 trillion, nearly a sixtyfold increase.

Growth was quite high even when adjusted for inflation and population increases: Real per capita spending rose from ¥24,804 in 1960 to ¥80,804 in 1970, ¥170,432 in 1980, and ¥232,061 in 1990.[10] In those terms, Japan's spending grew by 9.4 times in this thirty-year period, during which time American real per capita medical spending only tripled – hardly low growth in Japan.

It is important to realize, however, that Japan started from a very low base. In 1960 the average Japanese was getting only about $100 worth of medical care a year, and of course the standard of living was not very high in other respects as well. As people's living standards go up, we would expect that they would want more health care, and of course the income of providers will rise as well. At the level of the entire society, both cross-national and longitudinal evidence indicates that higher income levels (as measured by GDP) lead to a higher *proportion* of spending on health care. For most purposes the most informative measure of growth in health-care spending is its share of total spending, for an individual or for the overall economy.[11]

Figure 1.2 gives a picture of health-care spending growth as a share of national product for Japan in comparison with American data. Japanese spending stayed relatively stable in the 1960s. After health insurance benefits were improved in the early 1970s, particularly for the elderly, spending started to grow at an even higher rate than in the United States. It was in reaction to this explosive rise in spending (and the disproportionate burden on the public treasury) that the government instituted a series of cost-control reforms in the early 1980s. These succeeded in holding health-care spending as a fairly constant share of GDP throughout the 1980s and into the 1990s.[12]

Was this impressive result just due to Japan's very rapid economic growth? In a sense, yes. In the "income-doubling" era of the 1960s, real growth in GDP was averaging a remarkable 10 percent a year, meaning that medical spending could expand at a similarly rapid clip without showing any increase

---

10 These data are in 1990 prices, using OECD data (the 1993 Health Data File).

11 Robert J. Maxwell, *Health and Wealth: An International Study of Health-Care Spending* (Lexington, MA: Lexington Books, 1981), p. 29.

12 In the mid-1990s, however, the trend went somewhat upward because GDP growth slackened. The OECD estimate of this share for 1993 was 7.3 percent, up from 6.8 percent in 1990, even though the growth rate of medical spending was about the same as earlier. Early OECD estimates (experience indicates that recent estimates are often revised considerably later) were 6.9 percent for 1994 and 7.2 percent for 1995; the 1996 figure should be somewhat lower since GDP growth was healthy. Figures from the *OECD 1996 Health File.*

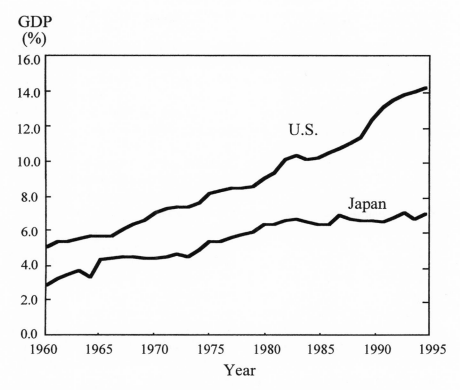

Figure 1.2 Ratio of Total Health Expenditure to GDP, 1960–95 [*Source: OECD Health Data 96* (1996)].

in share. This factor does not explain away the extreme contrast in health-care spending growth between the explosive 1970s and the placid 1980s, however, because the average growth rates of GDP in those two decades were almost the same.

It is clear then that a real change occurred in 1980 and that the Japanese achievement in constraining spending is real. This achievement is not unique: Germany, England, and France also kept health-care spending at a roughly constant share of GDP in the 1980s. It is worth noting, however, that in these nations the proportion of older people in the population stayed roughly constant in the 1980s, while in Japan it was rising rapidly. The elderly's share of national health-care spending rose in that period from 18 to 29 percent,

9

meaning that the relative cost of medical care for the rest of the population dropped.[13]

The clear contrast is to the United States, where health spending has sky-rocketed even though the population has not been aging, at least not in terms of the proportion of people 65 and over. Of course, the nation has been "middle-aging" as the baby-boom generation gets older, but individual health-care usage does not go up very much with age below 65. This fact has ominous implications for American health spending when that generation becomes elderly.

Our two main points are therefore well demonstrated: Japan's health-care expenditures are low, and their growth was leveled off quite sharply in the early 1980s. Both points are noteworthy in comparing Japan with other OECD countries and of course stand in stark contrast to quite the opposite performance in the United States.

POSSIBLE EXPLANATIONS

Why are health-care costs in Japan so much lower than in the United States? Unfortunately, no one has tried to answer this question in a systematic and detailed way, although several partial explanations were suggested by various researchers in our broader project. One participant, William Hsiao of Harvard, made some very crude estimates by adjusting American health expenditures in 1990 for various conditions in Japan. He suggested that about 25 percent of the gap was due to a lower incidence of disease (partially a matter of the social environment), 15 percent to less aggressive practice styles, 15 percent to lower hospital staffing levels, 10 percent to smaller administrative burdens, and 15 percent to the lower income of the majority of Japanese doctors who are on salary. The remaining 20 percent of the gap has various other causes.[14]

Whether these estimates are close to the mark or not, or whether they leave out some other important factors, the question remains: *Why* do Japanese behave so differently in these categories. Although available data do not

---

13   Naoki Ikegami and Yoshinori Hiroi, "Factors in Health Care Spending: An Eight-Nation Comparison with OECD Data," in *Containing*, pp. 33–44; and *Iryō Handobukku* 1995, p. 233.

14   William C. Hsiao, "Afterword: Costs – The Macro Perspective," in *Containing*, pp. 45–52. For another review of several such factors, see M.G. Marmot and George Davey Smith, "Why are the Japanese Living Longer?" *British Medical Journal* 299 (December 23, 1989), 1547–1551.

permit quantitative estimates even at Hsiao's rough-and-ready level, the most important general explanations seem to involve sociocultural and systemic factors, as discussed in the following sections.

Sociocultural Factors

Particularly in comparison with the United States, Japan looks like a rather placid society, lacking an undue number of health problems that should cause high medical spending. Japan has relatively low levels – and the United States has remarkably high levels – of such social maladies as drug addiction, violent crime, teenage pregnancy, high-speed traffic accidents, and poverty-stricken urban and rural slums. The incidence of such expensive conditions as severe trauma, low birth-weight babies, AIDS, and some other diseases is therefore markedly lower in Japan.

However, one should not jump to the conclusion that the only difference between Japanese and American health is that Japan does not have an "underclass."[15] With regard to the personal habits of ordinary people, Japanese eat healthier food and in smaller quantities than Americans. It is certainly interesting that although Japan has not seen as much of a fad for health foods and intense exercise as has the United States in recent years, its population has remained relatively lean, while the number of overweight Americans has increased at a record pace. On the other hand the Japanese diet tends to be high in salt, leading to high blood pressure. Japanese drink slightly less than Americans (and rarely drive afterward) but smoke much more. These personal-habits factors seem to be mixed but on balance may account for somewhat better health in Japan.

What about stress? Popular accounts in both Japan and the United States portray Japanese as intensely hard working, to the point of all sorts of psychological tension on the part of students studying for exams and of course the allegedly unique Japanese phenomenon of *karōshi* or death by overwork. That should lead to higher medical costs in Japan, but we are dubious. Any sort of quantitative evidence, on stress-related physical illness, diagnosed psychiatric ailments, use of various kinds of therapy including self-help groups, or consumption of psychotropic drugs, would indicate that it is Amer-

---

15 For example, the infant mortality rate just for American whites in 1993 was 6.8, much better than the 16.5 for African-Americans but still well above the Japanese rate of 4.3. *Health United States*, 1995, p. 102.

ican society that is more stressed. The far lower security of jobs, of family life, and of sheer survival in the urban environment in the United States makes this view more plausible. Actually, we think the work life of many Japanese is relatively relaxed, despite the long hours, and the rates of *karōshi* might well be higher in the United States if anyone counted it there. Here too, despite the conventional wisdom, differences in stress probably favor lower health-care spending for Japan.

We can also note some indirect sociocultural factors that might account for lower health-care spending in Japan than in the United States. Americans are widely held to be the most rights-conscious and litigious people on earth, and Japanese are among the least. The difference shows up particularly in health care. Malpractice suits are rare in Japan, and people generally seem to be willing to go along with what the doctor says without much explanation, although both tendencies may be changing today. American conservatives often see lawyers and pushy patients as the main cause of high health-care spending, directly through legal fees, enormous verdicts, and high malpractice insurance premiums, and indirectly through the practice of defensive medicine. They would take this difference as the main factor.

We are more inclined to agree with those who do not take malpractice so seriously as a factor in high American medical costs. After all, the great bulk of payments to the affected patients is used just to cover their direct medical and caretaking costs, which have to be covered somehow (note these would not be nearly so high in countries like Japan with guaranteed low-cost health-care coverage). We are moreover skeptical that many American providers would forgo all those profitable tests even if they were not so worried about getting sued.[16]

Incidentally, another point sometimes raised is that Japanese costs are lower because doctors are less likely to take heroic measures to prevent death, or families are less likely to demand them. This is a hard topic to investigate empirically, but we did ask some Japanese doctors who have experience in both countries what they thought the differences were. One neonatologist told us that he thought Japanese hospitals would go further in trying to save a low birth-weight baby than would usually be the case in the United States (except when the hospital or family were Roman Catholic). The difference

---

16 A 1985 estimate of the cost of liability insurance was $5.16 billion or 1.22 percent of health-care costs. Clark C. Haighurst, *Health Care Law and Policy* (Westbury, NY: Foundation Press, 1988), p. 700.

in spending clearly is that there are far fewer greatly premature babies in Japan. Even with regard to very elderly patients, in university hospitals and other elite facilities, we were told that there is a great reluctance to "pull the plug" in Japan and that quite often extreme life-prolonging measures would be taken. On the other hand, many elderly patients are housed in hospitals for the elderly that really are similar to nursing homes in the United States, and there a more "natural" death is more likely.[17]

It is true that one finds less heroic surgery performed on terminal patients in Japan, but then there is far less surgery of all kinds than in the United States – on average about one-third the amount.[18] Clearly low surgery rates themselves are a major factor in low medical spending. One reason that is explored later is that the fees for surgery are low enough to make operations rather unprofitable, but a cultural distaste for invasive procedures is also a factor. Indeed, the long tradition of Chinese medicine in Japan has led to a general preference for conservative rather than aggressive treatments.

Finally, many have noted the Japanese tendency to be quite mindful of their health – the unfriendly term is hypochondriac. Survey evidence indicates that Japanese are much more likely to take some sort of action at the first sign of some ailment, and their rate of visiting the doctor is much higher than Americans'.[19] Moreover, mass health screening is very widespread in Japan, being provided at school or work, or for several categories of citizens (the middle-aged self-employed, elderly retired people, pregnant women, and young children) by local governments. A remarkable number of people undergo an elaborate one- or two-day physical examination called a "human dry dock" (*ningen dokku*) every year or two.

The impact on health spending is uncertain. No doubt a significant number of illnesses are caught early when they can be treated at lower cost. On the other hand, all these visits and screenings are expensive in themselves, and they often lead to identifying health problems that are then treated even though they might well improve on their own if not discovered. The cost–

---

17 The practice of a "living will" is uncommon in Japan, and there are few hospices, although interest in these issues of dying naturally is growing.

18 Toshihiko Hasegawa, "Comparison of Hospital Admission Rates between Japan and the United States," in *Containing*, pp. 101–105.

19 See Hiroko Akiyama, "Paradoxical Comparison of Health Care Needs, Utilization and Costs between Japan and the United States," and Margaret Lock, "Keeping Pressure Off the Japanese Health Care System: The Contribution of Middle-Aged Women," in *Containing*, pp. 201–225.

benefit literature on preventive medicine in the United States has generally cast doubt on whether much of it is efficient, and those doubts should apply even more to Japan, where screening is much more popular.[20]

However, we would argue that screening has probably had at least two positive impacts on cost control. First, in a few areas, early intervention and intensive health education probably do have major payoffs. The outstanding example is Japan's aggressive prenatal and neonatal public health program, which in the postwar period succeeded in bringing mortality rates down from very high levels to about the best performance in the world. It appears that there have been significant cost savings by avoiding expensive medical treatments of mothers and children as well. Second, all the screening and frequent doctor visits perhaps lead indirectly to a positive attitude about health and even the individual's ability to help maintain it. People seem to be more oriented to taking care of themselves in Japan, and that consciousness may help to keep health costs down.

In sum, a lot of these factors are somewhat ambiguous, but on balance they probably do contribute significantly to the difference in heath-care expenditures in Japan and the United States (as Hsiao's estimates indicate). However, they cannot be the only answer. For one thing, such relatively durable characteristics of Japanese society can hardly explain why health-care spending was rising so rapidly in the 1970s but then leveled off so sharply in the 1980s.

Systemic Factors

For a comprehensive explanation, we must therefore also look to the institutional structure of the health-care system and how it has changed – the main topic of this book. We present here a quick overview emphasizing the flow of money through the health insurance system. Figure 1.3 is a schematic view.[21] The reader should be cautioned that many important details and exceptions are simply not mentioned here in the interests of clarity, though they will be found in appropriate chapters later.

The funds to pay for medical care come from citizens and employers in

20 Louise Russell, *Educated Guesses: Making Policy About Medical Screening Tests* (Berkeley: University of California Press, 1994).

21 For the various ways in which funds can flow through a health-care system, see Uwe E. Reinhardt, "Reorganizing the Financial Flows in American Health Care," *Health Affairs* 12 (Supplement, 1993), 172–193.

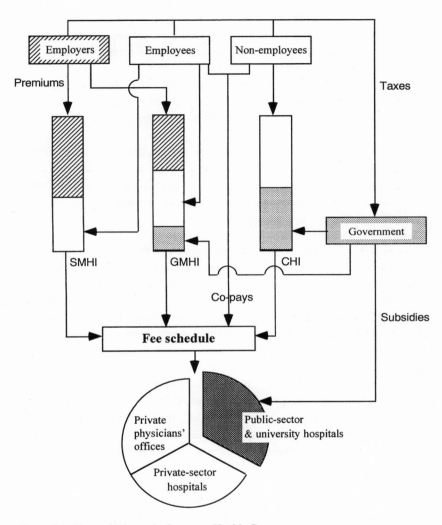

Figure 1.3 Flow of Money in Japanese Health Care.

three forms: taxes, health insurance premiums, and co-payments. Taxes are the ordinary income, corporate and consumption taxes, the general revenues of government. Premiums are paid to an insurance carrier, mostly under one of the three major categories of health insurance:

- Society-Managed Health Insurance (SMHI, Kumiai Hoken, often just called Kenpo) covers the employees of large companies and consists of 1,800 insurance pools at the firm level, administered by management–labor committees.
- Government-Managed Health Insurance (GMHI, Seifu Kanshō or Seikan) covers the employees of small companies and is a single pool administered at the national level by the Ministry of Health and Welfare.
- Citizens' Health Insurance (CHI, Kokumin Hoken or Kokuho, often translated as National Health Insurance) is the residual category that covers non-employees, such as the self-employed and retirees, and consists of 3,253 insurance pools at the city, town, and village level, administered by the municipal government.

As Figure 1.3 indicates, the revenue sources of these three categories are different. SMHI subsists on employer and employee premiums; the rate varies across industries and companies but averages 8.3 percent of covered wages (with half or more picked up by the employer). GMHI has a fixed premium rate of 8.5 percent nationwide, shared equally between employer and employee, but in recognition of the lower incomes of these employees, a set percentage of outlays (currently 14 percent) is provided from government general revenues. Finally, CHI premiums are figured by a formula that varies somewhat from locality to locality but is based on household income, assets, and number of members. About 50 percent of CHI outlays is provided from general revenues. The effect of this subsidy, though not its stated purpose, is that the government makes up for the lack of an employer. The general principle throughout is that government subsidies to the plans with lower-income enrollees are higher.

Co-payments, or out-of-pocket costs for medical services in general, are relatively low in Japan. Most treatments including prescription drugs are covered by health insurance. Co-payments are charged for everything, now ranging from 20 to 30 percent (less for the elderly), but "catastrophic" caps mean that the co-pay applies to only about the first $350 of total medical care per month.

The most important point about the Japanese system is that despite this multiplicity of financial sources and health insurance carriers, the payments to providers nearly all flow through a single faucet – the national fee schedule (*shinryō hoshū*), which applies to all patients regardless of which health in-

16

surance system they belong to, and regardless of where they receive services. The fee schedule lists all the procedures and products that can be paid for by heath insurance, and it sets their prices. It is revised every two years after negotiations between payers and providers that take place within the Central Social Insurance Medical Care Council (called Chūikyō), an advisory committee to the Minister of Health and Welfare.

Health-care providers in Japan fall into two groups, office-based physicians and hospitals. Hospitals can be further divided into those that are privately owned, public hospitals run by government mostly at the local level, and university hospitals. Actually, the majority of physicians are salaried employees of hospitals, which are virtually all "closed" in that private-practice physicians cannot attend their patients – a system that seems peculiar to Americans but actually is the most common practice in Europe and around the world. A more unusual feature of the Japanese system is that the same fee schedule applies to both private-practice physicians and hospitals.

With only one important exception, all the revenues of all Japanese health-care providers are determined by the fee schedule. For every hospital or private-practice physician, their operating expenses, capital expenses, and the equivalent of profit are derived entirely from volume times the listed prices for each service or product that they deliver to patients. The exception is that public hospitals also receive government subsidies in varying amounts to cover capital and, often enough, a portion of operating expenses.

The reader should be cautioned again that this description is extremely simplified – nearly every sentence would have to be qualified at length if it were to be completely accurate. The chapters that follow fill in the missing portions and note many exceptions as we try to explain why the Japanese system works as it does, and how its key features constrain health-care spending. With regard to the latter goal, it is worth highlighting five of the most important points now.

First, of course, is the fee schedule itself, which together with a prohibition on any extra charges (or "balance billing") both directly controls prices and indirectly influences providers' behavior through relative prices. The rates of surgery in Japan are low at least partly because the cost of many operations may not be fully covered by the fee. One might even say that the general principle has been to make relatively inexpensive procedures profitable, and expensive procedures unprofitable.

The dramatic leveling off of spending in the early 1980s was possible because the fee schedule was and is substantially though not unilaterally

17

determined by the government, and it covers nearly everything. In successive biennial negotiations, fees for services were raised very marginally and fees for pharmaceuticals were cut sharply. The interesting question of why these actions did not lead to a correspondingly sharp increase in the *volume* of goods and services is discussed in Chapter 6.

Second, the Japanese system is extremely egalitarian, not only in that everyone can go to any provider and get essentially the same treatment but because various mechanisms – premiums as a percentage of income, differential tax subsidies, direct cross-subsidization among carriers – ensure that premium levels are adjusted to the ability to pay. These are explained in Chapter 4. The advantage of an egalitarian system for holding down costs is paradoxically that it makes an improvement in benefits to any group extremely expensive because it must be provided to everyone. That prevents the familiar "ratcheting up" or demonstration effect in which some benefit goes first to those in a generous health insurance plan, and then pressure mounts from the less privileged in the system, which is one reason why in the United States, uniquely in the world, nearly all hospital patients now stay in at least semi-private rooms rather than wards.

Third, although Japan does not have a formal "global budget" for total medical spending, there is something of an equivalent. The government subsidies to CHI and GMHI are calculated as a fixed percentage of outlays as established by law, and so are not easily altered, and they come from the regular General Account budget. That means that before each revision of the fee schedule, the Ministry of Finance must approve the amount of the subsidy required and in effect impose a rough ceiling on total projected medical expenditure.

Moreover, the fact that the Health Insurance Bureau of the Ministry of Health and Welfare (MHW) is directly responsible for management of the single largest insurance pool, the GMHI system for small-business employees, means that its officials have to keep a careful eye on trends in their own outlays for medical care. If they miscalculate, they either have to raise premiums, which is as unpopular with politicians in Japan as elsewhere, or go hat in hand to the Ministry of Finance to beg for a rise in the subsidy rate or a special bailout. Neither is easy to get. The kicker is that the only method available to economize on GMHI outlays is through the fee schedule, which applies not only to GMHI members but to everyone in Japan. This important mechanism for controlling costs and how it has changed over time is discussed in more detail in Chapter 5.

Fourth, as is usually the case in Europe and other countries, the principle for setting fees is political rather than scientific. Fees are decided not by analysis as much as by consent of the interested parties. The biennial negotiations begin with the current fee schedule, and the payers and providers dicker back and forth item by item until both sides agree. This approach is very different from the elaborate research on "relative values" that is supposed to be the basis of the Medicare fee schedule in the United States. It is quicker, cheaper, and actually less likely to provoke conflict over broad principles or claims of scientific validity. As is discussed in Chapter 5, there used to be intense conflict over the fee schedule, but the practice of repeated negotiations over time among essentially the same small group of contenders has largely routinized the process.

Finally, the fifth point is the inhibiting effect of regulation on entrepreneurial behavior. As is described in Chapter 3, private hospitals lack enough surplus revenue to allow much capital investment for expansion, and they cannot sell their services to the highest bidder. Advanced high-technology medicine, except with regard to diagnostic machinery, is mostly in the domain of government or university hospitals, which can get subsidies for capital investment but typically operate more like bureaucratic organizations than entrepreneurial revenue maximizers. Aggressive private-practice physicians used to be a big factor in pushing up spending, but today they are aging and seem fairly content with their rather stable (and high) incomes. Health insurers cannot make profits and cannot compete for enrollment of low-risk, high-profit members. Pharmaceutical companies worry mostly about how to deal with price cuts (churning out marginally new products can bring high short-term profit margins, but their prices too are soon brought into line). Medical researchers rarely have access to large government grants, and even health policy analysts have little incentive to come up with daring reform ideas because there is not much of a market for them.

The Japanese health-care system thus does not appear as dynamic and interesting as that of the United States. On the other hand, it does a good job of keeping its population healthy, and it does so at remarkably low cost.

LESSONS FOR AMERICANS?

In our view, Americans should look at the Japanese health-care system today with as much interest as they analyzed the Japanese automobile industry fifteen years ago, and for similar reasons. In the early 1980s it became clear that the Japanese could make very reliable cars, even if they were sometimes a bit dowdy, at a much lower price than was then possible in the United States. After a decade of close study and major organizational reforms, today American cars are much closer to Japanese cars in quality and, depending on the exchange rate of the moment, may actually be less expensive.

Producing health care is a good deal more complicated and uncertain than producing automobiles, and the health-care system is more fragmented and more difficult to transform than a single car company or even the entire automotive industry. Moreover, as is amply shown in this book, a nation's health-care system has deep roots in distinctive cultural values and ways of thinking, and in social institutions that have grown up over decades. Nonetheless, as in the automotive industry, a few basic organizational structures can make all the difference in performance. We believe that these structures can be learned, even between two quite different cultures.

It is worth keeping in mind that the Pacific Ocean is just as wide looking West as looking East. In the nineteenth century, the 1920s, and again since World War II, Japanese have looked to America and Europe to find ways to make their economy and society work better. Often they just borrowed technologies, but the more fundamental process was the importation of organization – how to establish a modern military, a factory, a postal system, a joint-stock corporation, a research laboratory, even (to some extent) a hospital.[22] They found that many of these organizations did not work in Japan quite the same way as in their countries of origin but usually could be adapted and improved. Ideas about how to run a factory were improved enough to be borrowed back by the West decades later.

The motivating force for the Japanese was often a sense of crisis, a conviction that if they could not catch up with the advanced nations of the world quickly, their country would be overwhelmed. As a follower nation, Japan had many proven models of good organizations to pick from and adapt. We think that American health care is in just such a crisis, and today many models of systems that work much better are available for inspection, partial imitation, and adaptation. Japan's system is not the only potential model, of course, but it is worth a closer look.

22 Eleanor Westney, *Imitation and Innovation: The Transfer of Western Organization Patterns to Meiji Japan* (Cambridge: Harvard University Press, 1987).

20

2

Actors, Arenas, and Agendas in Health Policy Making

HEALTH care in any nation is a complex system, one that has been shaped over the years by social, cultural, and economic factors as well as by historical accidents. We try to explain these factors and their interactions later in the book. Our main focus is nonetheless governmental health policy, not because it is necessarily the most important aspect of the health-care system but because it is where deliberate decisions make the most difference, in Japan as in the United States.

HEALTH-CARE POLITICS IN JAPAN AND THE UNITED STATES

Before analyzing the substance of Japanese health policy and its impact on the health-care system, we need a sense of how it is devised. We begin therefore by asking: Who makes health policy in Japan? Where do they get together (and under what rules)? What do they talk about? A quick comparison with the United States indicates that Japan is different in terms of these three key aspects of governmental decision making. We then go into a bit more detail on the Japanese decision-making system, in general and as it operates in the health-care policy area.

Actors

When we begin to describe a decision-making system, we start with the individuals and (more often) organizations that have both enough interest in health care and enough political power to participate and have an impact. In the United States in the 1990s, we would think of the President (and perhaps his wife), the two political parties, a few Senators or Representatives (some long associated with health-care issues), and a long list of interest groups: providers (various groups of doctors and hospitals), insurers (big companies, small companies), consumers (AARP, the unions), employers (small business, big business), and so on. And then we could not understand what goes on without taking into account the attitudes and desires of the general public (along with the media that lecture at and purport to speak for it), and then all those experts with Ph.D.s who make a living by analyzing and endlessly debating health policy. State governors and legislatures are important as well. Almost as an afterthought, we might think about the Department of Health and Human Services and other national bureaucratic agencies. The relationships of conflict and cooperation among all these actors is quite complicated.

We can see right away that Japanese health policy making is different by observing that it has been dominated over the years by a long drawn-out conflict between just two actors, the Ministry of Health and Welfare and the Japan Medical Association (JMA). Some big players in the American context, such as the chief executive, a good many of the interest groups, and the academic experts, take little or no part in Japan, and some actors whom we find in both countries – parties, individual politicians, the unions – play somewhat different roles.

Of course, we must not fall into the easy trap of thinking it is the United States that is normal and Japan somehow unique. Actually the health-care decision-making system in Japan is not too different from most other advanced countries most of the time, while the American scene in the 1990s has been convoluted to the extreme. And even in the United States, if we went back to the 1950s and '60s to talk about health-care politics, no doubt we would start with the well-established confrontation between the American Medical Association and the Social Security Administration.

Arenas

Beyond the number and variety of participating actors, we need to know about the arenas where they act, or the rules of the various games of health-care decision making. In the United States, some important health-care policy changes have been decided essentially in a bureaucratic rule-making arena in which highly specialized knowledge is the ticket of admission (say, cost-cutting measures in Medicare like Diagnostic-Related Groups), while others are played out by party competition in Congress, where the arcane rules of legislative committees are quite important, or will be heavily influenced by the posturing inherent in the executive–legislative checks-and-balance standoff. In short, institutional settings matter a lot most of the time. Note however that American health policy making has also not infrequently gone into a

"crisis" mode where ordinary rules do not apply and the process is impro-
vised on the fly.

In Japan as in the United States, how policy making works depends heavily
on where it takes place, but the most important arenas are more stable. The
fee schedule is decided in a key biennial negotiation between insurers and
providers, and that forum – the Central Social Insurance Medical Care Council (Chūikyō) – has provided a mechanism for dealing with many recurring
issues in a routinized way with very restricted participation. Most important
policy changes such as new laws are fought out in a broader but still rather
structured "subgovernmental" arena in which the JMA's supporters in the
long-term majority Liberal Democratic Party play a major role. Only occasionally will conflicts spill over to engage heavyweight actors, with less
predictable results.

Agenda

Finally, we can have no good sense of policy making without understanding
what policy issues are being discussed. The immediate agenda is made up of
what are seen as important problems and plausible solutions, the issues that
are perceived as likely to lead to some policy change. Underlying those ideas
are the images of various actors about what the health-care system should
look like. Such images are generally a bit self-serving – they protect or
advance the interests of those professing them, and as such can be seen as
ideologies. However, they also must resonate with real values and norms in
the minds of people, or they would not be effective.

Health-care policy arenas in the United States are populated by quite a
variety of images and ideologies, including such traditional notions as compassion and the sacred doctor–patient relationship. However, particularly potent in recent years have been

- the image of *consumerism*, held by citizens and those who speak in
  their name: Good health care is when patients take responsibility for
  getting the best health care they can, and physicians supply lots of
  information.
- the image of *science*, held by providers: The measure of a good
  health-care system is the ability to cure the most difficult cases, and
  improved medical care depends on research and the diffusion of the
  practices proven to be most effective.

23

* the image of *health economics*, held by public officials and many policy experts: Good health care is achieved in an efficient market, and economic analysis is the road to wisdom.

Traces of all these images can be found in Japan, and health economics has been quite in vogue among Ministry of Health and Welfare officials since the early 1980s. Still, it is striking that much discussion of health-care issues has long revolved around a set of images that have endured for several decades:

* the image of *dedicated service*, held by ordinary citizens: Good health care is when doctors are selfless and think only of patient welfare (while nurses all act like Florence Nightingale).
* the image of *professional autonomy*, held by providers: Good health care is provided by ethical physicians learning through their personal experience how to practice medicine; this requires autonomy from government, from insurers, and even from scientific protocols drawn up by experts.
* the image of *public health*, held by government officials: Good health care is a matter of public programs provided to the population on an egalitarian basis.

Health-care politics in Japan, at least as compared with the United States, is thus played by fewer actors in more structured arenas, and it centers on a set of ideas that perhaps look a bit old-fashioned to Americans. However, old-fashioned ideas do not necessarily make for bad health care.

ACTORS

For many decades, Japanese health policy has been dominated by a struggle between the Ministry of Health and Welfare, with its public-health vision centered on government management of health care, and the Japan Medical Association, with its paradigm of professional autonomy. The conflict produces negative versions of the main images: to government officials, the private-practice doctors represented by the JMA look like avaricious shopkeepers, while the doctors see MHW bureaucrats as arrogant and power-hungry. But at the same time, each of these powerful actors depends on the other.

The Ministry of Health and Welfare

The usual image of the Japanese bureaucracy is that it is strong, self-confident, high in social status – and that it feels responsible for defining and pursuing the national interest. In short, it is similar to the bureaucracies of most advanced nations – particularly those of France and Germany, where administrative organs developed earlier than the legislature – and is very different from that of the United States.[1] It should be kept in mind that each individual Japanese ministry has its own historical tradition, personality, and sense of mission and that the bureaucracy is very fragmented, with little ability to coordinate policy across ministerial lines (or sometimes even across bureau lines within ministries).

The forerunners of the Ministry of Health and Welfare were the Social Bureau and Public Health Bureau of the prewar Home Ministry. The Home Ministry was in charge of local government and the police; its concern for social policy stemmed largely from worries about labor unrest and left-wing agitation. It developed a variety of programs in the Bismarckian mode aimed at attaching workers to their firms and stemming discontent, including health insurance for employees (passed in 1922).[2] Home Ministry bureaucrats carried reputations as being authoritarian, nationalistic, paternalistic, moralistic, activist, and concerned about "the people" (*kokumin*, which can also be translated as "the nation") more than about companies or other special interests.

The Ministry of Health and Welfare itself was created by splitting off and expanding these two bureaus in 1938. It has long had three major functions: pensions, social welfare, and health care. Pension policy is relatively self-contained, but social-welfare and health-care concerns interact on many fronts and have long been in rivalry. Social welfare (*shakai fukushi*) was the original "mainstream" function of the Ministry, logical given its origins and the predominance of poverty and other social problems in the wartime and immediate postwar periods. After a period of taking the back seat, it returned to prominence on the back of public worries about the "aging society" and

---

1 See Bernard S. Silberman, *Cages of Reason: The Rise of the Rational State in France, Japan, the United States, and Great Britain* (Chicago: University of Chicago Press, 1993).

2   E.g., Sheldon Garon, *The State and Labor in Modern Japan* (Berkeley: University of California Press, 1987), esp. chap. 1; and Andrew Gordon, *The Evolution of Labor Relations in Japan: Heavy Industry, 1853–1955* (Cambridge, MA: Harvard University Council on East Asian Studies, 1985).

today jostles with health care for control over old-age policy within the Bureau of Health and Welfare for the Elderly (Rōjin Hoken Fukushi Kyoku).[3] As is often true in Japanese organizations, each unit develops its own personality and strives for self-sufficiency, so conflicts flare up frequently across all these jurisdictional boundaries.

Another form of conflict or enduring tension cross-cuts organizational boundaries. Japanese upper civil servants come in two shapes: generalists (*jimukan*), who are most often graduates in law (especially from the Law Faculty of Tokyo University), and experts (*gikan*), who are trained in some technical specialty and take a different examination. In principle they are equal, but in practice the generalists are in a superior position, controlling most bureau director slots and the highest position of administrative vice-minister in nearly all ministries. In the Ministry of Health and Welfare, most of the experts are medical doctors, who control many division-chief posts plus the directorships of three bureaus.[4] MHW physicians come from quite varied backgrounds, often including study abroad (such as for a Masters of Public Health degree), and they pride themselves on their intellectual acuity.

Within the field of health care, the Ministry's main functions are supervision of health insurance, maintenance of standards for the medical profession, traditional public health programs including local Public Health Centers and environmental hygiene, management of national hospitals, and regulation of pharmaceuticals and medical devices. These tasks are carried out by various bureaus. The core agency for health policy connected with cost containment is the Health Insurance Bureau (HIB), particularly its Medical Affairs Division (Hoken Kyoku, Iryō Ka). Although this Division is headed by a physician, it is kept under close control by generalist officials. The Health Insurance Bureau occupies the key position in health policy making because of its multiplicity of functions: direct management of the national program covering all employees of small businesses, oversight for the health insurance

---

3 The social-welfare function had centered in the Shakai Kyoku (translated as the Social Affairs Bureau in the postwar period), which took on a health-care dimension in 1972 by establishing the Health Care for the Elderly Division to handle the new Free Medical Care for the Elderly program because the health-care bureaus didn't want it (Campbell, 1992).

4 Their relatively powerful position can be traced back to Colonel C. F. Sams, in charge of health policy during the American occupation, who believed that expert knowledge was required for good policy making and refused to talk with "unqualified" bureaucrats. See Sugiyama Akiko, *Senryōki no-Iryō Kakumei* (Tokyo: Keisō Shobō, 1995).

programs for large-firm employees and the non-employed, and main negotiator for the payers' side in the biennial fee-schedule negotiations. The fact that this Bureau is also the operational administrator of the fee schedule, and supervises the Social Insurance Agency (Shakai Hokenchō), which carries out the functions of the American Health Care Financing Administration and more, adds to its considerable power.

Despite the constant tensions across organizational boundaries and between different classifications of civil servants, over the years there had been general agreement within the ministry on broad policies in health care. This consensus centered around what we have called the "public-health paradigm." In fact, as is discussed shortly, the Ministry of Health and Welfare was more unified in its policy views than is often the case in the Japanese bureaucracy, precisely because of its long battles with the Japan Medical Association.

The Japan Medical Association

In the 1960s and 1970s, the JMA was the prototypical interest group in Japan. Journalists always ranked it with Nōkyō, the Federation of Agricultural Cooperatives, as a pressure-group *yokozuna* (grand champion in sumo wrestling), and Takemi Tarō, its president from 1957 to 1982, personified the role of a boss who could nearly always get his own way by the skillful application of money, connections, electoral muscle, rhetorical creativity, and sheer force of personality.

The accepted date for the creation of the JMA is 1916, when the Greater Japan Medical Association (Dai-Nippon Ishikai) was established under the leadership of Kitasato Shibasaburō, first dean of Keio University's medical faculty and a towering figure in both the scientific and organizational histories of Japanese medicine.[5] It followed several earlier attempts to organize physicians and was the product of conflicts both among medical practitioners (Western vs. Chinese medicine, elite university graduates vs. those qualified by apprenticeship, private-practice vs. hospital-affiliated physicians) and between the doctors and the government (including over the issue of whether physicians should continue to sell medications). The name was changed to Japan Medical Association (Nihon Ishikai) and membership made compulsory by law in 1923. The Association became more and more a tool of

---

5 This account relies heavily on William E. Steslicke, *Doctors in Politics: The Political Life of the Japan Medical Association* (New York: Praeger, 1973).

government health-care administration until the end of the war, but it still managed to retain its character as spokesman for Japan's private-practice physicians.

In 1947, the Association was reconstituted as a voluntary professional organization, as part of the effort by American Occupation authorities to democratize Japanese political and social life. Membership in a prefectural medical association is the condition for joining, along with paying dues. The JMA is governed by a House of Delegates elected by the prefectural associations. The Delegates elect the Board of Directors and the President for two-year terms. The internal politics of the JMA have often been stormy, centering on presidential elections, although during his years in office, Takemi generally exercised autocratic one-man control. The JMA purports to speak for all physicians, and in earlier years the association did in fact enroll most doctors although its ability to sign them up has since slipped substantially (in 1955 it enrolled 68 percent of all physicians, but in 1992 just 58 percent). Membership is far higher among private practitioners than among doctors employed by hospitals.

The political influence of the JMA, similarly to physicians' groups in other nations, rests on substantial resources. First, doctors – especially those in private practice – are deeply aware of the importance of public policy to their livelihoods as well as very well off financially. The combination makes for large contributions that can be converted into large official or unofficial donations to politicians. Moreover, the prefectural medical associations that make up the JMA became skilled in picking likely winners in each election district (in the multimember system in effect until 1996), which maximized the leverage of physicians.

Second, physicians are functionally necessary for the health-care system to work. That means the ultimate weapon of a doctors' strike (actually a mass refusal to accept health-insurance payments) can be a potent threat, although more so in earlier years when it was actually exercised occasionally. More important on a day-to-day level, it means that the JMA must sign on – or at least grudgingly assent – to nearly any important medical care policy if it is to be implemented successfully. This power is most often used within the many statutory or temporary government advisory committees to which the JMA sends representatives (and from time to time threatens to withdraw them).

What had Takemi and the JMA been after? William Steslicke lists both its formal and informal goals as of the early 1960s.[6] The formal goals, as might be expected, focus on medical ethics, advancement of science and education, maintenance of standards, and promoting national health. Its key informal goals were all about politics:

- Maintain autonomy, dominance over all providers, and veto power over policy.
- Protect or improve the position of private practitioners within the health-care system.
- Raise physicians' incomes.
- Protect the right of physicians to sell medications.

Although major shifts in the JMA's environment have brought changes in tactics and strategy, these goals have remained remarkably consistent in the ensuing decades and are still a good list of JMA objectives in the 1990s.

Supporting Players

Although the MHW and the JMA have been the main contenders in the long struggle for control of Japanese health care, each has also been surrounded by other organizations and groups that in effect have supported its interests, albeit in complicated ways. These other important actors in health-care policy can be seen as two opposing coalitions.

The MHW Side. The *Ministry of Finance (MOF)* is usually regarded as an antagonist of the spending ministries, and indeed every year its budget examiners go toe-to-toe with the MHW to fight about how much money will be allocated to social policy. Nonetheless, the MOF is a key ally of the Welfare bureaucrats in its struggles with the JMA because it can credibly say that no more money will be spent on medical care.

Finance officials' interests are easy to describe: They want to keep costs down, they especially want to keep government costs down, and most of all they want to keep spending from the General Account budget down. That is, the MOF has consistently backed up the MHW in its efforts to hold down medical fee increases, but when more money is necessary, Finance officials have generally sought to have it come from the private sector (increased co-

6 Condensed from Steslicke, pp. 61–68.

payments by patients, higher premiums) or from social insurance funds – even those managed by local governments or the Welfare Ministry itself.

The *insurers* typically fight against Finance Ministry economizing and try to get more public money spent on health care, an issue that puts the MHW in a mediating position. Most often, however, they unite with the Welfare bureaucrats in their mutual distaste for the JMA. The local governments that serve as the carriers for Citizens' Health Insurance for the non-employed are organized into one national federation, and the various mutual-aid associations for public employees are also represented, but the lead is taken by the Federation of Health Insurance Societies, or Kenporen.

Kenporen is made up of the more than 1,800 individual societies that cover employees in large firms. The societies are jointly run by management and labor, and the main constituency groups of Kenporen are the national employers' association (Nikkeiren) on the one hand and the labor peak organizations (today unified as Rengō) on the other. Despite their many conflicts in other issue areas, labor and management generally agree on health policy, opposing fee hikes and seeking more control over doctors. Kenporen hires retired MHW officials to fill several key jobs, and although its interests sometimes diverge from the official line, it is usually seen as closely integrated with the Health Insurance Bureau. In fact, the Kenporen Vice-Chairman (always a retiree from a very senior MHW position) actually serves as the sole spokesman for the payers' side – including the government – during sessions of the Central Council.

The JMA Side. The JMA side includes both *other providers* and the *Liberal Democratic Party*, who usually – though not always – cooperate with organized physicians.

1. *Other providers.* Along with its own formidable resources, JMA power rests on its claim to represent all health-care providers – an advantage that has leaked away for its counterparts in other nations. We note:

- Physicians' specialty organizations are not very well developed in Japan and are organized under the umbrella of the JMA itself. They do not publicly take independent positions on health-care issues.
- Salaried doctors, although they are a large majority of all physicians and their interests differ from those in private practice, have no organization of their own.

- Hospitals are too disparate to speak with one voice or generate much organizational power.
- Dentists and pharmacists have autonomy within their own areas. Their interests sometimes conflict with those of physicians, but they are usually susceptible to calls for unity from the JMA.
- Pharmaceutical manufacturers, nurses, and other groups that are influential in other nations have construed their interests narrowly rather than broadly and are not very active in overall heath-care policy making.

JMA dominance among providers is exemplified by its position in the main decision-making forum in health policy, the Central Council. The providers' side has eight members: two dentists, one pharmacist, and five doctors (all five named by the JMA). Until 1963 the main hospital group named a member, but because the Japan Hospital Association generally supported the government side, the JMA attacked this rule and succeeded in getting the right to name the hospital representative itself.

2. *The Liberal Democratic Party (LDP)*. From 1955 to 1993 Japan was ruled continuously by a single political party, the LDP, which in the most general sense was therefore responsible for a series of substantial changes in health policy.[7] Did the LDP have an overall philosophy, or at least a consistent viewpoint, on the big issues of how medical care should be delivered and financed? In a word, no. Only at one juncture could it be said that the conservative party was the prime initiating force in a major health policy change. That was the passage of "health insurance for all" (*kaihoken*) in the late 1950s, a key element of the LDP's early efforts to beat back a socialist challenge by expanding the welfare state.[8] Otherwise, rather than initiating policy, the LDP has served more as a ratifier, a broker, or a supporting player – albeit often a crucial one – in processes dominated by other actors.

Why has the majority party not played a more central role? First, although characterizations of the LDP as a catch-all party with no programmatic views

7 Indeed, even after losing its majority and being excluded from government in 1993, the LDP returned to power as part of a coalition in 1995 and took back the Prime Ministership in 1996.
8 There is no full account of this important policy change in English, but see Chapter 5 in this text and, for the social politics of that era, Campbell, *How Policies Change*, chap. 3, and Kent Calder, *Crisis and Compensation* (Princeton, NJ: Princeton University Press, 1988), chap. 8.

of its own are often exaggerated, as it happens health-care issues do not often impinge on the deep convictions and ideological passions of conservative politicians. Specifically, although many aspects of social policy can arouse profound disquiet among Japanese conservatives – rights of women and minorities, failures to inculcate traditional values in education, dependency, public programs for the elderly and their implications for the sanctity of the family – the specter of "socialized medicine" as endangering the free-enterprise system or the sacred doctor–patient relationship lacks the emotional wallop so dear to American conservatives.

Second, health policy fell easily into the well-understood pattern of clientelist politics for the LDP. The JMA has long been a key constituency group for conservative politicians. Individual candidates appeal for support from medical associations at the local level because doctors are seen as influential members of the community and good sources of votes – one politician credited the doctors' support as worth twenty seats to the LDP in the 1996 election.[9] The national JMA – or more precisely, its political-action wing called the Doctors' League (Ishi Seiji Renmei) – endorses candidates and provides substantial campaign funds, mostly though not exclusively to conservatives. For many years the JMA was the single largest on-the-record contributor to the Liberal Democratic Party and its candidates.[10] Physicians have also often been elected to the Diet with JMA sponsorship.[11]

From the viewpoint of conservative politicians, then, health policy would look similar to such fields as agriculture, retail business, veterans' benefits, and so forth. Instinctively they would think first about the wishes of a highly organized interest group, one that is active in their own constituencies as well as at the national level. The fact that the JMA had succeeded so well in dominating medical-care providers meant that a conservative politician rarely

---

9 Kamei Shizuka – note that he was speaking to a JMA meeting, and perhaps exaggerating a bit. *Asahi Shinbun*, Dec. 29, 1996.

10 Note that although no doubt some JMA contributions were under the table, the proportion was probably not as high for some other contributors, and most money from medical interests came through the JMA rather than being scattered among various groups, companies, and individuals. Certainly if one added up all the "political money" changing hands in Japan, doctors would fall far short of the construction industry and probably several other sectors (and indeed well short of health-care industry support of politicians in the United States in the 1990s).

11 Particularly to the Upper House, back when a large proportion of its membership was directly elected from a national list. From the 1983 election, this national list was replaced by a proportional representation system, and the number of JMA-sponsored physicians in the Diet has declined.

had to worry much about competing claims, so the JMA could usually count on consistent support by LDP backbenchers for its policies.[12]

Spectators

All the actors who normally participate in health policy making in Japan have been mentioned. We should also note some who, in other countries, might be expected to play an active role in health policy, but who tend to be on the sidelines in Japan. Partly this relatively narrow participation is due to how the political system has been organized (at least until recently) and partly to a lack of issues that would draw a wide range of participants into the process.

Opposition parties. The new political parties that emerged around the political change of 1993 have yet to reveal much character with regard to health policy (or to most other policy issues). Under the old regime, all the political parties that were in opposition to the LDP claimed that they were on the side of "the people" – for example, they criticized the introduction of small co-payments for the elderly in 1982 and for employees in 1985. With a few exceptions, however, they have not been initiators of policy, even in the sense of coming up with ideas that were later coopted by the bureaucracy or ruling party.[13] The main exception was the advent of "free medical care" for the elderly in 1972, which stemmed from a Socialist- and Communist-backed social movement in the 1960s, picked up by Tokyo's progressive Governor Minobe in 1969.[14]

The Japan Socialist Party (JSP) has always been the largest opposition party and moreover might be expected to take the role that has usually been ascribed to European socialist parties in building and maintaining welfare state policies. However, its position on many health-care issues such as financing has been complicated by its close ties with labor unions, which often have interests that conflict with non-employed people such as the elderly.

12 Since the JMA was fighting with the MHW much of the time, that meant that majority-party Dietmen would often be pitted against a bureaucratic agency rather than cooperating with it – a rather unusual configuration in the Japanese decision-making system. We return to this point in the section on arenas.

13 That has happened in other policy areas, such as social welfare, labor, and small business. See Calder, *Crisis.*

14 Campbell, *How Policies Change,* chaps. 4–5.

The fact that unions of hospital employees have organizational and financial ties to the JSP makes it harder still for the party to play a very active role.

Among other parties, the small Democratic Socialist Party represents the large-firm private-sector unions that have worked most closely with the management side within Kenporen; the party itself had not been active in health-care policy. The Clean Government Party, backed by the Buddhist Sōka Gakkai organization, has a populist image and often talks about health care and other social issues, but without much practical effect.

In a sense it is the Japan Communist Party that has been most committed to health-care issues over the years. Even before the war, radical doctors and medical students (particularly at Tokyo University) were active in providing medical care to the poor. In the postwar years Communists participated in establishing a number of cooperative hospitals and clinics that have been among the leaders in, for example, providing home health care to elderly patients. A radical critique of the medical-care establishment is shared by Communist activists and many progressive academics.

These phenomena should be seen more as products of a social and intellectual movement than as regular party politics, however. The JCP role in national policy making has been as a gadfly and as a representative of certain union interests, but the party is too small to have much impact. Of course, the fact that the LDP was in control meant that none of the opposition parties really had a chance to be responsible for policy. It is striking nonetheless that much of what they did do looked more like knee-jerk reactions without much real commitment rather than either impassioned critiques or pointed suggestions.

Interest Groups. We have already observed that the big labor union federations and Nikkeiren, the employers' association specializing in labor–management issues, are active constituents in Kenporen, the Federation of Health Insurance Societies. In that capacity they push, for example, to limit the amount of cross-subsidization to old-age health care (see Chapter 5) and to step up the reviews of health-care utilization in order to hold down medical spending (see Chapter 6). Similarly, small business representatives (such as The Japan Chamber of Commerce) have on occasion opposed hikes in the contribution rate in Government-Managed Health Insurance, and local government associations have been concerned about the fiscal health of Citizens' Health Insurance. The interesting point is that these and other big interest groups do not do much more.

That is, from the perspective of mid-1990's America, it is striking that major social interest groups are not much concerned with health-care issues except in the most narrow sense. In comparison with the United States, one important difference is that there are no major private health insurance companies with thousands of employees and vast amounts of money trying to defend their interests. Beyond that, groups representing big business, small business, farmers, the elderly, women, and other large or powerful groups in Japanese society have generally not perceived health care as vital to their interests.

Of course, one cannot compare a nation where the health-care system is seen as very problematic, especially when explicit reform efforts are high on the agenda, with a nation where the system is generally regarded as working. Still, even comparing Japan with other advanced nations with normal health-care systems, and looking at those periods when fairly substantial policy changes were in the offing, it is noteworthy that health care does not seem to be perceived as engaging vital social interests, at least as represented by organized groups.

Experts. Most of the noise in American health policy disputes comes from academic experts, mostly college professors or full-time researchers with graduate degrees in social science (or even humanities, among "ethicists") who write and talk about health care as their career. Substantial resources from universities, foundations, government, and various interested parties are available to pay salaries, research grants, and honoraria to these policy experts, who may be seeking scholarly prestige for their objective research, or may be grinding an ax belonging to themselves or another. This enormous policy community gives American fights about health care an intellectual air that amazes outsiders – elaborate theories and econometric models pile up on both sides of every argument, and a talent for academic debate has become a key political resource.

Japan has few health policy experts, and those tend to be quite divided. One group can be characterized as taking the traditional stance of Japanese academics or the intelligentsia, which is to criticize government policy from a progressive point of view. They attack the government for not providing enough money for health care and exerting too much power at the expense of patients, and they believe in equality and grass-roots participation. Leading experts from this viewpoint are Kawakami Takeshi, Maeda Nobuo, and Niki Ryū. Many journalists, particularly those associated with the *Asahi* newspaper and magazines, generally take this perspective in reporting on policy failures and scandals.

On the other side are a few insiders, whose views may well be critical but more from a technical point of view. Few economists with Ph.D.s regularly do real research on health care – the best known is Nishimura Shūzō of Kyoto University. Disciplines like hospital administration, medical-care organization, and health-services research barely exist in Japan. The Ministry of Health and Welfare and a few foundations (particularly those affiliated with pharmaceutical manufacturers) have sponsored some research projects related to health policy, but generally there is not much financial or organizational support for professional expertise. When "experts" are quoted in the press, they are often either medical doctors (often on the faculty of an elite medical school) or so-called "commentators" (hyōronka) who are mostly specialized journalists without much academic background. Recently, conservative economists have been speaking up in favor of constraints on social spending (including health care), but lacking expertise in the medical-care system, they have yet to come up with significant reform ideas on the supply side.

Whether this lack of experts is the cause or an effect, it is clear that there are many fewer health policy debates in Japan compared with the United States, and when they do occur neither theoretical arguments nor sophisticated data manipulations are very important in how they are resolved. It is true, as noted previously, that MHW bureaucrats take pride in their ability to diagnose problems and come up with solutions, but they rely mainly on monitoring a few basic data series plus common-sensical analysis (though there have been some recent exceptions). The more public rhetoric of discussions of health-care issues is usually rather unsophisticated and moralistic.

The general public. The lack of organized group interest is manifestly not because Japanese citizens are especially happy with Japanese health care. In fact, polls indicate that the Japanese are quite discontented. For example, in a 1990 five-nation Harris survey, Japanese were generally the *least* satisfied with such aspects of medical care as gaining access to advanced medicine, seeing a doctor or getting surgery promptly, and even being able to obtain quality care regardless of income (in most cases it was Americans who were *most* satisfied).[15]

---

15 Respectively, a survey by Louis Harris and Associates for the Harvard Community Health Plan, cited in *The Public Perspective* 5:1 (May/June 1994), 85; and *"Kenkōzukui to Iryō"*

Why are the Japanese so unhappy? One reason is that Japanese tend to be dissatisfied in general. In various cross-national surveys, workers have expressed unhappiness with their jobs and companies, and mothers with their children's schools, in much higher proportions in Japan than in the United States and other Western countries.[16] Those results pertain to institutions that by many accounts work better in Japan than elsewhere. And of course health care in Japan does have some serious quality problems (see Chapter 7) and a degree of public dissatisfaction is to be expected.[17]

Certainly the images that Japanese get in the media of their health-care system are overwhelmingly negative. Hospitals are portrayed as overcrowded and grubby, doctors as arrogant and overpaid. The most frequent stories are about financial scandals or some form of medical malfeasance. And despite the fact that Japanese health-care costs are extremely low by international standards, every year when estimates of total medical expenditures are released, the media play up high spending. The public clearly believes it: the Harris poll cited earlier indicated that Japanese were far more likely than Canadians and Germans to think that too much money was being spent on hospitalization, physicians, the terminally ill, and advanced technology, when in fact Japan spent considerably less than these countries. In fact, on the last two categories, about 55 percent of Japanese and only about 30 percent even of Americans thought that too much money was being spent.

So Japanese people-in-the-street apparently see their health-care system as scandal-ridden, poor in quality, and much too expensive. We might speculate that this dissatisfaction is partly due to a rather idealistic expectation that physicians should be selfless and medical care a domain of virtue. Another

ni kansuru Chōsa Kekka Hōkokusho (Tokyo: Kenporen, 1995). Note that the results of cross-national comparisons of public opinion data can vary considerably depending on question wordings and so forth. See, e.g., Robert G. Evans, ''Going for the Gold: The Redistributive Agenda Behind Market-Based Health Care Reform,'' *Journal of Health Policy, Politics and Law* 22:2 (April 1997), 427–465.

16 See Robert E. Cole, *Work, Mobility, and Participation* (Berkeley: University of California Press, 1979), and Harold W. Stevenson, *The Learning Gap: Why Our Schools Are Failing and What We Can Learn From Japanese and Chinese Education* (New York: Summit Books, 1992).

17 For example, according to a 1991 Gallup poll, the proportion of Japanese who highly rate the quality of service received from seven institutions (banks, airlines, auto repair, etc.) was on average about 14 percentage points lower than those of Americans and West Germans. However, for hospitals, only 18 percent of Japanese compared with 46–48 percent in the other two countries thought they got good service. *Public Perspective*, op. cit., 86.

reason is that few Japanese have any real basis for comparison through experience of medical care elsewhere. And note that although their feelings of dissatisfaction are clear enough, there is no way to know how *intensely* they feel about it.

In that regard, we note again that politicians and organized groups seem not to have seen health care as an issue that could mobilize many people, at least not since the expansion of the system was completed in the early 1970s. Trial balloons from the Ministry of Health and Welfare and other sources about improving quality do not seem to generate much enthusiasm. Medical care seems to be one of the many areas of life in Japan that induce constant complaints but not much action beyond a shrug of the shoulders.

ARENAS

We have now listed the main actors who actually or potentially are important in health-care policy making. But policy is not made in a vacuum: These actors interact in fairly structured spaces that we call "arenas," each with its own set of rules of the game that favor some interests or strategies over others. We take a brief tour of three arenas that are important in health policy, from the narrowest to the broadest.

The Spending and Regulations Arena

Periodically (in recent years mostly every two years), the fee schedule that covers nearly all medical goods and services in Japan is revised. Nearly always, the overall level of fees is raised, and relative fees are adjusted. The fee schedule is the main mechanism for cost control in Japanese health care, and as such it is discussed in more detail in Chapters 5 and 6. Here we briefly describe the decision-making process and the power relations among the key actors.

The arena is the Central Social Insurance Medical Care Council. It is a legally constituted advisory committee to the Welfare Minister, with its staff provided by the Medical Care Division of the Health Insurance Bureau. Unlike many other advisory committees in Japan, which either just give general advice or serve as ratifiers or rubber stamps for bureaucratic initiatives, the Central Council is supposed to make real decisions by forcing agreement between contending sides.[18] Its twenty members include eight on the provider side (five doctors, all picked by the JMA including one who is supposed to represent hospitals, plus two dentists and a pharmacist named by their associations), eight on the payer side (four insurers, plus two each from labor picked by the union federations and from management picked by Nikkeiren), and four "public interest" members (typically including a journalist and two or three academic economists).

Both the membership of the Central Council and its procedures – in particular, whether it could initiate its own recommendations or should merely react to those proposed by Ministry officials – have been the subject of sharp fights in years past. The JMA won the early battles, but the MHW regained the advantage in the 1980s (see Chapter 5). No matter which side has had the edge, however, the key point is that the Central Council mechanism has brought the contenders together in the same room on a regular basis to bargain over a very complicated deal. It handles overall levels of payment, relative payments across groups of providers, and a host of regulations.

In that sense, the Central Council negotiations resemble labor-contract bargaining in a firm. The interests of the two sides conflict in fundamental ways, but they get to know each other well, to the point that much of the outcome can be readily predicted by insiders. When that happens the process tends to get ritualized. And of course, as in a labor negotiation, each side needs the other, so there is constant pressure for agreement. On the other hand, each side retains the ability to say no if the deal is not to its satisfaction.

The analogy to labor contract bargaining breaks down a bit when we consider the larger context. In a free-market economy, a company's management and union are relatively free to decide what to bargain about, and if negotiations do break down and a strike results, the outcome will depend on a test of strength and will between the two parties. In national health-care bargaining, the issues are essentially matters of public policy, imbedded in laws that must be passed by the legislature, and requiring funds that are allocated through a very bureaucratic and political budgeting process. Moreover, a breakdown in negotiations does not just escalate the conflict between the two

---

18   For advisory councils in Japan, see Frank Schwartz, "Of Fairy Cloaks and Familiar Talks: The Politics of Consultation," in Gary D. Allinson and Yasunori Sone, eds., *Political Dynamics in Contemporary Japan* (Ithaca, NY: Cornell University Press, 1993), pp. 217–241.

parties; it throws the issue into a broader arena where other powerful actors are drawn into the fray.

Although the Central Council is the key institution in the spending and regulations arena, its meetings themselves are not the site of most important negotiations. Indeed they are usually brief, pro forma affairs that simply ratify decisions made behind the scenes – for example in last-stage bilateral negotiations between one MHW official and one JMA representative. However, any behind-the-scene deal has to be acceptable to the entire Council membership or it would not be ratified and the entire process would break down – as in fact did happen in the 1950s and '60s. Political struggles led to compromise and then gradual agreement on a set of unwritten rules-of-the-game. Under those rules the process today looks rather routine, as long as the results approximate those that would have resulted from an open conflict.

The Subgovernmental Arena

The Central Council process can be so routinized because it deals with such a narrow list of recurring issues. Wider participation and more flexibility is needed for broader issues. Most of these are handled in what can be called the health "subgovernment." In general, the national decision-making process in Japan is dominated by structures of a particular government agency (ministry or bureau), one or a few organized interest groups, and a set of LDP legislators who specialize in that policy area. The term "subgovernment" was coined by observers of American politics to describe the alliances of agency, interest groups, and Congressional committees characteristic of Washington (a similar term is "iron triangle").[19] The members may not always agree, but they usually share an interest in maintaining their policy area's portion of national resources, and they would rather work out differences among themselves than deal with the uncertain prospects of interventions by outsiders. Over time a common view of the world, a sense of what problems are important and what solutions are at least worth discussing, will grow up within the subgovernment and indeed the broader policy community

---

19 The nuances of these terms differ: For recent interpretations, see Paul A Sabatier and Hank C. Jenkins-Smith, *Policy Change and Learning: An Advocacy Coalition Approach* (Boulder, CO: Westview, 1993), and Michael M. Atkinson and William D. Coleman, "Policy Networks, Policy Communities and the Problems of Governance," *Governance* 5:2 (April 1992), 154–180. For Japan, see John Creighton Campbell, "Bureaucratic Primacy: Japanese Policy Communities in an American Perspective," *Governance* 2:1 (January, 1989), 5–22.

(including the specialized media and various policy experts as well as the bureaucrats, politicians, and interest groups at the core).

The subgovernmental pattern of decision making may well be even more important in Japan than in the United States, but there are some differences in how things work. One difference is that Japan is a cabinet–parliament rather than president–congress system and was ruled by the same party for decades. The political component of a Japanese subgovernment is not so much a Diet committee, which of course includes members of all parties, but rather a group within the Liberal Democratic Party. In terms of formal organization, the main group is a "division" (*bukai*) of the LDP's Policy Affairs Research Council (PARC), more or less one per ministry. Each PARC division reviews new policy initiatives by its ministry and is especially active at budget time, ensuring that political interests are included in the ministry's requests and then serving as "cheerleaders" (*ōendan*) to get the requests approved by the Finance Ministry.

Less formally, the three or four senior politicians who have gone through a long apprenticeship as specialists in a particular policy area become leaders of what are called "family Dietmen" (*zoku giin*; note *zoku* is sometimes translated as "tribe"). That usually means that they are close to the ministry, in terms of serving as its high-level fixers of political problems. Most often that involves going to bat for the ministry against other *zoku* in the interministerial (or intersubgovernmental) disputes that are the life-blood of the Japanese policy process. It also involves going back to the ministry to reconcile bureaucrats when their cause fails. Of course a *zoku* Dietman will often be quite influential in specialized policy making himself, although taking too strong a position on policy issues can vitiate his ability to be an effective broker.

These are patterns that hold through most of the Japanese governmental system. The health policy subgovernment is unusual because, as already noted, the Japan Medical Association has been in perpetual conflict with the Ministry of Health and Welfare and by strategic use of its voting and financial power has enlisted the Liberal Democratic Party as an ally. That means with regard to many issues that the LDP politicians who specialize in health policy will oppose the bureaucrats rather than the more usual pattern of cooperating with them. A nearly unique organizational pattern resulted.

That is, the regular PARC division remains allied with the Ministry, because that is normal for divisions and because its scope goes beyond the conflictual health-care policy area to include pension and welfare matters where there is little disagreement.[20] However, pro-JMA sentiments are also organizationally represented by "temporary" committees within the PARC, such as the Medical Problems Investigative Committee. Disputes between the JMA and MHW were thus replicated inside the LDP's policy-making structure.

These conflicting pressures have put the *zoku* leaders in a particularly delicate position, although they made their role as fixers even more important and probably added to their power – social policy has often been seen as more dominated by the specialized LDP "bosses" than have most other policy areas. From Nadao Hirokichi in the early years to Hashimoto Ryūtarō during the health insurance reform efforts of the 1980s, welfare *zoku* leaders have combined a long friendship with the JMA and an intimate relationship with MHW officials. In the midst of battle, they would go back and forth between the contenders to arrange the deals that solved the problem. Of course, conflict is only part of the story, and in many respects the health policy subgovernment functioned in an ordinary way to provide links among bureaucrats, politicians, and interest groups.

The LDP's role as the sole ruling party ended in 1993, and in the unsettled political situation since then, it has been difficult to discern how decision-making patterns will change. Ministry officials have had to consult with a larger number of politicians than earlier, but they probably have not had to pay as much attention. Still, we would expect a reestablishment of the basic pattern of most decision making being handled through established relationships among bureaucrats, politicians, and interest-group representatives who specialize in a particular policy area. Of course, in the future as in the past, some issues will spill over subgovernment boundaries and involve actors who usually pay no attention to specialized policy concerns – even those at the highest levels of the governmental system.

The General Arena

Although the great majority of policy decisions are made by specialized actors at the subgovernment level in all advanced nations, the most important issues have to be dealt with by "heavyweight" actors, the leaders in the

---

20 The PARC structure parallels that of Diet standing committees. For many years, only one Diet committee and therefore one PARC division handled both the MHW and the Labor Ministry, but they were separated in both cases in 1991.

executive and legislative branches plus top interest groups and the national media. What makes an issue important enough to demand the attention of these busy actors might be broad public interest, high cost, some new policy priority for the nation, or a conflict at lower levels that gets in the way of resolution in the usual fashion.

Subgovernmental-level conflict of that sort has not infrequently propelled some health-care issues up into the general arena, either because of an offensive campaign by the Japan Medical Association, or when the Ministry of Health and Welfare was about to win some point and the doctors protested. A good example of the former case is portrayed in Steslicke's *Doctors in Politics*: In 1960–61 a favorable political opportunity permitted several of the JMA's "long-smoldering demands to explode into a general political struggle."[21] Only after the threat of a doctors' strike could a deal be struck between Takemi, the Welfare Ministry, and the head of the LDP PARC. A decade later, 50,000 doctors actually did go "on strike" to fight against an MHW attempt to reform the fee schedule on its own terms, and the Prime Minister had to enter the fray.

In fact, for a substantial period, health care probably ranked only slightly behind matters of foreign policy or other highly ideological issues in its capacity to disrupt normal politics and bring on intense conflict. Of course, issues that affect the average citizen's pocketbook, such as increased contributions or co-payments, will often attract sharp attacks from the opposition parties in the name of the people's interest. The reasons beyond that are the intensity of doctors' feelings about several public policy issues, and the substantial resources commanded by the JMA once an issue goes beyond accustomed channels. As noted earlier, doctors could make a credible threat to go on strike, and they had the money and the influence over votes to get many LDP politicians on their side (both ordinary backbenchers and the *zoku* leaders who specialize in health and welfare matters).

But JMA power and its ability to disrupt normal politics was greater still because of Takemi Tarō himself. His mercurial disposition, which enabled him to shift from charm to bullying to principled eloquence at a moment's notice, always unsettled opponents and kept even his allies guessing. His close personal ties with many top politicians (including a strategic marriage alliance) and the large sums of cash he allegedly kept on hand increased his capacity to maneuver. Beyond that, as Steslicke observed, Takemi saw his

---

21 *Nihon Ishikai Zasshi* (November 1, 1962), an official JMA organ, cited by Steslicke, p. 70.

role as leader as ''to speak for, to educate, to arouse, and to mobilize his followers, but above all to maneuver, and in so doing to create new expectations and new circumstances.''[22]

General arena processes are by their nature unpredictable because they do not move through normal channels and because heavyweight actors, unlike the full-time specialists in a given policy area, can be quickly attracted to an issue but then just as quickly lose attention. In those situations, someone like Takemi is at his best, which is why just the threat to take an issue public was often an effective tactic for the JMA even within more routine, subgovernmental-level politics.

Or at least that was true while Takemi was in charge. After the late 1970s, health-care issues were not *pushed* up into the general arena at the initiative of the JMA; they were *pulled* up by heavyweight actors as a result of new national priorities. In 1981–85, the LDP top leadership (especially Nakasone Yasuhiro as Administrative Management Agency head and then Prime Minister), organized big business, and the Ministry of Finance combined to wage an ''administrative reform'' (*gyōsei kaikaku*) campaign of fiscal austerity and privatization. A substantial portion of the economizing of public spending came from health care, by revisions in the fee schedule and a variety of other measures including limitations on new hospital beds, cross-subsidies, and new co-payments.

The administrative reform campaign was highly publicized and was portrayed as energetic market-oriented reformers taking up the cudgels on behalf of the general public to sweep away bureaucracy, overregulation, entrenched special interests, and cozy deals. The wealthy and arrogant doctors were an obvious target. Rather than actively fighting back in public, however, the JMA played a more passive, rear-guard defense aimed at protecting as much as they could of their members' prerogatives and income.

In the decade since the mid-1980s, no health policy issue really reached the general arena agenda (until the proposal for public long-term-care insurance in 1996 – see Chapter 4). Why not? Mainly because the system has worked, in two senses. First, day-to-day disputes could be worked out within the confines of the Central Council or the subgovernmental arena. Second, no actor with much power has been dissatisfied enough to make serious trouble. Predicting whether the latter condition will continue to hold, or

22 Steslicke, p. 223. Also see Taro Takemi, *Socialized Medicine in Japan : Essays, Papers and Addresses* (Tokyo : Japan Medical Association, 1982).

whether health-care policy will soon face another period of upheaval and debate, requires a closer look at the ebb and flow of issues in this field.

AGENDA

Up to World War II, the initiative for forcing change in the Japanese health-care system was almost entirely in the hands of the government. It had to take political pressures from physicians and others into account, but it dominated the agenda. New ideas in health policy came overwhelmingly from bureaucrats and their allies, with other actors mostly just reacting. During the war, of course, the government had nearly its own way as it installed a top–down public system.

What would Japanese health care look like today if bureaucrats had continued to monopolize the policy agenda? The likely answer is a socialized delivery system, a British-style National Health Service. The Beveridge Report in wartime Great Britain had impressed social policy experts in Japan as elsewhere. The old Bismarckian social-corporatist notions of social policy, with their nuance of payoffs to the working class to avoid revolution, had been discredited by defeat, but they could well have served to pave the way for a more democratic-socialist conception of collective provision of public goods.

But the bureaucrats did not run things. American Occupation authorities, at first convinced of the virtues of the American way in this as in other fields, quickly dismantled the wartime medical-care apparatus and thereby obviated the possibility of a quick transition into a socialized delivery system. In the longer run, empowered by the strengthening of the institutions of parliamentary democracy, the Japan Medical Association asserted its own views of how health care should be organized.

This confrontation led to one of the sharpest and longest debates about public policy in Japan's modern history. Private-practice physicians challenged bureaucratic hegemony on a piecemeal basis during the Occupation period and into the mid-1950s, although the JMA did not formulate a coherent strategy for accomplishing its vision of Japanese health care until Takemi became president in 1957. The debate then raged until perhaps the early 1970s, when there was both a political standoff and a certain exhaustion of ideas – everyone in Japan must have gotten completely bored with the rhetoric of health policy.

Ideological Conflict: Public Health Versus Physician Professionalism

What was the debate about? As noted at the beginning of this chapter, the MHW took a "public-health" position, an ideal of universal good health across the population, assured by a variety of public programs. The origins of this view could be traced back to campaigns against infectious diseases such as venereal diseases, leprosy, and especially tuberculosis going back to the nineteenth century, and to the quasi-military organization of medical services in the wartime years.[23] Immediately after the war, the MHW even built a "model" public-health center in Tokyo, where a large staff of government-employed physicians and nurses would provide comprehensive health services. This policy failed, but hopes of a public health hegemony persisted. Doctors might not quite be public employees, but their behavior (and their incomes) would be directly regulated by government. There would be a heavy emphasis on screening and preventive care, and much medical care would be delivered through public-health centers and large hospitals.

In contrast, the physicians' view of health care was based on the ideal of professional autonomy. The ideology of JMA members was that they took the interests of the patient to heart, adhered to high ethical standards, and were competent to diagnose patients and to choose and carry out the best treatment. There was no need for the government to prescribe guidelines, nor for health insurance societies to examine physicians' records. The JMA wanted to get rid of employment-based health insurance because it allowed the government or the societies too much opportunity to interfere with physicians and burden them with paperwork. All Japanese should be covered under one system, community health insurance, administered by a government agency at the prefectural level that would be responsive to the needs of residents (and not incidentally of doctors).

This debate was hardly a high-minded exchange of ideas. In fact, each side spent less time extolling its own vision than attacking the other. From the vantage point of private-practice physicians, the MHW's image of health care looked like paternalistic bureaucratism at best or authoritarian control at worst. The JMA charged that the bureaucrats cared nothing for patients, only for their own power and the cold discipline of technocratic administration. From the vantage point of the government, the JMA's ethos of the profes-

---

23   See Margaret Powell and Masahira Anesaki, *Health Care in Japan* (London: Routledge, 1990) for a brief historical account.

46

sional looked more like the instinct of the shopkeeper. Bureaucrats would point for example to doctors selling drugs as the antithesis of the professional practice of medicine; the JMA's tenacious defense of that privilege proved that doctors cared only about money.

Actually, the confrontational rhetoric of this debate tended to obscure a substantial overlap between the two positions, at least when compared with ideas about health care found in some other nations. First, everyone in Japan accepted the legitimacy of the government's role in medical care, at least in organizing its financing. Second, equality was a dominant value both for the MHW and the JMA; in effect, both sides took provision of equal treatment as overriding other concerns, such as quality. Third, in the early years both sides (and almost everyone else) saw the main need in health care as expansion, providing more services to more people.

Because of these fundamental agreements, and despite the rhetoric, the specific issues in actual disputes usually came down to money and power rather than ideology. The money issues pitted the MHW's interests in cost containment (partly in order to finance further expansions) against the doctors' desire for income, and the doctors generally won. The power issues were more complicated; they pertained to the bureaucrats' desire to constrain doctors' treatment decisions on the one hand and the doctors' desire to participate in policy decision making on the other. The typical outcome was the pattern that Richard Samuels (in writing about government-industry relations) called "reciprocal consent."[24] The doctors could not win autonomy but achieved substantial influence over policy.

By the early 1970s it had become quite clear that the battles were ending in compromise. The political advantages of the JMA meant that they won most of the specific points, but they did not have enough power to defeat the MHW and reshape the overall health-care system. A truce was called on terms largely favorable to the JMA in terms of money but regaining some formal prerogatives for the MHW (see Chapter 5).

The impact of the ideological debate was thus less in the sphere of actual policy outcomes as it was in opening up the discourse about health care to ideas from a different source than the government – ideas that were not just

---

24 In brief, both sides are active at both levels, with the balance of influence shifting as environmental changes affect power resources. Richard J. Samuels, *The Business of the Japanese State: Energy Markets in Comparative and Historical Perspective* (Ithaca, NY: Cornell University Press, 1987).

the idle thoughts of intellectuals writing magazine articles but backed by real interests and political power. In that sense, the strong advocacy by the JMA was significant beyond the health-care policy arena in building Japan's post-war democratic system.[25]

Of course that impact came when the JMA's challenge to the government was fresh. As the confrontation continued in one specific battle after another, the ideas expressed by both sides did not change much, and the debate became ritualized. The fact that other actors had become subordinated to the JMA on the one hand or the MHW on the other meant that no one else was discontented or independent or powerful enough to voice new and different ideas about health care.

Health Economics

In fact, when a new ideology did emerge, it was inside the Ministry of Health and Welfare itself. The reason was two changes in the environment of policy making. First, the task of expanding health care had essentially been accomplished by the early 1970s. Second, in the late 1970s the issue of cost was coming to the fore. That concern had two roots: rapid increases in both health-care spending and the overall government deficit in Japan, and an intellectual and political movement against "big government" in general and in the medical-care field in several foreign nations, particularly Great Britain and the United States.

Thus, when young MHW officials came back from the United States fresh from exposure to the newest trends in health economics, their superiors were ready to listen. Of course, they heard what they wanted to hear: more about efficiency simply in the sense of cost containment, and less about the values of individual choice or of quality. Doctrines of health economics – evoked if not necessarily really applied – came to provide ideological support for the Ministry's new emphasis on holding down costs.

Although Takemi had often extolled the virtues of the free market, this new thinking was in no sense favorable to the JMA. A key focus, in the tradition of the Chicago school, was attacking the rent-seekers who could take advantage of regulations. The target was private-practice physicians. The leading exponent of health economics was Yoshimura Hitoshi, the brightest

---

25 Cf. Steslicke, chap. 9. Of course, the JMA played this role from within the conservative camp, not as a radical critic like the Japan Teachers Union.

and most pugnacious official of his generation in the MHW. Years ago, a study group that Yoshimura had organized to look into universal coverage had devoted much of its energy to thinking up strategies to defeat the JMA.[26] In a succession of high-level posts culminating as Vice-Minister, he led the successful campaign to restrain medical costs.

No parallel intellectual awakening occurred among the doctors. Indeed, now that the dominant problem had become high costs rather than expansion, no plausible argument was really open for the JMA. It in effect quietly abandoned its quest to transform health care or to increase the flow of resources into the system in favor of defending the private-practice physicians' substantial slice of the pie. The JMA's protectionist policy went so far as tacit support of the MHW's plan to limit the number of hospital beds in the mid-1980s. Such strictures had once been anathema to the JMA, but now aging doctors saw new hospitals as threats to their comfortable practices.

The initiative in defining the health policy agenda therefore passed almost entirely to the MHW, which in the first half of the 1980s proposed a series of cost-cutting measures. As could be anticipated, although the rise of economic thinking had provoked a lively debate within the ministry and helped stimulate the policy shift toward cost containment, the ideology of the health economists did not really take root. The new policies – bed limitations being just one example – generally tried to constrain costs by increasing rather than lightening regulations. The key strategy was to discourage overusage by moving some reimbursements away from fee-for-service toward bundled or per capita payments (see Chapter 6), but with little if any gesture toward increasing competition.

And, in fact, even the ministry's traditional public-health vision retained vitality in the period of austerity. An important step in the campaign to hold down costs was the Health Care for the Aged Bill, which the MHW sent to the Diet in May 1981. This bill added a small co-payment to what had been "free" medical care for the elderly, and it provided extensive cross-subsidization from employee health insurance to older people's coverage (see Chapter 4). At the same time, it established a substantial new set of targeted health services, including screening, prevention, education, and home health care not just for the elderly but for everyone over 40. The logic was that only by better health maintenance, requiring public programs, could long-

26 Tahara Sōichirō, *Nihon no Daikaizō: Shin-Nihon no Kanryō* (Tokyo: Bungei Shunjū, 1986), pp. 292–303.

term health-care costs be held down – a classic public-health argument. There was also a provision to build health-care centers for the elderly around the country.

Incidentally, the doctors were ready for this fight on a battleground they knew very well: Many local medical associations had already clashed with public-health officials over home health care (which was largely carried out by public-health nurses without direct supervision by physicians), and the health-care–centers idea was a direct threat to their practices. Political allies in the LDP and the opposition parties were mobilized to amend the bill, giving physicians a bigger role in the new programs, killing the centers, and assuring the JMA of a key voice in implementing the law.[27] The old debates could still arouse emotion and effective political action.

In short, the new health economics have not really transformed the health policy agenda in Japan, at least not so far. As has been noted, the MHW bureaucrats were really interested in using this ideology to legitimize efforts at cost containment. There was no natural constituency to pick up and amplify its broader implications, in that Japan has hardly any academic community devoted to health policy, nor for that matter much attachment to the "liberal philosophy" in general. The notion that a patient could get more choices if willing to pay more has been limited to quite narrow concerns.[28] In the near future, at least, health-economics ideas will probably continue to be used mainly as a justification for efforts to shift costs to patients.

Science and Consumerism

The new image that scholars and journalists in Japan and overseas keep expecting to dawn is consumerism. The survey research cited earlier makes it clear that dissatisfaction with the health-care system is widespread, and television and the newspapers constantly report on people's irritation with

---

27 That is, the venue for writing regulations under the new bill was switched to the Central Social Insurance Medical Care Council, which the JMA dominated, rather than a newly created advisory committee that MHW bureaucrats could control. For a case study of this bill, see Campbell, *How Policies Change*, pp. 288–297.

28 For example, at a 1993 conference on Japanese health care in New York, one leading official responded to a general question about the ministry's current policy priorities with a little speech about how removing hospital meals from insurance coverage would save money and would encourage consumers to demand more variety and taste. His listeners were bemused – the problem hardly seemed of a piece with their own worries about the many thorny problems plaguing the American health-care system.

long waits and overcrowding, the reluctance of Japanese doctors to share information, and periodic scandals of one sort or another.

Criticism from physicians and other experts, particularly those with overseas experience, is often still more pointed about the lack of a scientific regard for excellence in Japan. Wistful remarks about state-of-the-art surgery (as well as the plush facilities) at some famous American medical center are common. A few critics would go so far as some American commentators in claiming that the best health-care system is the one that can provide the absolute best treatment to any one patient, as measured by where some wealthy person would go to have a tricky operation. Others, more sensible, emphasize the lack of peer review and other routine mechanisms to institutionalize high professional standards among physicians.

However, although the lack of much informed consent and other failings of the Japanese health-care system from a consumerist or scientific point of view have been identified as social problems in Japan, it is not at all clear that they have really reached the national agenda in the sense that anyone expects significant change soon. Reasons include inertia, vested interests, and the persistence of ideologies – in particular, the attachment of physicians to the practice of medicine as an art form, which requires autonomy not only from government but from the strictures of purportedly universal scientific protocols (which tended to be associated with cost-cutting guidelines pushed by insurers). More fundamentally the key is that the underlying principle of the Japanese health-care system is equality, among patients and among providers, and equality and quality tend to contradict (see Chapters 3 and 7). Thus, a proposal for a major reorientation toward quality would have to contemplate massive organizational reforms and the prospect of confronting deeply held assumptions about how health care should work.

CONCLUSION

Japanese health politics in recent years certainly looks quite different from the intense political and ideological clashes that have occurred in the United States. Our brief review indicates that the active participants are fewer and more organized, the arenas in which decisions are made more routinized, and the issues under discussion less important. Why do these differences exist?

One set of explanations would focus on fundamental and stable differences between Japanese and American institutions and style. One might observe that Japanese political parties (and voters) are not much concerned with issues, interest groups are passive and hierarchical, bureaucrats outweigh both politicians and academic experts, decisions are made privately in small circles, and the process works by striving for consensus about small matters rather than sharp conflict over principles or comprehensive policies.

Such propositions can be helpful in understanding many aspects of Japanese politics in general and of specific policy areas like health care. But they can be profoundly misleading as well. Go back 15 or 25 years in the health-care area, and we find plenty of arguments about principles, sharp interest-group conflicts, and mobilizations of political power that forced significant compromises in public policy. The evolution of health-care politics in Japan was by no means a simple story of bureaucracy-led consensus.

Nonetheless, the key to later developments was that, within these struggles, the advantage lay with two key participants. The providers' side was dominated by private-practice physicians organized by the Japan Medical Association. How their role has affected health-care delivery in Japan is a main theme of the next chapter. On the payers' side, the Ministry of Health and Welfare has similarly prevailed, and the consequences of that pattern for the social insurance system and cost control will be explicated in Chapters 4 and 5.

3

Health-Care Providers

ONE reason why American health-care costs got so high is that the American hospital was so well organized for making money. Entrepreneurial coalitions of highly trained managers and savvy physicians alertly searched out every opportunity to maximize the revenues that brought them more money and power. Japan was different. It is not that Japanese physicians and others in the health-care system were more altruistic and less interested in money or power. They simply were more amateurish – or, to look beyond personality, they grew up in a more structured and regulated system, where the payoffs for entrepreneurship were limited, and the penalties for bumbling along were minor.

How did this system come about? Was it a far-sighted design on the part of the Japanese government, or more a story of conflict and compromise? The first half of this chapter is a brief history of how the health-care delivery system developed in Japan. The latter half is an overview of Japanese providers, illustrated by describing six prototypes. We then explore the cost implications of the Japanese pattern of health-care provision, with a few possible lessons for the United States. The key question of whether costs have been controlled in the Japanese system at the expense of quality will be taken up in Chapter 7, after taking a look at other aspects of the Japanese system.

THE LEGACY OF THE PAST

After even a brief encounter, Americans are often struck by such "traditional" aspects of the Japanese health-care system as long hospital stays and the heavy reliance on many (but not very potent) medications. Japan resorts to far less surgery and tends to choose conservative therapy in general. Such legacies are more than superficial in that the entire health-care system is very much a product of its own history. Note particularly that it was not really

53

transformed in the Meiji period, as many Japanese assume, nor during the postwar occupation, as many American observers believe.

The Indigenous System

Japan already had a well established network of practitioners in Chinese medicine by the middle of the eighteenth century.[1] Chinese medicine took a holistic approach, focusing on the need to restore the balance between the two opposing forces of *yin* and *yang* within the body. Medication was the main treatment, to the extent that these practitioners were often known as apothecaries (*kusushi*).[2] Payment was theoretically made only for the cost of the drugs – it was regarded as morally unacceptable to accept fees for performing a humane service, so practitioners were not supposed to bill patients. Once when a practitioner sued a patient for nonpayment, the municipal government of Edo (present-day Tokyo) came out with a verdict strongly condemning the plaintiff: The official view was that practitioners in medicine should not demand payment.[3] However, the unstated quid pro quo was that patients were expected to pay according to their ability, and therefore munificently if they had the means. This norm served a useful purpose for the government: It was absolved of the responsibility of providing public assistance for medical care because the practitioner's duty to provide services and the patient's obligation to pay were not directly connected.

Medical practice was an exception to the rigidly divided society of that time because it was open to all classes and there was competition based on skill.[4] Practitioners recognized a hierarchy among themselves, with those ap-

---

1 A very small minority practiced Western medicine, especially in the field of obstetrics and surgery. It had been introduced by the Portuguese in the sixteenth century and was one of the few foreign ideas that were allowed during the self-imposed policy of isolation that lasted from 1639 to 1854. See Sakai Shizu, *Nihon no Iryōshi* (Tokyo: Tokyo Shobō, 1982) for more details.

2 Chinese medicine (*kanpō*) is still quite popular as an alternative form of health care today. The medications are mostly sold over-the-counter by specialized pharmacies, although a few are included in the health-insurance fee schedule and are prescribed or dispensed by regular physicians. Acupuncture and other traditional practices are also widely used. See Margaret Lock, *East Asian Medicine in Urban Japan: Varieties of Medical Experience* (Berkeley: University of California Press, 1980).

3 Fuse Shōichi, *Ishi no Rekishi* (Tokyo: Chūō Kōron Sha, 1979).

4 For example, medical practitioners who were personal physicians to a feudal lord would be considered samurai, the warrior class (though of a low order within it), or would be raised to this class upon being appointed.

pointed as personal physicians to the feudal lord being ranked the highest. Despite the austere rule of not demanding payment from the patients, many practitioners were able to become quite wealthy. Indeed, it could be said that deemphasizing money was part of their strategy to advance their position in society, because if it became explicit that they depended on the practice of medicine for their livelihood, they would be seen as having the same low rank as an artisan. It was as scholars possessing knowledge of medicine that they would rank high, because their skills were esteemed in Confucian teaching (they fulfilled the sacrosanct filial duty of maintaining the health of one's parents).

Compared with Western nations, there was little development of guilds and professional identity among medical practitioners in Japan, and there was also little provision of institutional care for the sick and indigent either by religious organizations or by government. The selfless practice of philanthropy was not a religious duty for the popular Buddhist and Shinto sects, which promised the granting of secular wishes, nor was it a secular duty under the Confucian ideology favored by the rulers, which emphasized practical ethics. Care of the ill, disabled, and elderly was regarded as the responsibility of the family.

From the Meiji Era to the End of World War II

With the inauguration of the Emperor Meiji in 1868, the government embarked on a policy of rapid Westernization throughout society. The early years in particular were characterized by wholesale and enthusiastic adoption of Western ideas and institutions. In health care, the first edicts issued in 1875 proclaimed that in the future only Western medicine would be given official recognition, and eventually all practitioners would have to sit for a national licensing examination. The first step was to invite German physicians to come and teach at the new government medical school in Tokyo in 1871. In retrospect, these edicts were very radical compared with the development of medical care in other non-Western countries.[5] The Meiji leaders soon realized that they had to be more realistic, however. For one thing, little public money could be allocated to health care because the country was facing foreign aggression and internal discord. Available resources had to be in-

---

5   In China, Korea, and India, for example, parallel schools were established for the teaching of indigenous medicine.

vested in defense and building the industrial infrastructure (*fukoku kyōhei*, rich country-strong military, was the slogan). Moreover, to grant licenses only to physicians trained in Western medicine would mean that existing practitioners would be deprived of their livelihood, and most of the population would be denied access.

Compromises were therefore inevitable. First, most of the available resources were put into one medical school, that of the University of Tokyo. The students would be taught by German professors at the same high level as in Germany. After completing their training, they would be appointed as faculty at other schools. Later in the century some of these schools were raised to university level, but others (including most of the private ones) remained at the vocational-school level.[6] This pattern led to a difference in status among the physicians that in some ways reconstituted the hierarchical structure of the previous period. Indeed, many thought that university hospital physicians behaved exactly like retainers of feudal lords, if not like the lords themselves.

The second compromise occurred in 1882, the year before medical licenses were to be granted only to those who had studied Western medicine. The government "grandfathered-in" the existing practitioners of Chinese medicine – and even their sons – so they could continue to practice indefinitely. The pattern of medical practice was accordingly eventually transformed to the Western model, but the basic structure of the indigenous system was left intact.

In one area, hospitals, it was necessary to adopt a completely new method of delivering care. As noted earlier, before the Meiji era there had been virtually no public or religious institutions that could serve as nuclei for hospitals. This institution therefore developed quite differently than in the West. For one thing, hospitals had no association with care for the indigent (in fact, hospitals were the first to introduce regular fees because they were not constrained by the old rule of not demanding payment from patients). Another major difference was that since Japan had no tradition of community-based philanthropic activities, the task of establishing hospitals was taken on by the government on the one hand or by individual physicians on the other.[7]

---

6 An exception to the low status of the private-sector was the medical-school established by Keio University in 1920. From the very beginning, it was at equal standing with the national universities.

7 Exceptionally, a few hospitals were established by missionaries, such as one by the Salvation Army in 1911. A charity hospital was built in 1916 by the Saiseikai Foundation, endowed

Hospitals in Japan were therefore built for the following specific purposes. The first was for teaching and research. Since Western medicine could not be taught without studying patients, hospitals had to be built along with medical schools. The second was for the army and navy. The several rebellions and wars of the Meiji era created a pressing need for hospitals to treat combat-related diseases and injuries. The third type was established by the local governments for quarantine of communicable and venereal disease.[8] The fourth type, to become the most numerous, was built by private practitioners as extensions to their offices. In all four cases, the hospital was regarded as very much the doctor's workshop, and the physician as the director carried both clinical and administrative responsibilities. Hospitals therefore failed to develop an identity independent from physicians.

The independence of hospitals was further weakened by the control over their medical staff by the professors of prestigious medical schools. Physicians were rotated at the whim of the professor within the closed network of the university clinical department and its affiliated hospitals. Although this arrangement developed partly as a result of the acute shortage of physicians – hospital founders had to beg the professors to send physicians – it fitted very well with the vertical structure of the Japanese society. Hierarchical relations were formed among physicians within the close-knit, family-like network in each clinical department, presided over by the patriarchal figure of the professor. The strength of these vertical relationships made the development of professional organizations difficult. As a result, practice patterns tended to differ from university to university, or even within the same university if the physicians did not belong to the same clinical department.[9]

Another problem was that hospital physicians tended to be more concerned with research than with clinical medicine because their career advancement depended on the approval of the professor. Young physicians concentrated on obtaining the research degree of Doctor of Medical Science (*igaku ha-*

by the Emperor, from Bismarckian motives: The main objective was to head off the incipient socialist movement.

8   Following the central government's lead, some early teaching and community hospitals had also been established by a few prefectures. However, they were forced to close when the central government prohibited funding from local taxes in 1887.

9   The large clinical specialties of internal medicine and surgery were usually divided into the first, second, and third departments. Each was a self-contained, autonomous unit, encompassing all the subspecialties and having its own group of affiliated hospitals. This pattern has continued to the present day.

kase), which came to be regarded as a mark of professional competence by the public because there was no formal system of accreditation for specialists.

Despite the tensions inherent in this hierarchical system, most physicians were relatively satisfied with their positions. Attaining a senior position in a prestigious hospital was denied to anyone not a graduate of the elite medical schools, but to the vast majority of physicians, hospital appointments were only a temporary stage in their careers. Even the most elite graduates expected eventually to go into private practice, where a high income was almost guaranteed because of the continued shortage of trained physicians.[10] Doctors no longer had access to hospital facilities once they became private practitioners, but those who wanted to continue to perform surgical operations or provide inpatient care could do so by building small hospitals next to their offices. The most successful of these continued to expand until they rivaled the large hospitals in the public sector.[11]

There was thus a continuum from physicians' offices to small hospitals to large hospitals. There was also not much distinction between specialists and general practitioners. Those who went into open practice continued to regard themselves as specialists, but in fact they mostly provided primary care.

The general public did not see much change in medical care. Most went on seeing private practitioners and were treated mainly with medication obtained directly from the physician. Instead of herbal medicine, the most common form would probably be bicarbonate of soda for stomach upsets and other such simple but modern remedies. Payment was usually still made primarily for the medication,[12] and although some physicians started to adopt regular fees, others continued to accept whatever amount the patient was willing to give (until the full introduction of social insurance). People seldom visited hospitals, and even when they were hospitalized (except in military hospitals), nursing care continued to be provided primarily by family members who would bring in bedding and prepare meals. Nurses were trained

---

10 When income tax was introduced in 1887, physicians paid a full 16 percent of the total collected. About half of the physicians had annual incomes of over ¥500, more than four times that of elementary school teachers. Tatsukawa Shōji, *Meiji Iji Ōrai* (Tokyo: Shinchōsha, 1995), p. 95. The years around the turn of the century are known as the "golden age of the private practitioner" (*kaigyōi ōgon jidai*).

11 In the postwar period, some physicians actually succeeded in expanding their offices to medical-schools: The Kawasaki Medical School is one example.

12 The importance of dispensing was apparent from the fact that the consultation fee for a repeat visit could not be billed if medication was dispensed (until 1967 – see Chapter 6 for more details).

almost solely for the purpose of assisting physicians. University hospitals were looked upon with particular awe as they appeared to be reserved for the elite; ordinary people lacked the resources to be admitted unless they were certified as being needed for teaching purposes (*gakuyō kanja*). For the chronically ill and disabled, care within the household continued to be the norm. Even the introduction of social insurance for manual workers in 1927 did not lead to any major changes: It merely institutionalized the existing pattern of compensating private practitioners.

However, despite all this continuity, it is important to observe that the government eventually did succeed in changing the basis of medical practice from Chinese to Western medicine. Moreover, this transition was achieved with minimal cost and social disruption. It was only when the war with China in the 1930s brought pressure from the army to improve the health condition of conscripted men that the government changed its style of gradual adjustment. In 1942, virtually all the major hospitals were nationalized and placed under the newly created Japan Medical Corporation (Nippon Iryōdan). As well as managing existing regular hospitals and building new ones, the Corporation was given the responsibility of building more tuberculosis sanatoria (tuberculosis was the number one cause of death at that time) and improving access to health care in rural areas.[13]

The Limited Impact of Postwar Reforms

Japan's defeat in World War II led to the disbanding of the Japan Medical Corporation, which in effect closed a road that might have led to a system like the British National Health Service. This decision came in part from the American Occupation authorities' traditional hostility toward socialized medicine itself, but in a more general sense as part of the overall policy of dismantling the top–down controls of the war years. This move encountered little opposition within Japan because the Corporation was on the brink of bankruptcy, and many Japanese had come to see the central government as unsuited for managing operational day-to-day services in an area with such varied needs as health care.

The Americans, or in particular Colonel C. F. Sams, Chief of the Public

---

13 It is worth noting that despite the national emergency, the government had to explain to the medical profession that the Corporation would not interfere in any way with the existing system of private practitioners, nor with the university hospitals.

Health and Welfare Section, had strong ideas about how the Japanese medical-care system should be reconstructed. These efforts were part of a determined campaign by the Occupation to "democratize" the entire fabric of Japanese society, which often meant changes along American lines. The major attempted reforms were the following.

- Standardizing medical schools (on the lines of the 1910 Flexner Report, which had led to the closing down of substandard medical schools in the United States) so that they would all become six-year university-level programs.
- Establishment of an internship system and a national licensing examination, that would be mandatory for all graduates of medical schools. Formerly, only graduates of vocational-level schools had been required to take the examination.
- Prohibition of physicians from dispensing medications. That service would be performed by pharmacists.
- Improvement of hospital nursing and administration. The hospital was to become more focused on patient care rather than just medical treatment by physicians.
- Closing down substandard physician-owned small hospitals.

This program was quite ambitious and was part of a major experiment in social engineering that had an enormous impact. However, the health sector proved intrinsically more resistant to change than other areas of society. It could not be restructured by fiat as readily as was the case in agricultural land reform. Moreover, the Japanese medical-care system was charged with the immediate task of preventing the spread of communicable and venereal diseases among American soldiers, which meant that the existing machinery of the health-care system could not be shut down for a full overhaul.[14] Whatever the reason, it is clear that the attempted reforms fell well short of their objectives.

First, the two-tiered system of university plus vocational schools in medical education was in fact abolished, and many vocational-level medical schools, especially the ones created in the war years for military service, were closed

---

14 Efforts to control communicable diseases actually left a greater impression on the general public than did the reforms in the health-care system. Note that the title given to Col. Sams' memoirs when translated into Japanese was *"DDT Kakumei,"* or DDT Revolution (trans. Takemae Eiji); (Tokyo: Iwanami, 1986).

down. The hierarchical structure with the University of Tokyo at the top remained intact, however, and the professors of clinical departments maintained their control within the encompassing networks of affiliated hospitals. One reason was that the faculty of the elite medical schools was not purged, as politicians and industry leaders had been.

Second, an internship system was established but never really achieved its objectives. Eventually it was abolished after a medical students' strike in 1968 (an unusually successful outcome for such movements). One grievance of the students was that they had received little instruction from hospital physicians, who lacked the time, experience, and inclination to organize a well-structured internship program.

Third, the Japan Medical Association killed efforts to prevent physicians from dispensing after the occupation ended – the law was left in effect, but a fatal loophole was inserted to the effect that physicians could dispense if the patient preferred not to go to a pharmacy. This illustrates the problem of transforming a system without providing the necessary infrastructure. Japan had few dispensing pharmacies; the payment system was based on services including the price of drugs; and patients were accustomed to receiving their medication from physicians. To this day, despite determined efforts by the government, over four-fifths of private-practice physicians dispense in their offices, and almost all hospital outpatients receive their medication from the hospital pharmacy.

Fourth, perhaps the greatest success of these reforms was that nursing was improved.[15] Because reimbursement under the fee schedule was insufficient, however, it was mainly the subsidized public hospitals that could afford adequate staffing. Many private hospitals found it difficult to attract qualified nurses, given the low salaries they could afford, and continued to rely on the family and later on *tsukisoi* (aides privately hired by the families from an agency) to assist in nursing.[16] Hospital administration was less reformed. A national training institute was established in 1951, but it has remained small, and an independent profession of hospital administrators

15 One example is that the position of the director of nursing was created for the first time. Formerly, no one had managerial responsibility for nursing in the entire hospital, and the highest post that nurses could attain was unit head nurse, appointed by the chief of that clinical department.

16 *Tsukisoi* charges were mostly covered by health insurance, but in April 1996, this reimbursement was ended, and it is anticipated that the *tsukisoi* will disappear.

has not developed – for one thing, legal restrictions require hospital directors to be physicians.[17]

Fifth, as the first step toward the closing down of small hospitals, in 1948 inpatient facilities were divided into "hospitals," with at least twenty licensed beds, and "clinics with beds" or physicians' offices having less than twenty beds. The intention was to limit the length of inpatient care to 48 hours in the "clinics with beds." However, after pressure from the Japan Medical Association, this exclusion was made meaningless by adding the clause, "unless unavoidable for medical reasons." Japan still has many small inpatient facilities: "Clinics with beds" amount to one-sixth of the total number of beds, and hospitals having less than 100 beds constitute another one-sixth.

These largely unsuccessful explicit reform attempts may in fact have been less significant than what did *not* happen during the Occupation period. Under other circumstances, the organizational changes of the wartime years might well have paved the way to a government-dominated health-care system akin to the British model. Many Welfare Ministry officials held that vision, and indeed hold it in attenuated form to the present day, but their dreams were thwarted first by the more American notions of the Occupation authorities, and then by the newly established power of private-practice physicians. The result, similarly to the earlier process of the transition to Western medicine during the Meiji era, was that the basic structure of the delivery system remained largely intact during these years.[18]

We note particularly that both hospitals and specialist groups have failed to develop into major players in the health policy arena, so that providers' interests are still represented almost solely by the JMA. Professors in the elite medical schools have remained powerful, but they could not become a unified force because they were rivals in the narrow goal of trying to expand the hospital departments under their control. They became de facto allies of the JMA in opposing advances by hospitals and specialty boards because their development would weaken the professors' positions at the top of the hier-

---

17 For that reason, hospital administration courses are all offered within medical-schools. Even today there are only six full professors of hospital administration in Japan.

18 Sams also tried to introduce the U.S. system of office-based attending physicians in hospitals, but he quickly realized that this was impractical. He never pushed for the establishment of specialty boards because he had second thoughts about the increasing trend toward specialization in the United States, and because he felt that Japan had already gone through more than enough changes. Sams, op. cit.

archy. Thus, with no other serious contenders, confrontations between the Ministry of Health and Welfare, pursuing its goal of public health, and the JMA, with its ideology of professional freedom, dominated the postwar health policy scene.

Recent Developments

From the end of the occupation period until the beginning of cost containment in the 1980s, the JMA had the advantage. The Japan Medical Corporation had been disbanded, and the government simply did not have enough money to pursue its ideology of public health. Just as in the Meiji period, health was low in priority compared with rebuilding the country. Moreover, the JMA was led by the charismatic Takemi Tarō, who energetically protected the interests of private practitioners. However, despite the JMA's continued leading role during this period, insidious but deep-rooted changes occurred in the delivery system – some the indirect and often unintended effects of government policies, and some due to market forces. Their ramifications are still unclear.

The first trend is the long-term increase in hospital care. For the first time in Japanese history, hospitals became readily available to the general public, as the number of hospital beds per capita nearly tripled from 4.2 per thousand in 1953 to 13.5 in 1993. Most of this increase has come from the private sector, with its share increasing from 25 percent to 67 percent of the total number of hospital beds.[19] The expansion owed much to the establishment of a quasi-government corporation called the Medical Finance Corporation (Iryō Kinyū Kōko) in 1960, when credit was very tight, that gave low-interest loans for capital investment by private-sector medical-care institutions. Although this policy meant failure for the long-held goal of many officials to establish a public-sector-dominated delivery system, it fulfilled a more immediate objective – simply increasing the number of hospitals – at the low cost of merely subsidizing a small difference in the interest rate.[20]

---

19 Data from the MHW's Iryō Shisetsu Chōsa, 1955–93.
20 The Corporation was established as the result of JMA lobbying. Although larger hospitals compete with the JMA's private-practitioner constituency, owning a hospital was the dream of many doctors, one that seemed attainable in the high-growth era if the necessary investment were available. Incidentally, this process was similar to the expansion of higher education in the 1950s and '60s. In response to public demand, plus pressure from private university associations, growth took place by easing regulations for creating or enlarging

The second underlying change, a partial cause of the first, is the expansion of geriatric care. This trend had both demographic and policy causes: The proportion of the population 65 and over doubled from 6 percent in 1960 to 12 percent in 1990, and medical care was made essentially free for the elderly in 1973. The focus of care accordingly shifted, from curing the acute illnesses of the young working population to managing the chronic conditions of elderly retirees.

Moreover, for the first time in Japanese history, substantial numbers of the frail elderly could now be cared for in institutions rather than by their family – the current rate of institutionalization for the 65+ population is about the same as the United States, about 6 percent. Because few nursing homes were available, however, these older people mainly entered hospitals (the proportion of the 65+ population that was hospitalized rose from 0.9 percent in 1960 to 4.4 percent in 1990). As a result, nearly half of all hospital inpatients in Japan are now 65 or older, and one-third of these have been hospitalized for over a year. Nearly all of these long-stay patients are in private-sector hospitals, many of which have become the functional equivalent of nursing homes.[21]

The third change is an increase in the strength and importance of public-sector hospitals, especially those owned and subsidized by local governments.[22] The private-sector leads in numbers, as already noted, but the public sector has more prestige in health care as in the closely related field of higher education (where public universities have only a quarter of the students but are seen as the leaders). These advantages have increased in that private-sector revenue has been held down by cost-containment pressures on the fee schedule, while public hospitals have been able to finance their capital investment and even cover operational deficits through subsidies. Local governments have cooperated because hospitals are popular with the public, and

private universities at little cost to the government, rather than by creating new public universities. See T. J. Pempel, ''Higher Education: Aiding Privatized Education,'' *Policy and Politics in Japan: Creative Conservatism* (Philadelphia: Temple University Press, 1982), pp. 171–217.

21 The fact that most of the increase in hospital beds since 1973 has been in the long-term care field, rather than acute care, has meant that the impact on health-care costs has not been as great as one would expect.

22 National government hospitals have generally not become so important. Apart from their inconvenient locations (a legacy from their origin as military hospitals), they receive smaller subsidies, and their human resources have been tied up by a cap on total national-government employees.

so make good campaign promises, and because they are supported by powerful public–employee labor unions. The widening gap has increased the animosity between the two sectors and further hindered the development of a common front among hospitals.

The fourth trend is the gradual expansion of private hospitals into multi-hospital chains or medical-welfare complexes. The chains began in the 1970s, when reimbursement was relatively generous. A few entrepreneurial physicians embarked on establishing chains of new hospitals to serve communities where there appeared to be shortages of beds. In the cost-cutting 1980s, chains took over some small- to medium-sized private hospitals in financial trouble.[23] Several chains have installed centralized billing systems for maximizing revenue. These chains have naturally antagonized local medical associations, who fought back by being rigorous in reviewing their claims (see Chapter 6) and by pressuring local governments to deny their applications for expansion. Such efforts have been largely successful, and the overt expansion of chains has been curtailed, although the covert acquisition of hospitals continues.

Private hospitals also moved into the field of social services, often starting by establishing a ''health facility for the elderly'' (Rōjin Hoken Shisetsu) or sometimes a nursing home (Tokubetsu Yōgō Rōjin Hōmu), and then opening up other services such as day-care, ''visiting-nurse stations,'' and ''home-care assistance centers.'' The 1989 Gold Plan, aimed at improving both institutional and in-home long-term care, brought substantial new funds that encouraged many hospitals (particularly in rural areas) to develop into ''one-stop shopping'' complexes for elderly patients.[24]

The fifth trend is the decline of office-based physicians, who held the majority until 1976 but are now only one-third of all doctors. As Figure 3.1 indicates, this was partially caused by the bulge of wartime graduates, producing a large cohort now in private practice, plus the doubling of medical school enrollment in the 1970s, so that there are many young physicians who are more likely to work in hospitals. In any case, the average age of private

---

23 According to Niki, the expansion in the 1980s resulted by 1988 in a total of twenty-four private hospital chains, each with over 1,000 beds. Niki Ryū, *Fukugan de miru 90 Nendai no Iryō* (Tokyo: Keisō Shobō, 1991), pp. 104–111.

24 For these complexes, see the series by Niki Ryū in the magazine *Byōin*, November 1996–March 1997. The push for rapid expansion and the new money also brought on the worst scandal ever for the MHW, when a hospital owner in financial trouble bribed a high-level official, Okamitsu Nobuharu, to obtain subsidies to construct nursing homes.

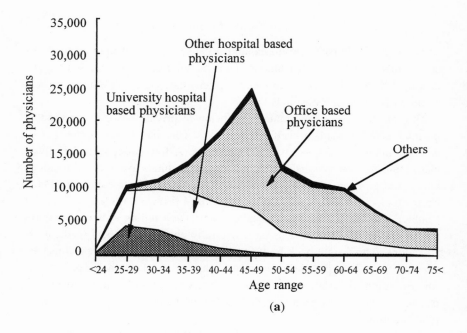

(a)

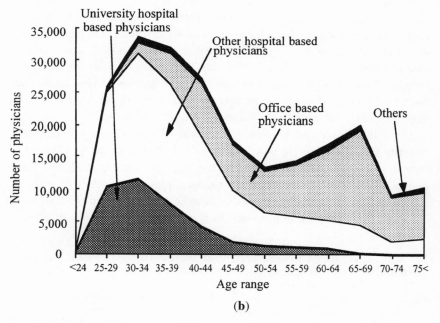

(b)

Figure 3.1 Age Distribution of Physicians According to Hospital Type and Office.
(a) 1972 [*Source*: *1972 Ishi, Shikaishi, Yakuzaishi Chôsa* (1974)]. (b) 1992 [*Source*:
1992 Ishi, Shikaishi, Yakuzaishi Chôsa (1994)].

practitioners is now over sixty, and many are retiring. Unlike the usual pattern in the past, so far their numbers are not being replaced by middle-aged doctors leaving hospitals for private practice to raise their incomes.[25]

What accounts for this change in physician behavior? On the one hand, training in medical schools has become more specialist-oriented, and the gap in the equipment available between large hospitals and office practice has widened, so younger physicians are relatively more attracted to hospitals. On the other hand, since a tax reform in 1979 that ended the large automatic business-expenses exemption for upper-income physicians, the enormous income advantage of private practitioners has been reduced somewhat, while the capital investment required for opening a practice has increased. Another factor is that patients have become more mobile and selective and have been deserting the local physicians' offices for large hospitals, so the prospects for attracting patients may not look too promising.

These five trends are leading to substantial changes in the Japanese provider system. Not incidentally, all of them have ominous implications for the power of the Japan Medical Association. Its response can be seen in its position on the Regional Health Planning Law of 1985 – in a major reversal of earlier policy, the JMA agreed to a proposal to cap the number of hospital beds. The immediate cause of the switch was the threatened expansion of hospital chains, but in a deeper sense it signified a basic shift in JMA strategy, from a positive interest in enlarging the opportunities of its members, to a negative concern with protecting what they had. As part of the bargain with the JMA, the government agreed that local medical associations would be well represented in the planning process to determine bed allocation for each region (indeed, the chair of the prefectural planning committee is always the chair of the local medical association).

The move to limit beds also signified a profound change in Japan's fundamental assumptions about health care. The system had depended on continuous expansion. The hierarchical pattern of university professors controlling appointments throughout a network of hospitals owes its existence mainly to the acute shortage of physicians, and it could work because of the continuous increase in the number of hospital jobs. Physicians tolerated the hierarchical system because they could either go into private practice (and dream of eventually expanding from office to hospital) or hope for career

---

25 Today even for physicians in their forties, hospital physicians outnumber office-based physicians. Data from MHW: *Ishi Shikaishi Yakuzaishi Chōsa,* 1992.

advancement within their university's growing network of affiliated hospitals. Now both ladders of success seem less attractive.

However, the significance of these recent developments has not been fully comprehended by individual physicians. This is partly due to the basic power structure of the Japanese system, which is still dominated by private practitioners on the one hand and university clinical departments on the other. Both have tried to ignore change. And as mentioned in Chapter 2, neither the MHW nor the JMA has been able to come up with alternative new conceptions of health care that could gain the full allegiance of even their own constituencies, let alone the general public. Regulations against the expansion of chains and the legal prohibition of for-profit hospitals have also contributed to maintaining the status quo.

Despite substantial underlying shifts in medical-care delivery, then, the system itself has yet to change very much. We can get a better sense of why this is so by taking a closer look at providers.

PROVIDERS: AN OVERVIEW

Looking at the Japanese health-care delivery system will give many Americans the impression of being in a time warp. The hallmark of modern medical practice is specialization and differentiation. In Japan, hospitals are not clearly differentiated from office-based physicians on the one hand, since they depend on outpatient care for profits, or from nursing homes on the other, in that so much of their inpatient population is the elderly getting custodial care (a patient just admitted for an emergency not infrequently will be lying right next to someone who has been hospitalized for over six months).

This lack of differentiation is not just a matter of facilities. Human resources also tend to be less specialized: Doctors are trained as specialists, but most function as primary-care physicians except in the largest hospitals. Virtually all office-based physicians are solo practitioners, each trying to deal with all the problems of every patient who comes through the door.

For other health personnel, too, the professional division of labor is not as extensive as in the United States. Nurses cannot earn professionally recognized credits for specialization, nor is there any formal process of accreditation for medical social workers or medical record librarians.[26] Moreover,

26 In 1996, specializations for psychiatric and cancer nursing were approved, but in the first round, only eight nurses received qualification.

even where licenses do exist, they tend to span a wider range of services than in the United States. For example, the "clinical test technician" (*rinshō kensa gishi*) license allows those qualified to perform both laboratory and physiological tests. Lastly, as noted, there are no professional schools for hospital administration; hospitals are managed jointly by physicians and a small, clearly subordinate administrative staff, all of whom get only on-the-job training.

Another major difference is that the Japanese health-care system has simultaneously more freedom and more regulations than the American system. For example, Japanese physicians have more freedom in that once they have set up their offices, designation as an approved social-insurance provider is perfunctorily given – nothing has developed along the lines of managed-care networks that pick and choose the physicians who will be reimbursed. Moreover, physicians are not restricted from performing and billing for any procedure listed in the fee schedule. On the other hand, *how much* they can bill is strictly regulated by the fee schedule. Moreover, should they choose to work in hospital settings, their income will be fixed, and especially if young, they may have to move to another hospital within the university clinical department network by order of the professor.

Hospitals are much more regulated than in the United States. As has been mentioned, there are regulations against multihospitals, and in many communities, private-practice physicians have effectively mounted pressure against hospitals establishing satellite clinics that could serve as their feeders. For-profit investor-owned hospitals are legally prohibited. Such regulations are not without loopholes – chains are a growing phenomenon, and investors are able to own the land and buildings of a hospital and lease them to a doctor to operate (mostly in the area of geriatric long-term care, where such investments are most profitable). The regulations nonetheless do severely limit the freedom of action of hospital owners. Moreover, hospitals are prohibited from advertising anything more than their clinical specialties (from the standard list), location, hours when the clinics are open, and so forth.

These restrictions have been imposed ostensibly for preventing the commercialization of health care and to ensure equal access to all. At the same time, by limiting competition, they have served to protect the interests of the private practitioners who are the dominant members of the JMA. These physicians have fought to maintain the status quo because corporate-style medicine would pose a major threat to their ideology of professional freedom, as well as their pocketbooks. Thus, the impression of being in a time warp can be at least partly ascribed to the JMA, and then to the Ministry of Health and Welfare as its counterpart in the policy making process.

Table 3.1 compares some basic characteristics of providers between Japan and the United States. Note the following highlights (all expressed in proportional terms):

* The numbers of physicians and nurses are fairly similar (total health employment in Japan is less than half that of the United States, but the difference is largely in other hospital staff). [27]
* Japan has about three times the number of hospital beds, and over twice the number when all long-term-care beds are included.
* The number of new admissions to hospitals in Japan is only two-thirds that of the United States (because there are so many more long-term-care admissions and only one-third the number of surgical operations).[28]
* Japanese visit a physician more than twice as often as Americans (the highest and lowest rates in the OECD countries).[29]
* The difference in the average length of stay in hospitals is enormous; much of it can be explained by the fact that Japanese hospitals also provide long-term care, but there is also a real difference for comparable cases.[30]
* Hospital administrative costs are about half that of the United States in percentage terms; so about one-quarter in absolute terms.
* Average physician incomes are somewhat lower in Japan.

Statistics can provide only an overview and are often misleading due to definitional problems and so forth. Therefore, rather than delving more deeply into quantitative data, we describe prototypical cases of the important types of Japanese providers. This is a synthetic exercise: The cases were con-

---

27 Note that in Japan 87 percent of physicians, and 97 percent of hospital directors, are male. To avoid a misleading impression of gender equality in the health-care system, we use only male pronouns for these professions in the descriptions that follow.

28 Hasegawa Toshihiko, "Comparison of Hospital Admission Rates between Japan and the United States," in *Containing*, pp. 101–105.

29 Earlier OECD estimates.

30 The stay for an acute myocardial infarction in Japan is about twenty-five days compared to nine in the United States. This does not necessarily make the U.S.'s hospital more efficient, in that they have five times the staff per bed when compared to Japan. See Naoko Muramatsu and Jersey Liang, "Comparison of Hospital Length of Stay and Charges between Japan and the United States," in *Containing*, pp. 184–192.

Table 3.1. *Provider Characteristics, Japan and United States*

	Japan	United States
Physicians/10,000 population	18.4[a]	24.3[b]
Qualified nurses/10,000 population	68.9[a]	75.5[b]
New physicians/10,000 population	0.4[a]	0.6[c]
Hospital beds/10,000 population	13.3[d]	4.5[e]
Hospital and long-term-care beds/10,000 population	24.2[f]	10.2[g]
Hospital admissions/population, percent	8.9[h]	13.0[h]
Visits to physicians per year	16.0[i]	5.9[i]
Average length of stay in hospitals, days	45.4[h]	8.8[i]
Private sector share of hospitals, percent	80[d]	74[g]
Private sector share of hospital beds, percent	67[d]	81[g]
Administration/total hospital expenditure, percent	5–7[j]	9–20[j]
Physician income/average income, ratio	4.0[k]	5.4[k]

Notes and sources: Some of these data are not strictly comparable; see original sources for qualifications.

[a] 1994 data. *Kokumin Eisei no Dōkō*, 1996.

[b] 1993 data. *Health United States*, 1997.

[c] 1994 data. Ibid.

[d] 1995 data. *Iryō Shisetsu Chōsa*, 1997.

[e] 1993 data. AHA Hospital Statistics, 1997.

[f] 1995 data. Includes Tokubetsu Yōgō Rōjin Hōmu and Rōjin Hoken Shisetsu beds. *Shakai Fukushi Shisetsu Chōsa Hōkoku*, 1997; *Rōjin Hoken Shisetsu Jittai Chōsa*, 1997.

[g] 1991 data. *AHA Hospital Statistics*, 1997.

[h] 1994 data. *OECD Health Data*, 1996.

[i] 1992 data. Ibid.

[j] 1991 data. Naoki Ikegami, Jay Wolfson, and Takamori Ishi, ''Comparison of Administrative Costs in Health Care between Japan and the United States,'' *Containing*, pp. 80–93.

[k] 1990 data. OECD Health Data, 1993. OECD's more recent estimates are quite different, but its basis for calculation is not clear; these figures are consistent with other estimates.

structed by taking representative aspects from numerous health-care facilities that we have observed. There is much more variety in Japanese health-care delivery than can be conveyed here, but we are confident at least that nothing in these descriptions would strike observers familiar with the Japanese system as surprising.

71

University and Public-sector Hospitals

We begin with the category that has played an increasingly important role in Japanese health care. University and public-sector hospitals have the advantage over other providers because they have access to financial support in addition to revenues obtained through the fee schedule. It comes directly as subsidies from government (or university) budgets, or indirectly as in not having to pay corporate or property taxes. They can therefore invest more in facilities and equipment and can deliver services that would not be feasible for other hospitals. For example, although university and public-sector hospitals constitute only 41 percent of the total number of general hospital beds, they perform 75 percent of the surgical operations requiring general anesthesia.[31] As shown in Table 3.2, public hospitals have the majority of registered nurses and proportionally more physicians than the private-sector.

Because they are perceived as providing better-quality care, these big hospitals have become increasing popular with the general public for ordinary primary care as well as high-tech tertiary care. This growing share in ambulatory care has driven total spending up because, even though their fees are the same, big hospitals tend to order more diagnostic tests and imaging than do smaller hospitals or, especially, private practitioners.[32]

As a group, university hospitals are much more homogeneous than the other types. Under Ministry of Education regulations, every medical school must have its own hospital of at least 600 beds, needed because virtually all undergraduate clinical education and over 80 percent of the residency training takes place there. However, there are still variations in staffing levels and the extent of research orientation. The most prestigious university hospitals go back at least to the early twentieth century, but nearly half of the total were established in the 1970s as the result of a Ministry of Health and Welfare policy to increase the number of physicians.

Public-sector hospitals range from small rural hospitals of less than 50 beds to urban medical centers with over 600 beds. They include hospitals owned by prefectural and municipal governments (56 percent of all public

31 Ikegami Naoki, "Iryō Kikan no Kōzōteki Yōin to Shinryō Tokusei narabini sono Hiyō Kanren no Nichibei Hikaku," in *Herusu Risaachi wa Iryōni dō Kōken Suruka* (Tokyo: Pfizer Health Research Shinkō Zaidan, 1995), pp. 24–27.
32 N. Ikegami and S. Ikeda, "The Paradox of Decreasing Prices and Increasing Costs for Diagnostic Testing, Imaging and Drugs in Japan," *International Journal of Technology Assessment in Health Care* 13:1 (1997), 99–110.

Table 3.2. *Provider Characteristics by Ownership, 1993*

	Public sector		Private sector		University		Total	
Hospitals	1,909	(19)	7,935	(81)	170	(2)	9,844	(100)
Beds	550,923	(33)	1,130,029	(67)	91,869	(5)	1,680,952	(100)
Physicians' offices	5,360	(6)	78,768	(94)			84,128	(100)
Physicians' offices' beds	7,060	(3)	258,023	(97)			265,083	(100)
Physicians in hospitals	69,785	(45)	85,875	(55)	37,736	(24)	155,660	(100)
Physicians in physicians' offices	7,738	(7)	100,291	(93)			108,029	(100)
Registered nurses in hospitals	226,306	(54)	190,402	(46)	47,417	(11)	416,708	(100)
Registered nurses in offices	10,049	(15)	57,388	(85)			67,437	(100)
Practical nurses in hospitals	51,071	(21)	191,323	(79)	4,538	(2)	242,394	(100)
Practical nurses in offices	6,600	(5)	125,361	(95)			131,961	(100)
Nurse aides in hospitals	28,145	(19)	116,883	(81)	6,032	(4)	145,028	(100)
Nurse aides in offices	436	(0)	52,143	(99)			52,579	(100)
Others employed in hospitals	171,982	(36)	307,092	(64)	43,343	(9)	479,074	(100)
Others employed in offices	24,882	(9)	258,149	(91)			283,031	(100)

Notes: Numbers in parentheses are percent of total. Figures for university hospitals are also included in the two previous columns, but separate data for public and private university hospitals are not available.

Source: Iryō Shisetsu Chōsa, 1993.

hospitals), the national government (21 percent), the Red Cross and other old established voluntary organizations (16 percent), and the big health and public pension insurance carriers (8 percent).[33] Some of the prefectural- and municipal-government hospitals date back to the old quarantine hospitals, but most were built after the war partly as a way for local politicians to gain popularity and votes. National hospitals, owned by the MHW, are mostly former military or tuberculosis hospitals (many remain rather marginal), with a few high-quality exceptions such as the National Cancer Center and the National Cardiovascular Center. The voluntary hospitals were nearly all established before the war. Most of the hospitals owned by social insurance organizations were established before or shortly after the war for the benefit of their members but are now open to the general public.

University Hospital, Prototype A. Our synthetic prototype case for a university hospital can be called Hospital A. It has 1,000 beds and is attached to an old established private medical school that is part of a comprehensive university.

For inpatient care, the hospital operates at full capacity, with an average length of stay of twenty-five days. There is usually a waiting list to get admitted, which can be six months or more for cataract surgeries (outpatient surgery is very uncommon in Japan). Most waits for admission are shorter, and urgent cases are either admitted immediately or referred to an affiliated hospital. The formal attending physician for an inpatient will be the clinical department chief, the only full professor in each department. However, apart from his weekly rounds, actual care will be in the hands of a team headed by an assistant professor or associate professor (*kōshi, jokyōju*) and including several assistants and residents.

For outpatients, the hospital has an average of over 3,000 visits per day, 90 percent coming for repeat visits. Patients needing specialized tertiary care are a minority; many come directly to the hospital for all their medical problems because they think the quality is better (or because it is fashionable).

33 MHW, *Iryō Shisetsu Chōsa*, 1995, p. 98. Hospitals owned by national voluntary organizations such as the Red Cross are classified as being in the public sector and referred to as "hospitals having public sector characteristics" (*kōteki seikaku o yusuru byōin*) in Japan. Like government hospitals, they are exempt from having to pay taxes, but unlike government-owned hospitals, any deficits they run will not be covered from public funds. Hospitals owned by public universities are also technically public-sector hospitals but have quite different characteristics.

About 30 percent of the first visits have referrals, mostly from medical-school alumni in private practice, not from other local physicians. Thus, the majority of first visits are self-referred, attracted by the reputation of the hospital or a particular physician, or dissatisfied with the care received elsewhere.

Outpatients may ask for the physician of their choice, at no extra charge, but that physician can decide whether to see the patient himself or not. The outpatient clinic operates mainly on a walk-in basis: All first visits and about two-thirds of repeat visits come without an appointment. The typical outpatient visit conforms to the popular image of "waiting three hours for a three-minute consultation." However, the three hours include the time spent waiting to pay the co-payment and for the medication to be dispensed by the hospital pharmacy.

The hospital director is the professor of neuropsychiatry, who also serves as the chief of his department. Having graduated and spent his entire career in the university, he considers his appointment by the dean to be an honor but laments the time he must spend on administration. He is assisted by two vice-directors, also both chairs of clinical departments, and by the business manager (*jimuchō*), who has had no specialized training and indeed had previously worked not in the hospital but as head of the university's personnel department.

The 250 full-time faculty positions in the clinical departments are virtually all filled by alumni. Thirty are full professors and department chiefs; below them are associate professors (*jokyōju*), assistant professors (*kōshi*), and then assistants (*joshu*), who compose about half of the total. All are paid on the same pay scale as the rest of the university faculty. For example, a 40-year-old assistant professor would have a yearly income from the hospital of about ¥8 million ($45,000 at our PPP rate of ¥180 = $1), though he might make as much again working part-time at other hospitals. In principle, all faculty positions are tenured and their number is strictly limited by the university budget. For that reason, in order to handle the workload, the hospital employs about 300 minimally paid residents and unpaid assistants, who work to gain experience. There are also 850 nurses, and 700 other workers. The total number of staff per bed would be about one-fifth of a U.S. university medical center.[34]

Physicians are allowed to work a day and a half a week in outside hospitals

34   For more details, see Matthew Holt et al., *Medical Ivory Towers and The High Cost of Health Care* (Stanford, CA: Stanford University Asia/Pacific Research Center, 1993).

(the only earnings for the unpaid staff). Another source of income for experienced faculty members are "gifts" (*orei, sharei*) from patients, which might go as high as about $3,000. Gifts are usually paid only by patients hospitalized in one of the hospital's 300 private rooms (which cost an extra $200 per day).

The medical school has 100 students, who pay ¥5 million ($28,000) in tuition for each of their six years of undergraduate training. It is headed by a dean who is the professor of pathology. On the same campus is a three-year junior college of nursing, the president of which is a former associate professor of surgery. Despite operating at full capacity, both the medical school and the hospital run at a deficit and in effect are subsidized by the other schools of the university.

It is often said in Japan that to become successful a medical-school professor will have to spend 80 percent of his time in research, 19 percent in clinical practice, and 1 percent in teaching. Although research is the major focus for many faculty, the grants they receive bring no financial benefit to either the school or the hospital. Grant money can pay only for direct expenses, including neither faculty salaries nor administrative overhead. The incentive to do research, apart from its intrinsic interest, is to advance one's position within the university clinical department and to bring more prestige and power to the professors in the outside world.

Public Sector Hospital, Prototype B. As a public-sector hospital prototype, we describe Hospital B, owned by a prefectural government and situated at the center of a major city. From a 30-bed hospital established just after the war, it has grown to become a comprehensive medical center with 500 beds, covering all the specialties; it serves as a regional center for complicated surgeries and examinations.

Hospital B also operates at full capacity of inpatients, with an average length of stay of twenty days. It has 1,200 outpatient visits per day, over 85 percent for repeat visits. About 40 percent of new patients have letters of referral from local practitioners, the result of a deal with the local medical association (the hospital agreed to refer patients back to their former physicians once they become stabilized). There is a waiting list for elective surgeries, though acute cases can get admitted more quickly than in the university hospital. Outpatient waiting and consultation times are about the same.

The director of the hospital is a former professor of a prestigious medical school, where most of the clinical department chiefs also graduated. Medical staff is often exchanged between this hospital and his old university hospital. The business manager previously worked as chief of the prefectural public works department, and his present position is his first hospital appointment, given as an honor just before his retirement. The total number of full-time physicians is 65, nurses 330, administrative and clerical staff 85, and the rest 125. Many earn seniority-based wages; for example, a nurse's aide about to retire might earn about ¥8 million ($45,000 at our PPP rate), about twice the salary of either the head nurse (in her thirties) or a young physician on the regular staff. This apparent anomaly is because the hospital must comply with the established wage scale for all public-sector employees (the labor union's slogan was "same age, same wage"). That is one reason why the hospital's operating expenses are more than 15 percent higher than its revenue from providing care. This operating deficit is covered by the local government, as are most of capital expenditures.

Some of the deficit is due to the fact that the hospital is providing high-tech care, which often must be done at a financial loss in Japan. However, we should also note that physicians do not have much incentive to maximize revenue because all are paid a fixed, seniority-based salary. Their salaries are not even linked to the financial performance of the hospital as a whole or of their clinical department, let alone their individual efforts. The average salary of Hospital B physicians would be about double that of medical-school faculty, but because they are officially not allowed to work in other hospitals (except for weekends and nights), and receiving gifts from patients is strictly prohibited, any actual gap in income is probably small.

A nursing school attached to the hospital has a yearly enrollment of forty. The school's director is a male physician (an internist) who is one of the vice-directors of the hospital. Nursing students do not have to pay tuition fees, and most are paid an allowance, as virtually all are expected to work in the hospital once they have graduated.

Private-sector Hospitals

Private-sector hospitals are usually owned by physicians as their personal property, or by a nonprofit corporation. In the latter case, except for the relatively few chain hospitals, the hospital director normally also serves as the chairman of the governing board, and care is taken in choosing the board members so that control remains within the physician's family. Therefore, in many respects, most of the private-sector hospitals operate as family businesses.[35] They are usually taxed in the same way as for-profit enterprises, and their capital investment must be financed by debt or from accumulated revenues. The hospital directors generally work under great pressure. Not only do they have to manage the hospital and purchase drugs, but, especially in the smaller hospitals, they are the primary generators of revenue through their clinical practice. Virtually all of these hospitals have developed from a physician's office.

Private-Sector General Hospital, Prototype C. Private-sector Hospital C is a hospital of sixty beds, in a town of 200,000 population. It has a mix of acute and long-term-care patients. The average length of stay is fifty-five days, reflecting the fact that many of the cases are chronic. The outpatient department is busy, with about 200 visits a day. One factor that makes this hospital popular for outpatients despite its somewhat squalid appearance is that it is open until eight in the evening. Moreover, the waiting time for an appointment is usually less than thirty minutes, and there is no waiting list to be admitted. The staff is well trained to be courteous to all patients.

The present director had opened an office with ten beds in 1965 after resigning from his position as the chief general surgeon of a public hospital in the same area (he had previously been sent to this hospital by his university clinical department because it was in his home town). He added another twenty beds in 1970, thereby becoming a hospital, and expanded further to the present size in 1975.

One of his reasons for expanding was in order to perform more specialized surgery, beyond routine appendectomies. Today the hospital performs few surgical operations, but it is active in emergency care and owns a CAT scan machine for diagnostic purposes. Many of the patients are elderly people with chronic conditions that have been exacerbated by acute episodes such as pneumonia, but there are also middle-aged patients with diagnoses such as gall stones. The inpatient occupancy rate has dropped to 70 percent because younger patients prefer the nearby public-sector hospital.

Occupancy could be raised if the director would allow chronic-care patients

---

35 Hospitals owned by the following organizations would also be classified in the private-sector: most philanthropic and religious organizations (6.9 percent of all private hospitals), private medical schools (0.9 percent), and corporations (0.8 percent). The last are hospitals that originally served company employees but are now open to the local community.

to stay longer. However, if the proportion of the elderly came to exceed 60 percent, the hospital would then be designated a "hospital for the elderly" (see next section). The average length of stay would increase, which would lead to a lower reimbursement rate. The director would like to avoid both the lower fees and a blow to his professional pride; moreover, he would thereby lose all hope of getting his son, who is presently specializing in cardiac surgery at a university hospital, to come to work in his hospital and eventually succeed him.

The hospital has a staff of three full-time and two part-time physicians, eight qualified nurses (three registered), four aides, and ten others. This staffing level just barely passes the minimal staffing requirements laid down by the government. Of the three full-time physicians, the surgeon is a younger graduate of the director's university clinical department, but the other two (an internist and an orthopedic surgeon) were recruited by advertising in journals. Night duties are performed by young residents from the university. All the physicians are paid a salary negotiated on a yearly basis, so they face some indirect pressures to maximize the hospital's revenue.

The three registered nurses have returned to work after bringing up their children, but the five licensed practical nurses are young graduates of the nursing school run by the local medical association. When a patient requires heavy care, the family is asked to help with the nursing or hire an aide (*tsukisoi*) from an agency. The business manager of the hospital is the wife of the director, and she is assisted by five clerical workers. The physicians are paid about 20 percent more, but the rest of the staff about 20 percent less, than in a public-sector hospital. The hospital shows a small profit, partly due to the fact that very little capital investment has been made. However, the director hopes to improve facilities in the near future in hopes of attracting his son; he prays that remodeling will bring in enough new business to cover the costs.

Private-sector Hospital for the Elderly, Prototype D. The hospital we call D is a 400-bed hospital located in a newly developed area on the outskirts of Tokyo, specializing in long-term care. It was built by a group of investors for that purpose in 1979 in response to the surge in demand that followed the provision of "free" medical care for the elderly in 1973. The property on which it stands is leased from a local construction company. Hospital D was officially designated a "hospital for the elderly" (*rōjin byōin*) in 1983 when the government adopted a new reimbursement plan under the Health

79

Care for the Elderly Law. Virtually all hospitals for the elderly are in the private sector.

The occupancy rate at Hospital D is always nearly 100 percent, and 80 percent of the inpatients have been hospitalized for over one year. The outpatient department is small: Only about thirty local residents visit it a day because the hospital is inconveniently situated. About one quarter of the inpatients are rated as independent in their activities of daily living (ADL). There is a fairly active rehabilitation program and more medical intervention than would occur in an American nursing home; in general, the patients appear to be well cared for physically, but there is not much in the way of social activity programs for them. The rooms are crowded, with an average of 12 patients in each. Only 40 of the 400 patients are in extra-charge single rooms.

The hospital director was recruited for the job from a university hospital, where he had been working as an orthopedic surgeon, because he had family connections with the investors.[36] Although government regulations specify twelve full-time physicians, the hospital fills some of its quota with part-time physicians, most rather elderly retirees from active duty in other hospitals. Important decisions such as admission and discharge are usually referred to the director, whose earnings are linked directly to the hospital's profit margin. The director relies on the business manager, who was recruited from the local branch of a major bank, for routine administrative decisions. Nurse staffing is more adequate than in Hospital C, with sixty-eight nurses and fifty aides. The hospital is prohibited from asking the family to hire a *tsukisoi* aide because that practice is prohibited under the new inclusive per diem fee schedule that was introduced in 1990, and voluntarily chosen by Hospital D in 1991.

On top of the reimbursement from health insurance (which amounts to about ¥320,000 or about $1,800 a month), the hospital bills the patients for services that are ostensibly not covered, such as diapers, laundry, and so forth, amounting to an out-of-pocket charge of about ¥90,000 ($500) a month, paid by the patient along with the small official co-payment (only ¥40,000, or $220). The hospital has a waiting list of several months due to the shortage of long-term-care facilities, particularly of facilities perceived as high quality. Because serious cases cannot wait so long, and also because the hospital is

36 The specialty of physical medicine, which is basic in rehabilitation, is not well developed in Japan and is often provided by orthopedists who have some training in this subject.

paid essentially the same amount for all patients, those who do manage to get admitted tend not to require very heavy care. The hospital runs at a healthy profit by Japanese standards, about 5 percent of revenue.

Physicians' Offices

Private-practice physicians' offices are the most numerous health-care facilities in Japan (there are about 85,000), and one can be found within a few minutes walk in most urban neighborhoods. Nearly all are solo practices, partly due to legal restrictions on sharing equipment or staff.[37] Most practices employ only two or three staff, but the one-third with inpatient beds (up to 20) would of course need more (although unlike hospitals, there are no minimal requirements for staffing levels). In urban areas, with the exception of obstetricians' clinics, these beds are now rarely used.[38] In rural areas, however, such clinics often function as minihospitals. Typically, the physician has his residence in the same building, although the recent tendency has been to set up independent practices in multipurpose buildings.

Traditional Physician Office, Prototype E. Our first prototype is Physician Office E, located in an urban residential area. The physician, an internist, opened his office in 1960 when he was 35 years old, after receiving his Doctor of Medical Science degree and working in a public hospital for a time. His office is open 9–12 A.M. and 2–6 P.M., during which times he sees about fifty patients. Most are elderly, with hypertension and other chronic complaints (although an outbreak of influenza would quickly fill his waiting

---

37 The lack of professional standardization due to the exclusivity of university clinical departments may be another inhibiting factor. Incidentally, group practices are also rare for lawyers. Perhaps because it is so hard to opt out of hierarchical organization in Japan, those who manage to do so seem wary of putting themselves in a situation of dependent human relationships where they would have to worry about their relative ranking. Cf. John Owen Haley, *Authority without Power* (New York: Oxford University Press, 1991), p. 113. Recently, a few group practices have sprung up in urban areas, for the purpose of providing quicker and better diagnosis of patients with problems that cross specialties, so private practitioners can compete better with big hospitals. Nihon University Health Care Management Professor Ōmichi Hisashi argues that such practices are the wave of the future: *Asahi Shinbun*, Jan. 13, 1997.

38 Normal delivery is not directly covered by social insurance in Japan, although mothers receive a lump-sum payment for giving birth, so these private practitioners compete on patient amenity and prices. Note that there is also a small private market for cosmetic surgery, and some of these practices have beds.

room with young patients). Normally, patients wait less than ten minutes if at all, and although his consultation time averages about three minutes, that may be sufficient given the fact that many of his patients visit on a regular two-week basis.[39] After the consultation, a patient would pay the co-payment and wait a few more minutes for the medication to be dispensed. Anyone needing specialized care or inpatient care is referred to the nearby public hospital, or to the university hospital where the physician graduated forty years ago. The physician no longer makes home visits because the work became too demanding, and there appeared to be little demand; nor does he usually answer night calls. He has already given up hope of persuading his son, who is now working as an internist at a Red Cross hospital, to succeed him in his office practice, so he will probably soon start to retire gradually by cutting back on the number of days he sees patients. Physician E's net income, after all expenses have been deducted, is about ¥25 million ($140,000), which incidentally is more than that of the director of Public-Sector Hospital B.

New Type Physician Office, Prototype F. Physician F has his office on the second floor of a seven-story building in a commercial business district in a major city. He opened his office in 1980 while still in his early thirties, after working as an Ear, Nose, and Throat surgeon at a public hospital.[40] His office hours are the same as Physician F's, but he sees more than eighty patients a day. Most of them have seasonal problems that afflict all ages, such as chronic sinusitis and allergic rhinitis. He does minor surgeries, such as myringotomies for acute otitis media, but would no longer think of doing tonsillectomies under local anesthesia as was the custom twenty years ago. Patients requiring inpatient care are referred to the public hospital where he used to work. Although he is relatively satisfied with his practice, he sometimes gets annoyed when he hears from colleagues that one of his patients went to a

---

39 See Ruth Campbell, "The Three-Minute Cure: Doctors and Elderly Patients in Japan," *Containing*, pp. 226–233. Under the fee-schedule regulations, the maximum amount of medication that can be prescribed and dispensed is usually for a two-week period. This limitation was imposed to keep physicians from dispensing too much medication.

40 The other specialties that are common among office-based physicians (other than internal medicine and general surgery) are ENT, ophthalmology, dermatology, orthopedics (mostly focused on physical medicine), obstetrics and gynecology, and urology. Such physicians have worked as specialists in hospital settings before going into open practice and confining their activities to ambulatory care. Most also deliver ordinary primary care including internal medicine.

university hospital without his referral and was seen by a physician many years his junior. His income, after all expenses (including the rental cost for his office) have been deducted, is about ¥30 million ($170,000).

Other Examples

As noted at the outset, these prototypes are just snapshots of typical cases, and there are many other kinds of providers. For example, some private-sector hospitals are similar in size and functions to Public-Sector Hospital B. Although they do not have access to public subsidies, they have managed to survive by innovative efforts: for example, promoting preventative services,[41] expanding home-care services (taking advantage of reimbursement increases), providing newly authorized "welfare" functions such as day-care for the elderly, or holding down labor costs by limiting seniority-based increases.

We should also note the special hospitals for treating cancer and acute stroke patients in both the public and private sectors, and the private multi-hospital chains mentioned previously. Psychiatric hospitals have not been described, although the number of their beds constitutes one-quarter of the total. They have many features similar to Private-Sector Hospital D, but few, if any, are leased because they were mostly built in the 1960s when this form of financing did not exist in the health sector. Because they cannot levy extra charges from the patient, many are in precarious financial conditions.

Finally, we have not attempted to depict innovators in the health-care professions, although their significance is greater than their relatively low numbers would indicate. For example, not a few dedicated office-based physicians have been active in making home visits to the elderly, as well as trying to persuade local medical associations to take a responsible role in establishing community home-care networks. Some nurses have become vice-directors in progressive hospitals, and others are establishing visiting-nurse "stations." Still, despite the considerable variety in health-care provision in Japan, its main characteristics are generally captured in these thumbnail accounts.

---

41 Preventative services are not listed in the fee schedule, so their fees are not covered by health insurance and can be set by the provider at whatever the market will bear. They have become an important source of revenue for many hospitals. Most expensive is the one- or two-day "human dry dock " (*ningen dokku*), which offers an intense battery of screening examinations.

CONCLUSION

Many characteristics of the Japanese health-care system are quite different from those of American providers. Japanese hospitals lack a clear identity in that they overlap into both long-term care and primary ambulatory care. The most expensive part of health care, acute inpatient care, is not a main product line except in some university and public-sector hospitals (the only ones with human and physical resources at all comparable to the United States). Even these providers behave more like bureaucracies than efficient revenue maximizers or entrepreneurs, given their reliance on subsidies and their staffing by salaried doctors working at a fixed pay scale. All hospitals are directed by physicians who have not received any formal education as managers, and except in a few multihospital chains, the administrative staff is clearly subordinate to physicians.

Why is Japanese health-care delivery structured this way? The immediate answer is government regulation, particularly the fee schedule, as is explained in Chapter 6. It reduces the rewards for entrepreneurship, discourages functional differentiation by paying all providers the same way, and makes inexpensive primary care relatively profitable and expensive high-tech procedures unprofitable. All these factors help hold down costs.

But we need to go one step further and ask why the payment system has been structured this way. We then discover that the fee schedule developed in the way it did largely in response to the way health-care providers were organized in Japan. That is, because there was little functional differentiation among hospitals, and between hospitals and physicians' offices, the logical way of payment was through a single fee schedule.

Clearly, today's system is not the product of some farsighted design of the government, but more the result of history. Western medicine was introduced in the Meiji period in a top–down fashion due to the perceived need for rapid Westernization. This accounts for the greater resources and prestige in the public sector, a pattern found in other aspects of Japanese society as well. Unique to the medical sector is that university clinical department chiefs have continued to control the appointment of physicians within their affiliated network of hospitals, while in contrast to this hierarchical system, private-practice physicians have had a great deal of freedom in setting up their offices and expanding them to hospitals. Thus, on the one hand, it was difficult for physicians to form collegial networks, and on the other, no clear distinction emerged between hospitals and physicians' offices, and a natural animosity developed between the public and private-sectors. Given this situation, it is not surprising that the development of specialty boards and hospital organizations has been greatly impeded in Japan.

Looking back, the way health-care providers are presently organized appears contrary to what most government officials had in mind. Heavy reliance on the private sector does not fit into their public-health model, which calls for a well-planned network of large public-sector hospitals and health centers. The major factor in the development of the current system was the power of the Japan Medical Association and its success in uniting the private practitioners and dominating other providers. A secondary factor was simply the lack of enough money to realize the dreams of the bureaucrats.

Nonetheless, government policy has had enormous effects on the delivery system in less abrupt and direct ways. These can be seen in five periods:

- Meiji to the 1930s, to transform medicine from Chinese to Western.
- During the wartime years, to nationalize the delivery of health care.
- The Occupation period, to redesign the system according to the U.S. model.
- The 1950s through the '70s, to improve access by increasing supply.
- Around 1980 to the present, to contain costs.

The government was generally successful in meeting its objectives in the first, fourth, and fifth periods: Medicine was transformed from Chinese to Western, hospitals were made readily accessible, and costs have generally been kept quite low. However, it has had much less success in the second and third periods, despite the fact that, or more likely *because*, these goals were pursued with great energy, speed, and ideological conviction.

We draw two lessons from this Japanese experience. First, although health-care institutions are difficult to change, government policy can have a big impact if it is pursued with a long-enough time frame. It is true that the glacial pace of change in Japan may partly be the result of the greater weight given to reaching consensus, but the main factor is that the health-care provider system there, as elsewhere, is an aggregation of institutions with their own histories and interests, plus the complicated relationships that have developed among them. Neat, rapid, large-scale reform is therefore very difficult. Reformers hoping for magic-bullet solutions, as seen so often in the United States, are probably doomed to disappointment – a big reason why few goals in health-care policy have been achieved.

Second, the Japanese record indicates that incremental adjustments in financial incentives are often the best way to induce change. The relative amounts and ways of paying fees to providers, adjusted little by little, can affect behavior substantially over time. Such measures are particularly effective when, as in Japan, they are used to maintain the balance and status quo of the health-care system as a whole. The continued dominance of office-based physicians in Japan is at least partly due to the fact that the fee schedule is tilted to favor their primary-care services. We should note that this covert pressure through the fee schedule creates less antagonism than explicit rationing of positions – for example, of surgical residencies – because it enables physicians to continue to identify themselves as specialists.

This is not to say that the Japanese system is free from troubles. We have noted the rapid increases in inpatient care and particularly long-term geriatric care, the growing strength of public-sector and university hospitals, the incipient spread of private hospital chains, the decline in private-practice physicians, and, in a general sense, the end of the era of continuous expansion. We think these developments need careful handling by government, although probably not the sort of drastic overhaul of the system that Americans like to contemplate (if not carry out). However, we postpone the explication of our suggestions until the last chapter because other key aspects of Japanese health care need to be explored further.

4

The Egalitarian Health Insurance System

THE Japanese approach to health insurance is quite different from that of the United States. These differences can be seen most clearly by contrasting two fundamental principles of insurance that amount to different ways of conceptualizing fairness. One can be called the "investment principle," and the other the "equality principle." Other dichotomies that convey this distinction include "equity" versus "uniformity," "risk rating" versus "community rating," and "casualty insurance" versus "social insurance."[1]

The investment principle means fairness in the sense that individuals should get out what they put in – get their "just desserts." If they have a higher risk of whatever is being insured against – death, auto accidents, illness – they should pay a higher premium or receive a lower benefit. Equality means a different kind of fairness, as in the classic socialist formulation "to each according to his needs, from each according to his means." In terms of values, these differences relate to an ethic of individualism versus an ethic of social solidarity.

The difference is easily seen in health insurance. Those who believe in investment would assert that people who exercise and don't smoke should not have to subsidize those who lead riskier lives, and they ask why people with money should not be able to buy superior medical care. Those who believe in equality would argue that poor sick people should not be deprived of the medical care they need and so must be subsidized by others. As a practical matter, the contradiction between the two principles is most acute in health care precisely because the people who need the most medical care are often those who are least able to pay for it, with the elderly being the obvious example.

---

1 For lucid discussions, see Joseph White, *Competing Solutions: American Health Care Proposals and International Experience* (Washington, DC: Brookings, 1995), pp. 23–27, and Victor R. Fuchs, *The Future of Health Policy* (Cambridge, MA: Harvard University Press, 1993), 207–209.

If a group of people, or a nation, would pick one or the other of these conflicting notions of fairness, it would be easy enough to devise a health-care system to match. Fairness as investment would be maximized by straight free-market medicine without insurance, or its close relatives, individual policies with "experience-rated" premiums or "medical savings accounts" that allow enrollees to keep unspent money. Such systems could be run with minimum government intervention *if* people found it acceptable for large numbers of people not to be able to afford health insurance. Fairness as equality would have universal entitlement to all medical services, with the costs paid from progressive taxes. Here, clearly, strong government compulsion is needed to prevent the healthier and wealthier people, who would feel themselves unfairly treated or "exploited" in the investment sense, from simply dropping out.

In the real world, no nation is single-mindedly devoted to one type of fairness to the exclusion of the other, so neither of these ideal types can be found. However, nations do vary in how close they are to one or the other pole in this continuum from investment to equality. The policy choice is one of degree as to whether health care should be seen more as a private or a public good – for example, as more like housing or more like primary-school education. It is usually assumed that wealthier people will live in nicer houses, but primary education is generally seen as important to the nation and an entitlement for all children that should be paid for by all citizens.[2]

Among the industrialized nations of the world, the United States is closest to the investment pole in health insurance, and in the mid-1990s, it was moving more in that direction. Japan is closer to the normal case. It would seem to be somewhat more investment-based than systems with tax financing and no co-payments for care (as in Canada and the United Kingdom). That is, as in the United States, health care in Japan is financed by numerous insurance organizations that are formally independent; they can set their own premium rates, and they also have some flexibility on benefits.

In terms of outcomes, however, the Japanese system is actually quite egal-

---

2 Both are usually mixed, of course, with public housing for the poorest people, and private education for the wealthy (who nonetheless must pay school taxes). We would hazard a guess that in nearly every nation, housing is more investment-based and primary education more egalitarian, with health care in between the two. We would also guess that in all three of these policy areas, the United States is closer to the investment pole and Japan closer to the equality pole than most if not all of the other OECD nations.

itarian. Everyone is covered by health insurance, and the regulations imposed by the Health Insurance Bureau of the Ministry of Health and Welfare are so pervasive that insurers have little scope for autonomous decisions on the most important issues. All insurers are nonprofit, they all offer the same benefit package with regard to medical care per se, and with very few exceptions, they have no ability to choose their members. Japanese can go to any hospital or physician they want, with no difference in cost, and providers have no reason to discriminate among patients. These characteristics have allowed the Japanese to achieve "fairness" in the sense of substantial equality in health care.

EGALITARIAN MECHANISMS

If benefits are more or less equal, what about burdens? Less healthy people are bound to consume more care, and less wealthy people cannot pay as much. Assuming that these characteristics vary together, if they are unevenly distributed across health insurance pools, some pools should be in very comfortable circumstances and some in dire straits.

In fact, these characteristics do vary quite systematically across Japanese health insurance pools. A simplified picture, ignoring some smaller categories and many administrative details, includes seven separate groupings.[3] (The parentheses include the usual name in Japanese of each system, the abbreviation we use in this discussion, and the percentages of the Japanese population enrolled, including dependents).

- Government or quasi-public employees, relatively young and well paid, in several large nationwide Mutual Assistance Associations (Kyōsai Kumiai, MAA, 10%).
- Employees of large firms, also relatively young and well paid, in

---

3   The main groups not categorically specified in this list include seamen, with a separate employment-related system; day-laborers, with a different financing system under GMHI; low-income households not receiving public assistance, who are covered by CHI but pay lower premiums and co-payments and have a lower ceiling for "catastrophic" coverage; and certain occupational groups in CHI Associations, discussed later. The numbers are for 1993 and are from Iryō Hoken Seido Kenkyūkai, ed., *Me de Miru Iryō Hoken Hakusho*, 1995 ed. (Tokyo: Gyōsei, 1995), p. 66, and Kōsei Tōkei Kyōkai, ed. and pub., *Kokumin no Fukushi no Dōkō*, 1994 ed. (Tokyo, 1994), pp. 104–105.

hundreds of insurance "Society-Managed" Health Insurance pools at the company level (Kumiai Kenpo, SMHI, 26%).

* Employees of small firms, not so young and not so well paid, in a single nationwide "government-managed" Health Insurance pool (Seikan Kenpo, GMHI, 30%).
* The self- or non-employed, including farmers and small shopkeepers, who on average are older and have lower incomes, in "Citizens' " (formally but misleadingly called "national") health insurance pools in each locality (Kokumin Kenpo or Kokuho, CHI, 34%).
* Retired people not yet 70, who are within Citizens' health insurance but pay lower co-payments and have separate financing (Taishokusha, about 4 million people, or 3% of the population, but included in CHI).
* The elderly over 70, who are members of the other insurance pools but have their own special financing system (Rōjin Hoken, about 11 million people, or 9% of the population, but included in other of the foregoing systems).
* The poor, those on public assistance often for reasons of mental health disability (Seikatsu Hogo, about 660,000 people, or half of 1% of the population).

It is easy to appreciate that need rises and ability to pay diminishes as one descends this ladder of social groups.

Three egalitarian policies counteract these inequalities. First, Japan like most other industrialized nations collects health insurance premiums as a percentage of wages (up to a ceiling). Even Citizens' Health Insurance, where most enrollees do not receive wages, bases its premiums on a combination of household income and assets (and indeed about one-quarter of CHI enrollees pay reduced premiums because their incomes are low). Within each pool, therefore, the burdens of health insurance are adjusted by ability to pay.

However, while proportional or progressive financing can equalize burdens in this sense across an entire population in a single-payer system like that of Canada, more complicated mechanisms are necessary where there are many insurers, as in Japan. The Japanese approach is to employ two types of cross-subsidization: subsidies from general revenues, and direct transfers between insurers.

Both mechanisms are illustrated on Figure 4.1, which includes all these groups except the poor (because their financing does not come from social

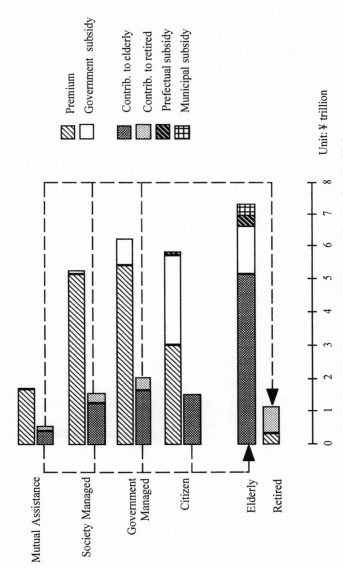

Figure 4.1 Cross-Subsidization in Health Insurance, 1994. *Note*: For the four health insurance programs, revenues are the upper bars, and expenditures on subsidies are the lower bars. The bars for the elderly and the retired are total revenues. [*Source*: National Institute of Population & Social Security Research, *Social Security Data Base* (1997)].

insurance).[4] The four groups listed first are the pools for public, large-firm, and small-firm employees, and the self-employed. For each, the bar on top is revenues, with the largest portion representing income from premiums (shared between employee and employer for MAA and Society- and Government-Managed Health Insurance). The portion to the right represents the government subsidy from general tax revenues. This amounts to only a small portion of administrative costs (under 1 percent) for the Society pools, but is set by law at 14 percent of outlays for Government-Managed Health Insurance, and at 50 percent of outlays for Citizens' Health Insurance (where the government in a sense picks up the employer's portion). Note that if the poor were included on this chart, 100 percent of their medical care would be paid from general revenues.

The bottom bar for each of these groups shows the direct transfer payments into the old-age system and, for the three employment-related systems (MAA, SMHI, and GMHI), into the system for younger retirees as well.[5] These transfers amount to a substantial sum: over ¥5 trillion, or about $30 billion at our $1 = ¥180 Purchasing Power Parity rate. For large firms and their employees, over 28 percent of the premiums they pay is transferred out to subsidize the retired and elderly – not counting the portion of their taxes that goes to this purpose.

The result of these two forms of subsidy is a pattern of great variation in how much health insurance participants get for what they pay. Specifically, using 1991 figures, large-firm employees got back ¥60 in health-care benefits for every ¥100 they paid in premiums (including the employer's share, which in economic terms should be seen as part of wages). Small-firm employees in Government-Managed Health Insurance got back ¥78 for each ¥100 of contributions. The self- or non-employed, on the other hand, on average received ¥170 in health-care benefits for every ¥100 yen of contributions.[6] This ratio cannot be calculated for the retired and elderly groups for technical reasons, but clearly they receive far more in benefits than they pay in pre-

---

4 They are drawn from various tables in Shakai Hoshō Seido Shingikai Jimukyoku, ed., *Shakai Hoshō Tōkei Nenpō*, 1993 ed. (Tokyo: Hōken, 1993). Our thanks to Yasuo Takagi and Mikitaka Masuyama for assistance with these calculations.
5 The retirees whose costs are subsidized in this way all belong to Citizens' Health Insurance, so it has no transfer payment to this group. A Health Insurance Society has the option of keeping its own retirees enrolled until age 70 and thereby avoiding this subsidy.
6 Calculated from Table 4–1 in *Iryōhi Handobukku*, 1994 ed., p. 246. The ratio is the outlays for medical care (*hoken kyūfuhi*) divided by the income from contributions, times 100.

miums. The poor on public assistance get all their health care without payment.

Minimizing Protest

The Japanese pattern is extremely fair in the sense of promoting equality – the healthy and wealthy subsidize the poor and sick. One would expect, however, that those who are paying much higher premiums than they receive in benefits would feel exploited by the system. They would believe that fairness in the sense of the investment model had been violated, and that others were benefiting unjustly. That should make for difficult politics.

Interestingly enough, at least until recently, the perception among Japanese citizens about who is treated fairly or unfairly tends to be exactly the opposite. Large-firm or public employees are always viewed as the most advantaged, as getting the best deal, while the self- or non-employed covered by Citizens' Health Insurance are regarded as disadvantaged. The main reason is that the amount of the co-payment is different.

That is, regular enrollees of Citizens' Health Insurance pay 30 percent of their medical bills directly to the doctor or hospital. Those in employment-related health insurance (SMHI and GMHI) paid only 10 percent for themselves, and 20 percent (inpatient) or 30 percent (outpatient) for their dependents. In addition, large-firm employees may have an additional break compared with small-firm employees in that quite a few societies have been rich enough to reimburse part of the co-payment and to provide free or subsidized health examinations (which are not covered by health insurance). Many large-firm insurance societies even own rest-and-recreation facilities (*hoyōjo*) at hot springs or other resort areas, or they provide small subsidies for members taking family vacations to rejuvenate themselves.[7] Big companies also often pay more than the required 50 percent of the premium, up to 80 percent.

It should be noted that while these differentials are real, the size of the gap in benefits is substantially mitigated by two facts. First, medical fees in Japan are low compared with the United States, so the difference between a 10 percent

---

7 In 1991, ¥543 billion ($3 billion), or 12 percent of total expenditures for the health insurance societies went to "other expenditures," including such extra benefits as well as investment in facilities. *Iryō Handobukku*, 1994, p. 246. Note that these nonstatutory benefits are rarely the result of demands from employees – unlike U.S. practice, neither premium payments nor benefits are the subject of labor–management negotiations in the private sector.

and 30 percent co-payment for an average doctor visit (including prescriptions and so forth) would be only about ¥1,000.[8] Second, Japan has "catastrophic" coverage, or a cap on monthly out-of-pocket spending (called the Kōgaku Ryōyōhi Seido). Any co-payments over ¥63,000 per month (¥35,400 for low-income households) are covered for members of all health insurance systems.[9] That means that no one should pay more than roughly $350 a month for covered medical care, and lower-income people would not pay more than about $200 (in terms of our Purchasing Power Parity rate of $1 = ¥180).

The differences in co-payments and extra benefits are quite out in the open, but the differential ratios of premiums to medical benefits are rarely mentioned. In fact, few employees either know or care how much their premiums are. Accordingly, people naturally view large-firm employees (and government employees, who are similarly treated) as the best off. At least, that is the assumption in public discourse, and when proposals are made to make the system more fair, the usual suggestion is to equalize co-payments. Indeed, for some time it has been the official Ministry of Health and Welfare policy goal to have all co-payments set at 20 percent, and the employee co-payment was actually raised to that level in late 1997. We might imagine, however, that the actual differences in costs and benefits are sufficiently known, or at least suspected, to mitigate feelings of unfairness on equality grounds.

One is reminded, in fact, of what is often cited as a key to political support for Social Security pensions in the United States: The premium (or Social Security Tax) is regressive, favoring upper-income people, while the benefits are progressive, favoring lower-income people. It is difficult for participants to judge whether they are being exploited or are exploiting others. In short, a degree of confusion caused by cross-cutting principles and interests can be very helpful in maintaining support or, at least, inhibiting resentment and protest.

Gifts

Finally, what about the wealthy? Aside from whether they might feel exploited by having to subsidize those with lower incomes, would well-off people not resent being forced into the same standard of medical care as

8 The average outpatient visit cost (including the co-payment) for 1991 in Government-Managed Health insurance was ¥5,075, or about $28. *Iryō Handobukku*, 1994, p. 258.
9 These are 1994 figures. In order to share the risks to individual insurance pools, catastrophic coverage is reinsured within both the SMHI and CHI systems.

everyone else? After all, in a system that is both low-cost and egalitarian, the level of services provided cannot be very luxurious.

In other nations with egalitarian health-care systems, mechanisms have developed to accommodate the desire of people with sufficient means to opt out of the regular system and get quicker service, more comfortable amenities, and what they will at least perceive as higher-quality medical treatment. Upper-income Germans buy separate, essentially private health insurance. British patients cannot disenroll from the National Health Service but they can avoid long waits for elective surgery by entering a private hospital wing and seeing a "consultant" physician who is paid directly. Canadians have no such option at home, but those who can afford it sometimes go to the United States for high-class medical care.

These alternatives are not available in Japan. First, foreign countries are too far away for anyone but extremely wealthy people who need the most sophisticated treatments. Second, the principle of compulsory enrollment cannot be violated in Japan because opting out of the established system would not only introduce serious problems of adverse selection, it would also disrupt the intricate pattern of cross-subsidization we have just described.

Third, and perhaps most difficult to understand, Japan has not seen the development of hospitals and physicians to serve patients desiring special treatment by providing services outside the regular payment system.[10] One reason is that compulsory enrollment, income-proportional premiums, and the prohibition on balance-billing mean that a wealthy patient would both have to pay heavily for mandatory health insurance for no benefit and then face the full cost of treatment. No doubt, a few rich people would be willing, but apparently not enough – a sizable market would be needed to warrant the substantial investment necessary to provide first-class medical care.[11]

Another reason is that two relatively minor "escape hatches" do provide some relief to the wealthy. First, hospitals are allowed to set aside some of their rooms as "extra charge" private or semi-private rooms. Recently, the

10 There are several exceptions, services covered inadequately or not at all by health insurance: some dental work, cosmetic surgery, normal childbirth (for which health insurance pays a lump-sum to the enrollee rather than reimbursing the provider), abortion, and the preventative physical examinations called "human dry-dock" (*ningen dokku*). In these areas, providers compete on price, amenities, and perceived quality.

11 Here, too, there is an exception: A few medical clinics have been established in big cities mainly to serve expatriate executives who do not speak Japanese. They do not accept Japanese health insurance and are extremely expensive.

ceiling for such rooms was moved up to 50 percent of total beds for all hospitals, although very few other than university hospitals go that high. In ordinary hospitals, the extra charge runs from about ¥5,000 a day in the provinces to ¥10,000 in Tokyo. University hospital charges will occasionally be as high as ¥70,000 a day, although the average is about ¥25,000 in Tokyo and half that outside the big cities. It is interesting that the demand for these extra-charge beds has not been excessive – many fairly affluent Japanese apparently do not think it is worth an extra $2,000 or so to spend two weeks in a semi-private room rather than one with three to five companions. But for those willing and able to spend more, at least some improvement in amenities to get above the average level is possible.

Second, wealthy patients often make "gifts" (*orei* or *sharei*) in order to be treated by a particular physician. In fact, such gifts to physicians are seen as normal for the minority of patients who opt for an extra-charge bed – better amenities call for special medical attention as well. There are no good data on such under-the-counter payments because they are not legal. It appears that they can range up to about ¥500,000 for difficult surgery by a department head in a famous university hospital, but the average amount is more like ¥100,000 (about $550). Typically, a patient's family will ask another doctor at the hospital to act as a go-between (for a fee of about 10 percent). Although the amount of the gift is not really negotiated, a certain amount of back-and-forth may be needed to decide how much is appropriate. In that sense, something like a market price probably prevails at least for a particular doctor, or perhaps within a given hospital. In most cases, the gift is handed over after treatment is completed (leading to some uncertainty in case the treatment is unsuccessful).

Although it is impossible to determine how much money changes hands in these transactions, our rather generous estimate for 1990 is that it amounted to some ¥270 billion ($1.5 billion), or less than 1 percent of total health expenditures (see the discussion in Chapter 1). Such payments are a sizable expenditure for some patients and an important source of income for a minority of physicians, but they are not all that significant as a factor in aggregate health-care expenditures. It is worth noting that the gift plus the insured hospital charges would hardly ever amount to as much as the normal cost of the same treatment in the United States.[12]

12 Note also that gifts of this sort, which are clearly payments for a specific service, should be distinguished from the New Year or summer presents of salad oil, a bottle of whiskey,

"Gifts" are clear violations of the prohibition of balance-billing, and for public employees – physicians in local or national government hospitals, or the hospitals attached to public university medical-schools – they amount to bribery, a serious offense. Public hospitals often post big signs stating that the practice will not be tolerated, and usually the rule is strictly enforced (not only by management but by the hospital employees' union, which is often very powerful in a public hospital and will be vigilant in looking out for someone taking special advantage). The attitude of society at large is probably that these gifts are wrong in principle, but in practice they are the way the world works – the *tatemae-honne* distinction that characterizes so much slightly shady behavior in Japan.

Questions of legality and morality aside, to an economist such payments are merely the market working to align supply and demand of a scarce resource, medical care of higher perceived quality. They are similar to paying a scalper a high price for tickets to a sports event. To a political scientist, the function of such payments for the overall health-care system is to dampen potential disaffection by a particularly powerful segment of society. Allowing a few people to buy something extra is in that sense necessary for maintaining what in most respects is a rigidly egalitarian system for the majority.

Why not make such practices legal? Some Welfare Ministry officials, influenced by the market orientation of American health economists, would like to move in that direction; indeed, since the mid-1980s, the number of allowable extra-charge beds has been expanded, and hospitals are allowed to charge directly for better meals. One goal has been to stimulate more variety and higher quality through competition. However, such proposals to date have not gotten too far.[13]

In general, it is very difficult for such market-oriented policies to be expanded enough to have a major impact on quality. Politically, violations of the principle of equal access draw quick criticism from progressive politicians and the media, followed by what appears to be substantial resonance among

---

or perhaps some money, which routinely come to doctors and other high-status people in Japan's reciprocity-based society.

13   For example, almost no hospitals thought that providing special meals would be worth the trouble. In 1994, partly to save money, the fee-schedule amount for a hospital stay was reduced by the cost of materials for meals (a measly ¥600 a day), and hospitals started charging this amount (or more) directly – the logic is that patients have to eat anyway whether in or out of the hospital. This issue has received a remarkable amount of attention within the MHW for a decade.

the general public. But more to the point, the Japanese health-care system is fundamentally based on the principles of a fixed fee schedule and on equal access to all providers by all patients. These principles, basic to equality, can be nibbled at the edges but not violated wholesale.

HEALTH INSURANCE MANAGEMENT

Another principle of Japanese health insurance, just as fundamental, is restricting choice. Individuals cannot be permitted to shop around for the most attractive plan. By the same token, insurers cannot be permitted to go after attractive healthy and wealthy members, or to discourage older or poorer people from enrolling. Allowing more choice in insurance would inevitably diminish equality in benefits and burdens. The principle of mandatory enrollment without choice has generally been followed rather closely, although four exceptions are worth noting.

First, about 4.6 million self-employed people and their dependents are enrolled in Associations (confusingly, also called *kumiai* as in SMHI) within Citizens' Health Insurance, based on their trade or profession. A few of these Associations actively solicited for members by offering lower premiums and were able to attract younger and healthier members, although such practices are frowned upon by the Ministry of Health and Welfare. In fact, the Ministry has not permitted the formation of any new Associations since 1958.[14]

Second, the proprietor of a growing company has some discretion over when to disenroll the firm from GMHI and form an SMHI Society. Most do so when they reach about 700 employees, because the switch will usually make sense economically despite forgoing the subsidy. That is because a growing company will usually have a young labor force that will use medical care less than the GMHI average – probably enough less to allow some extra benefits, pleasing the employees. Incidentally, once made, the decision to form a Society is irreversible.

Third, many Japanese purchase supplementary private health insurance. Mostly this is the "dread-disease" type, usually called "cancer insurance,"

---

14 There has been criticism of the fact that relatively high-income doctors usually enroll in one of the Associations, where the ratio of benefits to premiums will be attractive because most members are relatively high-income, healthy people (although note that the public subsidy to the CHI Associations can be as low as 33 percent rather than the 50 percent in regular CHI). See Okamoto Etsuji, *Kokumin Kenkō Hoken – Kanyūsha no tame no Hon* (Tokyo: San'itsu Shobō, 1988).

that pays a fixed amount per day for hospitalization. It is sold along with life insurance by Japanese companies, or as a stand-alone product (and quite a profitable one) exclusively by foreign firms. There is also a form of indemnity or "disability" insurance (*songai hoken*) that reimburses out-of-pocket costs such as extra room charges, uncovered high-tech procedures, a portion of the co-payment, and sometimes travel costs. It is sold by fire and marine insurance companies and is profitable though not particularly popular. The relatively low patient's liability for medical costs, plus an MHW regulation that at least a small deductible must be paid directly for medical care, has inhibited the growth of such private "gap" insurance (and note that the higher-income people who might be the most attracted to extra insurance have the lowest co-payments).

Fourth, because there is no effective enforcement of mandatory enrollment, and because CHI premiums are paid directly to the local government rather than being deducted automatically from income, it is possible (albeit illegal) to opt out of health insurance altogether. A non-enrollee who gets sick can then get coverage under CHI by paying up the back premiums. However, although this practice seems to be popular among young American business people who reside for two or three years in Japan, it appears that only about 7 percent of those who should be enrolled in CHI engage in such free-riding. That is not a large enough proportion to create major problems of adverse selection, in which only people who are likely to use a lot of services sign up for insurance.

Aside from these four exceptions, which are not very serious, there is not much choice in Japanese health insurance. What, then, are the functions of the managers of the insurance carriers, and do their actions matter? Actually, decisions made by those who run the giant GMHI system, officials in the Health Insurance Bureau, are quite significant for the "macro" management of health insurance as a whole, and this is discussed in the next chapter. Here we briefly describe managers in the two big systems made up of local insurers, SMHI and CHI, and also look into differences of behavior among the insurers.

First, who are the managers? The SMHI Societies in large firms are run jointly by management and labor, meaning that the Management Committee (*rijikai*) is made up of an equal number of representatives of both sides. In practice, however, the administrator and staff operate as offshoots of the firm's personnel office. A typical administrator is a regular employee of the firm, about 40 years old, who has held a variety of jobs perhaps with some training in personnel matters. The staff, in a firm with 4,000 employees, might be two full-time clerks plus part-time assistance from another five or so personnel-department staff members. No one in the office has had extensive training in insurance or health-care management.

CHI is managed at the city, town, or village level, by a regular division (usually called the Kokumin Kenkō Hoken Ka) housed at the city hall. The division chief is a regular municipal civil servant who has previously served in many parts of the government, probably with no experience with insurance or health care. Some of his staff (probably about five officials in a city of 100,000 population) similarly rotate from job to job within the entire municipal government, while others are permanent.

In both cases, most of the work is simply processing documents. The jobs of maintaining enrollment data and receiving premiums is totally routine in a company Society because all employees are enrolled, and each pays the same percentage premium, up to a ceiling set by law, by automatic deduction from wages. It doesn't matter whether the employee has any dependents or not, or for that matter whether he or she is covered as a dependent by someone else in the household. The only slightly tricky point is when family members become non-dependents because they work part-time, but actually that is not a difficult decision because the general rule sets an annual income ceiling of ¥1.1 million (about $6,000 at PPP rates) in order to be exempted from payment.

Both these jobs are trickier in Citizens' Health Insurance. First, by law, everyone in a municipality who is not covered by one of the other insurance systems is supposed to enroll in the local CHI pool, but the officials have no records on who is covered by what, and in practice a new resident or someone who loses coverage has to come to city hall to sign up. As noted previously, some simply do not, and they go without health insurance until they get sick. When they then come to enroll, it can be tricky to determine the amount of premiums due from since they were last covered.

Second, the amount of premium paid by each household is determined by a somewhat complicated formula that includes income, assets, and number of household members (regardless of age). The necessary documents must be provided by the applicant, and they need to be checked (in particular against local tax records). Many applicants are entitled to a reduction or a total forgiveness of premiums because of their low incomes.[15] All of these

---

15 The formula is complicated, but a household of three with a total income under about ¥2.1 million (about $11,500) would be eligible for at least a 20 percent reduction of its premium, based on number of members, and would pay no income-dependent portion. The elderly are treated more generously in that a portion of their pension income is exempt.

decisions are governed by strict rules, not administrative discretion, but the rules are complicated, and their application cannot be completely routine.

On the benefits side, the great bulk of the work at insurance carriers is simple processing of the claims that come from the financial intermediaries in each prefecture who actually pay the providers. The main task is checking whether the patient is enrolled and that there is no double-billing. However, SMHI managers have more to do here than their counterparts in local government because the extra benefits that many companies provide are processed by the Society itself (with payment directly to the provider or the employee). There may be tricky points about eligibility for a physical examination or, for that matter, a vacation subsidy. CHI programs never offer extra benefits, so the payment side is normally quite routine.

In both SMHI and CHI, however, this processing of individual claims can be made more problematical if the managers decide that they want to get tough. As will be described in Chapter 6, the main responsibility for reviewing claims – to see if the charges are legal and appropriate – lies with the intermediaries, but the insurance carriers have the right to make a second review. Managers can decide in effect whether to take an aggressive stance. The purpose is not so much to save money by rejecting claims as to send a signal to providers and others.

Usually, the most important policy decision open to insurance managers and their superiors (company management and to a lesser extent the union for Societies, the mayor, and ultimately the municipal assembly, for CHI) is deciding the premium level. This decision is easier for Societies, where the premium rate will not change except when the revenue-expenditure balance is altered substantially, and even then in most cases, the decision is a fairly straightforward one of how much to adjust the rate (about 7% of SMHI societies raised their premium rates in 1995). If the managers are worried about costs, they can cut back on extras and can also shift some of the burden from the company to workers by decreasing the employer's share of the premium.[16]

A key point here is that the factors that affect revenues and expenditures – principally participants' incomes, and their propensity to consume medical care as determined mainly by age – tend to be fairly constant within a given

16   Most companies pay more than the 50 percent requirement – the unweighted average across industries is that the company pays 4.7 percent and the employee 3.6 percent of wages up to a ceiling, which was ¥980,000 per month (about $5,500) in 1995. *Kenkōhoken Kumiai no Genjō*, 1995.

industry. Companies that compete directly with each other and their employees therefore do not usually have different contribution rates. On the other hand, there is substantial variation between industries in a way that – particularly during the high-growth era – tended to favor "sunrise" over "sunset" industries. This point can be illustrated by comparing contribution rates (the employee and employer shares combined) across several industries. Those with high rates, logically enough, are those with aging labor forces (such as steel, at 9.2%, and local government, 8.9%) or that pay low wages (textiles, 8.7%). The highest is mining, that has both factors (aging and low wages) plus a high rate of illness (9.2% for metal mining, 9.5% for coal). Growing industries tend to have lower rates, with younger workers (electrical manufacturing, 8.2%) or higher wages (publishing and communications, 7.8%).[17]

The problem of contribution rates is much more complicated in CHI, and the range of variation across municipalities is much wider, to the extent of causing some serious policy problems. For one thing, a local government has a fair amount of discretion in establishing its formula for premiums. The Ministry of Health and Welfare has a guideline that the formula should be one-half by flat rate (simply determined by the number of household members) and one-half related to financial strength – a combination of income and assets. However, many localities have chosen a more progressive formula, which weighs financial strength more heavily, and have adopted a rather steep scale of premiums relative to income and assets. Such choices often date back to a time when a mayor supported by the progressive parties was in office, but they have tended to persist even when more conservative mayors came into office and despite informal pressure from the MHW.

Even more important than such differences in policy choices is the great variation in the age and income structures of municipalities. An extreme case is an executive bedroom community outside a big city, where the population is relatively young and with high income. Unlike in the United States, where a move to an upscale suburb might make for higher medical costs because providers would charge more, health insurance premium rates in suburban Japan for a household with a given income is relatively low because infrequent usage is reflected in smaller total expenditures, and then these are shared among more affluent people. The other extreme is the rural village, where most of the younger workers have left for the city and the population is dominated by retirees and marginal farmers. Here rates can be extremely

17   Ibid., Table 1–3.

high – particularly if there are many low-income people, whose premiums are forgiven in part though they still draw benefits.

Of course, the impact on the individual household can be much greater when these demographic and policy factors intersect. A locality with many low-income people can be tempted to adopt a progressive formula that puts higher burdens on higher-income people, but given low average incomes, the definition of "high income" might have to be rather modest or there would be nobody to pay the higher premiums. Cases like the following are not uncommon: A company employee retires and moves with his wife from the city to his rural home town; he finds that just on the basis of his Employees' Pension benefit and his savings, he is in the highest bracket for that town and must pay very high premiums – up to ¥520,000 a year per person, or about ¥87,000 (almost $500) per month for himself and his wife together. That rate might not seem too unreasonable to some American couples, but it is perceived as extremely high in Japan.[18]

For municipalities with the oldest populations and the lowest revenue base, no manipulation of the contribution formula can produce enough revenue to cover expenditure. It is necessary for the national government to provide an extra subsidy to those in the worst financial condition. It was noted earlier that the Treasury subsidy to Citizens' Health Insurance is 50 percent; that figure represents the average subsidy, but the basis for allocating it among municipalities is that those in comfortable shape receive 40 percent of their expenditure, while those in financial trouble can be subsidized up to 80 percent.[19] Also available is the cross-subsidization from the special old-age system already described. So, all in all, only a tiny portion of the benefits paid

18 This figure of ¥520,000 per year, or about $250 per month in PPP terms, is the maximum that can be charged any individual for Citizens Health Insurance. Depending on the locality, a household income as low as the $40,000 range could trigger this highest rate. As for the highest possible payment per person in SMHI, an unmarried company employee might have to pay as much as ¥833,000 a year or under $400 a month himself – matched by his employer – if his salary is at or above the ceiling in an industry with relatively high contribution rates. If he were married, of course, the cost per person would be half that.

19 The principle is quite similar to the way General Revenue Sharing (Kōfuzei, usually translated as Local Allocation Tax) is calculated in Japan – a formula including demographics, income, and so forth is used to determine the "fiscal capacity" of the local government; the weaker ones get a larger allocation. Note that both CHI and SMHI also have "reinsurance" plans in which all insurers contribute to a pool that will cover high-cost patients. Such plans are necessary to limit risks for the smaller insurers, but they do not have a major redistributive effect because the contributions are calculated mainly on an actuarial basis.

103

by the most deficit-ridden localities is coming from the contributions paid by their members (as low as 5 percent in extreme cases). Note that the MHW attaches conditions to this extra subsidy, mainly that the locality must follow the guideline that no more than half of its contribution formula be income related (i.e., it is forced to have lower-income people pay what the Ministry sees as their fair share).

Managers of private-sector SMHI and public-sector CHI health-insurance programs thus do have important roles, but compared with their counterparts in the United States, their scope is quite limited. Executives in the American health insurance industry are paid, and very well, to be entrepreneurial. On the one hand, they go after the members they want and subtly or not so subtly avoid those they don't; on the other, they negotiate directly with providers for lower costs. They can tailor both their premiums and their benefits to appeal to their key customers (mainly large corporations). They expect individual rewards if they can maximize profits. Japanese health insurance managers have access to few if any such choices, and their incentives lead to an orientation much more that of a chief clerk than of an entrepreneur. For insurers as for the providers described in the previous chapter, this routinization and rigidity are key factors in maintaining Japan's low-cost system.

EVOLUTION

To emphasize stability and routine, and how effectively protest has been preempted or dampened, is not to claim that the system has been free of conflict. Quite the contrary: When we look at how health insurance developed in Japan, it is clear that, first, various social groups attained their degree of relative equality largely as the result of political struggles, and second, resentments about fairness have led to many marginal adjustments in relative burdens. Figure 4.2, which shows the percentage of the entire Japanese population covered by the major categories of health insurance, can help us trace the evolution of the system.

Early Developments

Health insurance in Japan began with coverage of military and other government personnel plus employees in a few paternalistic private companies from late in the nineteenth century. The Factory Law of 1911 established a com-

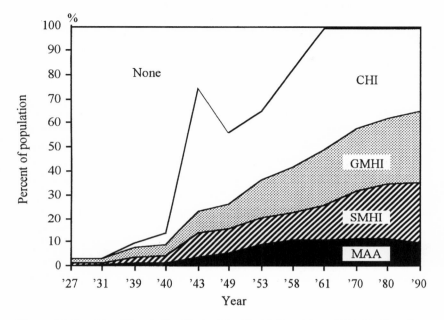

Figure 4.2 Percent of Population Covered by Health Insurance, 1927–90. *Note*: Data for the wartime period are approximate. [*Source*: Yasuo Takagi, "Kokumin kenko hoken to chiiki-fukushi – Choki nyuin no zehi to kokuho anteika taisaku no jissai to mondaiten," *Kikan Shakai Hosho Kenkyû* 30(3) (1974), 239.]

pulsory Workman's Compensation system. Then in the 1920s, partly as a response to fears about labor unrest, large companies were required to provide medical care for their blue-collar workers. This apparent benefit was resisted by nearly everyone involved.

That is, employers did not want to pay their share of the premium and worried that workers would malinger if they were paid for being sick. Workers did not want to pay any premiums and resented that occupational injuries would not be paid from the Workman's Compensation fund (all paid by the employer) and instead would come from health insurance. Doctors did not like the system because the fees it would pay were lower than their normal and customary charges. None of these three groups saw the longer-range payoffs that years later would be taken for granted: worker attachment to the firm for businessmen, more health care for workers, and increased demand for physicians. The plan was forced down everyone's throat by bureaucrats in the Home Ministry, the "industrial statesmen" sort of business leaders, and Kitasato Shibasaburō, the highly connected doctor who led the Medical Association of the day.

Compared to other nations, an unusual feature of the development of health insurance in Japan in the 1920s was that blue-collar workers in small firms were covered at the same time as large-firm employees. The reason was not political demand; it may have been simply bureaucratic in that small-firm employees had been covered by the same Workman's Compensation system as workers in large firms, so some change was needed. In any case, since small firms did not have the management capability or sufficiently large pools to manage their own systems, the government had to provide health insurance for them directly – the origin of the GMHI system.

This role of the government as one among a variety of direct providers of health insurance, rather than just as a coordinator of direct providers on the one hand or as the sole provider on the other, is the most distinctive element of the Japanese health insurance system even today. It was more an accidental result of the situation of the time than a deliberate strategy, but in the postwar period, it led to the Ministry of Health and Welfare taking the lead among insurers (for example, in bargaining with providers) rather than the Associations of large-firm or of local government carriers stepping out in front.

As Figure 4.2 indicates, in 1927 only about 3 percent of the Japanese population was covered by these employment-based systems, but the number increased rapidly as the Japanese economy was organized for war. Employee health insurance coverage was then extended to white-collar employees, and to dependents, in 1941. Meanwhile, the far larger number of farmers presented more difficult problems. They had no employers to contribute and, indeed, no wages from which to deduct their own contributions. Grass-roots medical cooperatives had been founded in a growing number of villages in the 1920s and '30s, and the national government in 1938 officially supported (and subsidized) rural health care in 1938 with passage of the Citizens' Health Insurance Act.[20]

Again, the motive for the new health insurance system was hardly compassion. The proximate reason was that the military had become concerned

20 Kokumin Kenkō Hoken Hō – again, the usual translation is "National" Health Insurance. See the excellent account by T. Higuchi, "Medical Care through Social Insurance in the Japanese Rural Sector," *International Labour Review* 109:3 (1974), 251–74.

about the physical condition of recruits and, by extension, of potential mothers of recruits. The number of localities participating in CHI grew slowly until World War II expanded into the Pacific Theater, but the system was then expanded dramatically by the government. In 1943, more than 70 percent of the Japanese population was covered by some form of mandated health insurance. However, financial problems toward the end of the war, and in the immediate postwar period, caused many localities to drop out, and the covered population had fallen to under 60 percent by 1948.

Health Insurance For All

As the economy recovered, more and more localities reestablished Citizens' Health Insurance programs. Municipal-level governments administered their programs in various ways. Many simply collected the premiums and paid private-practice physicians and hospitals on a fee-for-service basis. Somewhat less common was a pattern that went back to the prewar cooperatives, where the local insurer actually owned and operated its own clinics or even hospitals, using social insurance contributions plus government subsidies to cover the expenses (with doctors on salary). In 1958, 2,797 clinics and 451 hospitals were managed directly by local governments (or their insurance carriers); some provided free medical care as well as public-health services to residents, and many of these organizations were successful in stimulating grass-roots participation in health care.[21]

Along with the growth of employment-related health insurance, the expansion of these community-level programs – spurred by increasing government subsidies – had led to nearly 90 percent coverage of the population by the late 1950s. That meant that covering the remainder would not be too radical a jump, and at the same time, political pressures for universal coverage had been building. The socialist and then the conservative parties had been unified in 1955, and the two new parties competed for votes by calling for "*kaihoken*" or "health insurance for all." After some contention, the necessary legislation was passed in 1958 for full implementation by 1961.

Coverage was now universal, but it was far from unified. The government mandated that a Citizens' Health Insurance program be established by every municipal government. However, it passed up the chance to channel all health insurance through these locally managed programs. That alternative could

21   Ibid., p. 265.

have provided equal coverage for all, and indeed over time might have led to something like a national system of American-style HMOs (health management organizations). But labor and management did not want to give up the financial advantages of the existing employment-related programs, and neither the Ministry of Health and Welfare nor the Japan Medical Association cared to leave so much power, and so much possibility for idiosyncratic variation, in the hands of local leaders.[22] The provision that CHI would cover only those not covered by other programs was thus written into the new law. At the same time, this reform took away the possibility of effective independent management of CHI programs, to the lasting regret of many progressive academics and others who cherished the virtues of grass-roots participation and local initiative.

That is, the achievement of "health insurance for all" was a major step toward equality of treatment under centralized control. It was at about this time that the uniform fee schedule was made mandatory for all providers, disallowing both balance-billing and any discounts (e.g., for residents of a given community or employees of a company). All consumers could now go to any doctor or hospital in Japan and expect the same treatment, and no provider would have any reason to discriminate for or against any patient. This step was thus the culmination of a long process of bringing all medical-care provision under a common umbrella and much more subject to government policy – notably the cost-containment policy instigated two decades later.

Expansion

Although universal coverage was the longest step toward an egalitarian health insurance system, fundamental inequalities remained. Because CHI members, the non-employed, were on average less healthy and wealthy than enrollees in employment-based health insurance, the potential financial burdens on government at the local and national level dictated a 50 percent co-payment for services (while employees had no co-payment for themselves in their systems). These high out-of-pocket expenses particularly affected the elderly,

---

22   The JMA at various times called for eliminating employee health insurance in favor of a "regional" system, but it remained tactically vague about precisely what level of region it had in mind. For similar politics around "pensions for all" in the same period, see Campbell, *How Policies Change*, chap. 3.

most of whom at that time were receiving no meaningful pensions at all. Statistics indicate that the usage of medical facilities by old people, inpatient or outpatient, was far lower than for the middle-aged in the 1960s even though they were afflicted with more illness.

This inequality was substantially redressed in the early 1970s, which not coincidentally was another period of intense political party competition. In the period often called the "dawn of the welfare era" (*fukushi gannen*), the largest co-payments were reduced to 30 percent, and the "catastrophic" cap on out-of-pocket costs was introduced on the same basis for all health insurance systems. Most dramatically, a big new program of "free" medical care for the elderly – coverage from general revenues of the entire co-payment for most people aged 70 and over (plus the bedridden from age 65) – was established by the national government in 1972. The stimulus was initiation of a similar program three years earlier by the progressive Minobe administration in the Tokyo Metropolitan Government. Adoption of this initiative by a large number of other localities, many of them also with progressive leadership, led to an intense pressure-group and media campaign at the national level that amounted to an "old people boom."[23]

These early 1970s reforms marked the high point of the first form of cross-subsidization, in which the general population paid various proportions of the health-care costs of needier people by means of direct payments from tax revenues. These egalitarian reforms had their intended effect: The less well off in general, and older people in particular, began going to the doctor much more often. Not so intended was the development that a sizable number of the elderly also moved into hospitals because they now could get essentially custodial long-term care at virtually no cost to themselves or their families.

The cost of the government subsidy for old-age medical care accordingly rose sharply, more than doubling in the second half of the 1970s to reach nearly one trillion yen by 1980. Giving "free" medical care to the elderly became the most visible symbol for conservatives of public spending going out of control. It was inevitable, then, that health care in general and the program for the elderly in particular would become targets of the "administrative reform" austerity campaign that got underway in the early 1980s.

---

23 Pensions and other social programs were also greatly expanded in this period. See ibid., chap. 5.

Egalitarian Rationalization

The Health Care for the Elderly Law (Rōjin Hoken Hō, passed in 1982 and implemented in 1983) was one of the early steps in this campaign. It did cut the government's burden, but the interesting point is that its most significant provision was not a major reduction in spending on old-age medical care but rather a new form of cross-subsidization. This most expensive sector of health policy would now be covered mainly by direct transfer payments from employment-related insurance rather than from general revenues. Each insurance pool was assessed its fair share of supporting the increased burden of old-age health care.[24] Inevitable complaints from the relatively young large-firm employees were undercut by the large surpluses that many SMHI pools had developed, a result of the drastic 1981 policy of capping medical fees.

It is common enough in austerity campaigns to cut government expenditures by transferring costs to consumers. Increasing premiums and co-payments for Medicare in the United States is an example. Such reforms make the system less egalitarian (though perhaps more "fair" in the "investment" sense) because burdens tend to be increased for those with the lowest incomes and the greatest need for care, so that the cost to the general public can be limited.

In Japan, however, this old-age health-care reform, as well as the somewhat similar program for retirees created in 1985, actually made the system more egalitarian. The tax burden on the general population was lightened, but the bulk of the costs were transferred not back to the elderly but to the group that was the most healthy and wealthy, the employees of large firms. In fact, the firms with the lowest ratio of elderly members were required to transfer the most.

Oddly enough, an aspect of the Health Care for the Elderly Law of 1982 that in financial terms seems a backward step, away from equality in terms of transfers to less well-off groups, actually was a step forward toward equality in symbolic terms. This was the abandonment of the principle of "free" medical care by establishing a co-payment for the elderly. The fact that older people had been getting health care "for free" (*tada*), and also seemed to be overusing facilities, was widely resented. The elderly were seen as having unfair advantages that were not shared with the rest of the population. Intro-

---

24 The formula required each insurer to pay the amount it would bear if its proportion of elderly enrollees was the same as the national average.

ducing a co-payment seemed to redress the balance, even though it was almost trivially small – initially ¥300 per day in the hospital and ¥400 per month per provider for outpatient care. (These co-payments were later hiked gradually, and in 1997 they were raised to ¥1,000 a day inpatient, and ¥500 per outpatient visit up to a cap of ¥2,000 per month.)

Such changes, and the introduction in 1985 of a 10 percent co-payment for employees who hitherto had been getting free care (raised to 20 percent in 1997), were incremental adjustments in the balance of costs and benefits, real or symbolic, in response to perceptions of unfairness as well as to immediate financial problems. In another such move, more recently, the government marginally increased its general revenue contribution to old-age health care, in order to provide a measure of relief for the Health Insurance Societies, many of which had gone into the red because of the burden of cross-subsidization. In short, the cross-subsidization system is complicated enough, and flexible enough, to allow adjustments in response to immediate problems of financing or of perceived fairness – in terms of either "equality" or "investment." Grievances could be assuaged without major changes in the entire system.

Insuring Long-term Care

Such incremental change would not be enough, however, to deal with the problem of long-term care for the elderly. As far as one can tell from newspaper and television coverage, for several years the number-one problem facing Japan has been its "aging society" (*kōreika shakai*). The population is currently moderately old (a bit above the United States but below several European countries), but it is getting older, and getting there faster, than anywhere else. The proportion of the population aged 65 and over doubled from 6 percent in 1960 to 12 percent in 1990, and it will double again to about 25 percent (the highest level in the world) by 2020. Although hardly anyone argues that longevity is a bad thing at the individual level, there is much pointing with alarm at the economic and social implications of having so many elderly people. Currently, the most publicized problem is long-term care, the biggest dilemma for health policy in Japan, as in many other advanced nations.

From around 1990, the government started to deal with these problems in a high-profile way – for example, with the "Gold Plan" for a marked increase in both institutional and community long-term-care services. On the financial side, a bold plan for public Long-Term-Care Insurance (Kaigo Hoken, LTCI) was proposed in late 1994. It called for a brand new social insurance fund to which everyone over 40 would contribute, and from which (along with a matching amount from tax revenues) older people judged disabled or frail would pay for either community or institutional long-term care. The idea came from Germany (and originally the Netherlands), though it is noteworthy that the proposal for LTCI in Japan was announced before the German scheme had been even partially implemented, in April 1995.

The LTCI proposal should be seen mainly as a response to the general problem of population aging, but it was also aimed at some specific policy problems of health insurance. First, although as noted in Chapter 1, overall health spending had not been increasing much relative to GDP, the future burden of medical care for the elderly was a growing worry, particularly because the most rapidly growing component was institutional long-term care that in many cases went beyond purely medical needs. Politically, protests were growing from large-firm employees whose SMHI premiums were being hiked solely to cover increases in the cross-subsidy to the old-age and retirement health insurance pools.[25] Under LTCI, many of these old-age costs to health insurance would be covered under the new system.

Second, an immediate difficulty was the virtual bankruptcy of the Citizens' Health Insurance pools in many rural towns and villages hard hit by demographic trends. As described earlier, the costs of long-term care along with a lack of households that could afford to pay high premiums had made many municipal systems completely dependent on extra subsidies. The new LTCI system would alleviate this problem because, even though it would also be managed at the municipal level, the funds flowing into each pool would be fully risk-adjusted by age – that is, its budget would be proportionate to the number of elderly in the community.

The third nagging problem was the inequity inherent in Japan's fragmented long-term-care system (see Chapter 7). Patients are admitted to nursing homes

25   The SMHI average premium in 1995 was 8.34 percent, up from 8.25 percent in 1992. The protests became particularly vehement if a society's rate went above the 8.3 percent charged in GMHI. This complaint ignored the point that 1 percent of employee bonuses (usually about five months' salary each year) is collected by GMHI, so that its effective rate is about 8.5 percent of wages up to a ceiling. Note that the proportion of Society expenditures being transferred into the old-age and retirement systems had risen from 28.7 percent in 1991 to 30.5 percent in 1994. During this period, the Societies as a whole went from a surplus of ¥312 billion to a deficit of ¥77 billion, the latter about $4.3 billion at our PPP rate. *Me de miru Iryō Hoken Hakusho*, 1996, pp. 61, 78–79.

by application to the local welfare office, but they are admitted to hospitals simply by decision of a physician. The amount they or their families have to pay varies enormously even when the level of care actually delivered is similar, depending on the type of facility. For example, the quasi-legal extra charges required at most high-quality hospitals for the elderly, avowedly to cover diapers or laundry, can bring monthly out-of-pocket costs as high as ¥200,000 (about $1,100, although the average is about one-third that) while most nursing-home patients are paying very little. With LTCI, all three forms of institutional care – nursing homes, health-care facilities for the elderly, and hospitals for the elderly – would be covered under the new social insurance scheme, as would services provided at home. That is seen by officials as a crucial rationalization of policy in this high-priority area that will allow more sensible management in the future.

After a long period of deliberation with much debate among specialists on specific provisions, long-term-care insurance was formally proposed by a Welfare Ministry advisory committee in April 1996; the Ministry itself then watered the proposal down, and a day or two later, word leaked from the Prime Minister's residence that the bill might not be introduced into the Diet very soon after all. The main problem was resistance from rank-and-file conservative Dietmen, worried that an election would have to be called within a year and that voters might be upset by a new social insurance premium that would look like a tax. The idea was therefore shelved temporarily, but after some additional revisions the bill was passed by the Cabinet and submitted to the Diet in December 1996. It was then passed by the Lower House, but the legislative session ended in June 1997 before it was acted on in the Upper House; final passage was expected that fall.

CONCLUSION

The principle of equality has been central to the Japanese health-care system. The main reason that health insurance in Japan works as well as it does is not some cultural predilection to cooperation, nor the political skills of Ministry of Health and Welfare bureaucrats, although arguably both have been helpful. Most important is that the system is perceived as fundamentally fair in *both* the senses previously discussed. Equality is primary, and today it is accepted as natural that all Japanese are entitled to roughly the same health care at equivalent cost. As such, the major role played by the government in regulating the system is nearly unquestioned in Japan.

The investment principle has been secondary but important. To some extent, the lack of strong resentment about being exploited can be attributed to clever packaging, but those who contribute more do get marginally better treatment and have no reason for severe dissatisfaction. If the pattern of allocation somehow seems to be getting inequitable, adjustments can be made on an ad hoc basis.

More such adjustments were being talked about in the mid-1990s, in response to financial problems, particularly those facing Society-Managed Health Insurance. The main action was to raise employees' co-payments from 10 to 20 percent and to impose a larger co-payment for pharmaceuticals. For the longer run, some are calling for more radical changes in the direction of American-style market-based reforms. The likelier outcome, in our view, is a rearrangement of social-insurance and budgetary support for various forms of health care in the context of the proposed new public Long-Term-Care Insurance system. Although out-of-pocket payments by patients will become somewhat more important (see Chapter 7), the main mechanism for allocating burdens will still be cross-subsidization, via public spending and health insurance.

We see this pattern as interesting in the context of possible American health-care reform, precisely because it is unlikely that the United States will move to a "single-payer" system with the national government as sole insurer. It is also unlikely that health-care needs and ability to pay can be evenly distributed across insurance pools, particularly if large firms continue to self-insure their own employees. If extreme inequality of burdens is to be avoided, therefore, some form of cross-subsidization across groups will be required. The Japanese approach is an attractive alternative to the ideas currently being advanced by American experts. It can be summarized as follows:

* Contributions that are proportional to income help ensure equality within insurance pools. Catastrophic coverage with a low ceiling helps ensure equality across all individuals and households in the nation.
* Subsidies go to insurance pools based on employment status, not to individual participants. Both direct subsidies from tax revenues and transfers between richer and poorer pools are provided; the formulas are renegotiated periodically to provide flexibility.
* The complexity of the subsidization and the fact that participants in the richer pools receive marginally better benefits help obscure the

inevitable "unfairness" in investment terms – better-off participants do not complain much about bearing the heavier burdens.

- A movement toward equality needs to start by bringing up the bottom to decent levels, before imposing limitations on the top. That will probably mean increased public spending at the start, but cross-subsidization can then be used to keep the burden on the Treasury manageable.

At a more specific level, it might also be noted that a single national pool for small-business employees – or in the American context, perhaps one pool for all small-business employees in each state – offers a better solution for subsidizing health insurance for this difficult population than a sliding scale based on size or average wages of a firm, or on the individual employee's income. The fact that GMHI is directly managed by the government, giving the officials the leading role among health insurers, has also been helpful for cost control, as is noted in the next chapter.

The extreme emphasis on equality and the distinctive GMHI system aside, health insurance in Japan is generally quite similar to the systems of the majority of the other industrialized nations of the world. The key provision is mandatory enrollment in a given system based on employment or residence, with very few exceptions. That condition is necessary to avoid competitive enrollment via "medical underwriting," or "cherry-picking" for the most attractive enrollees. In general, the environment for Japanese insurers is even more regulated and routinized than that for Japanese providers, a major factor in holding down the costs associated with entrepreneurship.

Finally and most generally, we observe once more that the entire Japanese approach is based on underlying egalitarian values that can be observed in the tax system and other aspects of Japanese policy as well. America, too, has egalitarian traditions, although in the field of health care they have tended to be overshadowed by worries about fairness in terms of individual-level investment and by the health-economics approach to policy. The challenge for health-care reformers is to build on those traditions in order to bring about a more sensible system for the United States.

115

5

The Macropolicy of Cost Containment

DURING the 1970s, Japanese health-care costs exploded, but since the early 1980s, they have been contained within the growth rate of the overall economy. The next two chapters explain how this success was achieved. The story must be told at two levels. In Chapter 6, we take a "micro" approach to see how costs can be controlled, even in a fee-for-service system, by affecting the behavior of individual providers through constraints and incentives built into the fee-schedule and claims-review systems. In the present chapter, however, we focus on "macro" decisions about overall health-care expenditures – the equivalent of what is often called "global budgeting."[1] Japan's way to make such decisions is a unique hybrid of the approaches found in "single-payer" and "all-payer" systems that we call the "bellwether" approach.

The fact that Japan does use something like a "global budget" has often been missed. For example, the U.S. General Accounting Office concluded in a 1991 report on spending controls in France, Germany, and Japan that limitations on overall health-care budgets, in conjunction with price controls, were more effective than price controls alone in moderating spending growth in France and Germany.[2] The report claimed that Japan does not impose enforceable budget limitations but relies simply on price controls through the fee schedule and broad policy pronouncements about keeping total spending down by the Cabinet or the Economic Planning Agency – presumably carried out through "consensus" since there is no enforcement mechanism.

This interpretation does not bear up when looked at more closely. First,

---

1 This term has been used in various ways, some quite technical, but we simply mean deciding on meaningful (if not necessarily completely binding) figures for total spending on medical care.
2 U.S. General Accounting Office, "Health Care Spending Control: The Experience of France, Germany and Japan" (GAO HRD-92-9), p. 39. The report discusses budget limitations of several types over both physician and hospital spending.

the fee schedule is a necessary, but clearly not a sufficient, condition for spending restraint. The fee schedule was already well established when health-care spending was growing explosively in the 1970s, and the introduction of successful spending limitations in the early 1980s was carried out without any reform of the fee-schedule system itself. Second, the Japanese government often issues proclamations about policy goals in many fields, but most have no discernible effect on actual behavior. As illustrated at several junctures in this book, the health-care sector is characterized more by political pulling and hauling than by anything resembling consensus, and it certainly would not respond to idealistic policy pronouncements that lack institutional mechanisms for enforcement.

In fact, Japan's success in holding down health-care costs is similar to that of other nations in the sense that it relies on a set of institutional mechanisms – albeit unusual ones – to decide and enforce a rough ceiling on expenditure. These have evolved over a long period of time, and most of this chapter is devoted to tracing the historical process by which their necessary features were put into place. Before doing that, we examine how the system works today by focusing on the biennial process to determine the growth rate of health insurance expenditures – the key decision about overall health-care spending. This is a murky and complicated story that we have gleaned from repeated conversations with officials and others who know the process well.

BUDGETING HEALTH CARE

Abstractly speaking, the trick in constraining spending is to make those in charge of expenditure decisions also worry about revenues, so that the pleasure of spending money is directly linked with the pain of raising money. Indeed, the problem in the United States for most of the postwar period has been that many decisions on how much to provide have been effectively insulated from decisions on where the money will come from. Effective cost containment anywhere requires a concrete mechanism that links spending and revenue decisions:

- In a pure market system, these decisions would be linked by individual consumers, who would spend no more than they could afford.
- In a tax-based single-payer system, the government (national or provincial) knows that any concessions on spending must be matched by increased taxes or deficit spending.

117

- In Germany, and similarly in other "all-payers" systems where associations of insurers or "sickness funds" negotiate fees with providers at the provincial level, increased spending is soon reflected in higher premiums, so strong resistance to higher costs is automatic.
- In American "managed care," each Health Maintenance Organization must figure out how to provide health care efficiently, or see its monthly per-person fee rise to an uncompetitive level leading to an immediate loss of business.

In Japan, it is the Health Insurance Bureau (Hokenkyoku, HIB) of the Ministry of Health and Welfare that makes this crucial link. On the expenditure side, its Medical Care Division (Iryōka) oversees preparation of the fee schedule that governs nearly all the goods and services provided by physicians and hospitals in Japan. On the revenue side, its Planning Division (Kikakuka) is responsible for setting premium levels in the single largest health insurance system; it also takes the lead in the decision about the annual subsidy from general revenues.

The HIB hardly has absolute power on its own: It must negotiate with providers (mainly the Japan Medical Association) about expenditures and with the Ministry of Finance about the subsidy portion of revenues; more broadly, its decisions must be acceptable within the Ministry, to the Cabinet, and to the legislature. Still, it "has the action" throughout, to use the American bureaucratic phrase. The key choices are made every two years at the time the fee schedule is revised.

The Decision

These choices are essentially top–down, not bottom–up. It is true that the fee schedule itself is a detailed listing of all approved goods and services and their prices. However, the process of figuring out how much spending will rise does not rest on any sort of item-by-item cost accounting that is added up to a total. Rather, the total comes first. This can be seen clearly in the sequence of events: The growth rate in spending has to be decided before the budget is sent to the Diet, normally in December, while the fee schedule itself with all the individual fees is worked on afterward and published in March. This latter process of dividing up the pie is covered in the next chapter – here we are concerned with how the size of the pie is decided.

In concrete terms, the decision on spending growth is embodied in a report (later ratified as a law) by the Central Social Insurance Medical Care Council (Chūikyō), which as noted in Chapter 2 is a formal advisory body to the Minister of Health and Welfare. It is made up of insurers, providers, and public-interest members. Its report states how much in percentage terms the average fees for services should rise (divided between medical and dental facilities and retail pharmacies), and how much the average prices for pharmaceuticals should fall. For example, in the 1996 revision, the Central Council recommended (in December 1995) that medical fees would go up an average of 3.6 percent, dental fees 2.2 percent, and fees paid to pharmacists for their services (not the drugs themselves) 1.3 percent. Medical fees are by far the largest part, so the weighted average was a 3.4 percent hike in fees for services. Pharmaceutical prices were to be reduced by 6.8 percent, a reduction that would amount to 2.0 percent of total health-care spending, plus an additional 0.5 percent for the special reductions (*saisantei*) of the prices of top-selling drugs. The 3.4 percent hike in service-fee expenditures minus the 2.6 percent savings in pharmaceutical expenditures would mean a 0.8 percent hike in total expenditures.[3]

That is the decision. How is it reached? The process actually involves five different choices:

1. How much new money will providers need?
2. How much of that will come from a "natural increase" in their incomes rather than increases in prices through the fee-schedule hike?
3. How much of the fee-schedule hike can be covered by savings elsewhere, mainly in pharmaceutical spending?
4. How much additional revenue into health insurance will come from premiums?
5. How much additional revenue into health insurance will come from budget subsidies?

The five choices can be described in this logical sequence, although the actual decision-making processes overlap considerably in time. Moreover, each choice affects the others – in particular, consideration of the first is substantially shaped by the other four.

3   *Shakai Hoken Junpō* 1896 (December 21, 1995), 25.

1. How Much New Money? The first logical task for HIB officials is to figure out how much additional money is needed for the health-care delivery system to continue to function. The tool for doing so is the "Survey of Medical Institution Finances," which collects cost data for both private practitioners and hospitals, in four categories.[4] That is, officials calculate the proportion of provider expenditure used to pay physicians, to pay other staff, to purchase pharmaceuticals, and to purchase other materials. They then estimate how much each of these categories should be rising by applying the projected percentage growth in, respectively, GDP, wages, an index of actual pharmaceutical prices, and the Consumer Price Index. These are first added up separately for private practitioners and hospitals, and then divided by their numbers, in order to determine figures for the average costs facing each physician and hospital.

Actually, the process is not quite so cut and dried: Because estimates of current growth in these indicators are necessarily uncertain, the HIB actually comes up with ranges rather than precise numbers for the expenditure estimates. In figuring out which way to lean, the logic is that if a category of practitioner had been doing all right, it might not need quite as much this time, but if it had been facing difficulties, it might need more. "Doing all right" and "difficulties" is a matter of both substantive and political concerns.

On the substantive side, the main concern is hospitals. They are not directly represented on the Central Council and have never been unified enough to apply effective political pressure, so obtaining their consent to the decision about how much to spend is not a major worry. On the other hand, if many hospitals started going bankrupt, or turned to extreme cost cutting that would dramatically impair quality, the health-care system would fall apart. It was noted in Chapter 3 that hospital finances are inherently precarious in that they have no way to cover capital expenditures, such as for construction or equipment, except through their revenues under the fee schedule.[5] In fact, in the

---

4 Iryō Keizai Jittai Chōsa (lit. Empirical Survey of Medical Care Economics), conducted every two years based on questionnaires sent to a large sample of institutions. The methodology of this survey and even whether it should be carried out at all used to be a bone of contention between the JMA and the Welfare Ministry, and even today it can be conducted only under condition that the results are published only at a very aggregate level.

5 Except for public hospitals subsidized by governments, and university hospitals with their access to outside funds such as donations – a key reason for the lack of unity among hospitals.

period since austerity was imposed in the early 1980s, many hospital balance sheets turned red, and the HIB must ensure that enough funds are provided.

Political concerns are more relevant for office-based physicians. Here the key data are income trends mainly as affected by the previous revision. Welfare Ministry officials assume, with justification, that private practitioners' incomes on average are ample to cover costs and a comfortable standard of living. However, they also know that the Japan Medical Association, which dominates the providers' side in the Central Council, pays close attention to its members' interests, in terms of both income growth and their share of medical spending. That means that hospital needs cannot be met by transferring resources from office-based physicians. HIB officials take all this into account in formulating their estimates of how much additional revenue will be needed by health-care providers.

2. *How Much "Natural Increase?"* Back in the 1970s, it had been assumed that all of the additional income that providers need would have to come from a hike in the fee schedule. Critics pointed out, however, that providers' income was rising even in years when the fee schedule was not increased, due to more patients being seen (largely due to population growth or aging), or increased "intensity" – quantity or quality – of the treatments given each patient (partly due to technological improvement). Piling a hefty fee increase on top of such growth in fact had led to very rapid growth of health-care spending in that decade.

Japanese health policy makers now think of new revenues that are *not* caused by fee-schedule increases as the "natural increase" (*shizenzō*) in health-care spending.[6] The "natural increase" since the previous fee-schedule hike is used to estimate what it will be in the coming two years. The basis of this calculation is the estimate of "National Medical Care Expenditure" (Kokumin Iryōhi), compiled annually by the MHW from social insurance spending data. Since 1981, the "natural increase" has in effect been *deducted* from the increase that would seem to be necessary in the light of wage or price trends.

The logic is that physicians and hospitals should be able to maintain their real income, so the fee-schedule hike should cover only the portion of their increased costs that is not offset by higher incomes – that is, if their income

---

6 See Yoshinori Hiroi, "The 'Natural Increase' and Cost Control," in *Containing*, pp. 53–72, for details on differing definitions of the "natural increase" and how it is calculated.

goes up because they are serving more patients or because they are providing more services, then they will not need as much in the way of fee increases. Conveniently for cost-cutting officials, incidentally, this formulation ignores any higher costs to the provider for increasing services. It is not clear why this point has not been made controversial by the JMA or the hospitals – for the most part, the logic of deducting the "natural increase" seems to have been accepted as technical and not subject to political debate.

The estimated cost increase minus the estimated "natural revenue increase" becomes the Medical Care Division estimate of what percentage hike is needed for the medical fee schedule. Again, because the underlying calculations are a bit soft, this estimate is really more of a range (perhaps as wide as 0.5 to 1.5 percentage points) than a precise figure. In any case, it is figured out around November and becomes the starting point for two discussions: with the Japan Medical Association in the Central Council about whether the amount of the increase is adequate, and with the Ministry of Finance in the budget process about whether there is enough money to pay for it.

3. How Much Savings? Not all the new spending has to be paid for with new revenues, however; some of it can be financed by making cuts elsewhere – specifically, cuts in spending on drugs by reducing their prices. That is possible because it is assumed that, in the period since the last fee-schedule revisions, the pharmaceutical manufacturers and wholesalers will have been reducing or discounting the prices that they charge providers, so the gap – the difference between the fee-schedule price that providers receive from health insurance when they dispense drugs, and the amount they actually pay to buy them – will have widened significantly.

The tool for deciding how much can be saved in this way is the Pharmaceutical Price Survey, which investigates the actual market price for each product listed in the fee schedule.[7] A formula is applied to bring the fee-schedule price down to an appropriate level relative to the market price. The announced savings from pharmaceuticals is mainly the weighted average percentage reduction in the prices of all these drugs produced by this formula. Also, an additional small reduction has been added in recent years to take advantage of drops in raw-material prices. Another recent practice has been

---

7 Yakka Chōsa, carried out every two years. It relies mainly on questionnaires, but in recent years it has been supplemented by site visits and checks of financial records (see Chapter 6).

to cut the price of a given top-selling drug more than is called for by the formula, to tap what is seen as "excessive profits."

Such actions that single out a particular product can lead to sharp conflict with a manufacturer (see Chapter 6 for an example), and more generally the MHW has faced opposition from the pharmaceutical industry as a whole as well as from physicians because it has gradually tightened the price formula to capture more and more "profits" by narrowing the gap. For the most part, however, the biennial decision on how much to reduce drug prices has been relatively nonpolitical, probably because the industry is not represented on the Central Council and has little clout with the HIB, and because use of the survey and a systematic formula makes the results appear technical and objective.

4. How Much Premium Revenue? After deducting the "natural increase" and the savings from drug price cuts, some new real money is still needed to finance the fee-schedule hike. Most of it will come from increased premium revenue, since roughly 55 percent of total medical-care spending comes from premiums. The logic is that the proportion of medical cost increases that is caused by rising prices and wages will be more or less automatically offset by increased premium revenue, since premiums are largely proportional to wages or other personal income. Such calculations are carried out by the Planning Division of the HIB, concentrating on Government-Managed Health Insurance for the small business sector.

An estimated shortfall in premium revenues would immediately raise a caution flag in the negotiations about fee-schedule increases, because the HIB would not lightly entertain the idea of raising premium rates for GMHI. It requires legislative approval and might be strongly opposed by small-business groups and politicians. The largest hike was in 1981, from 8.0 to 8.4 percent of wages (up to a ceiling; shared equally with the employer). The rate was adjusted slightly in both directions in succeeding years; in 1997 an increase to 8.7 percent was proposed by the government, but legislative pressure forced it down to 8.5 percent.

5. How Much Subsidy? Finally, a share of the expenditure increase will come from an increase of the subsidy provided from general tax revenues. That allocation amounts to about 25 percent of total medical-care spending: specifically, 50 percent of outlays for CHI and 13 percent for GMHI, plus 14.2 percent for the special financing program for the elderly. It is the fact that the estimated amount of the subsidy must be included in the annual budget that drives the timetable for making these macropolicy decisions. That is, the Central Council report that announces the amount of the expenditure increase comes in December, very shortly after the Welfare and Finance ministers meet for the final negotiation on the amount of the subsidy.[8] Because the budgeted subsidy must approximate a fixed percentage of estimated expenditures, in effect the Finance Ministry has to sign off on the size of the fee-schedule hike, which gives it considerable influence even over deliberations within the HIB.[9]

Why It Works

These five choices, taken together, determine how much will be spent on health care and where the money will come from. Following are a few additional observations.

First, in the 1994 and particularly the 1996 revisions, the process as outlined here has been violated in that the amount of the fee-schedule increase has not been fully accounted for by specified revenues or savings. Only vague promises were offered to achieve greater efficiencies within the fee-schedule system (such as more "bundling" of lab tests). Such promises lack credibility and indeed contradict the very logic of the process, which starts from an estimate of how much additional income is needed by providers. Any efficiencies (and similarly the portion of savings on drug spending that affect doctors and hospitals rather than the pharmaceutical industry) would have their effect only by reducing provider income.

Second, as noted earlier, in actuality all the numbers need not add up too precisely because the entire procedure is more a matter of estimating future expenditures rather than writing an enforceable budget. Even the subsidy portion, although written into the budget document, is really an entitlement

---

8   It is included in what is called the Ministry of Finance Draft (*Okura gen'an*) of the budget, which is subject to a week or so of final negotiations on unsettled items before being submitted to the Diet. The medical-care subsidy cannot be left to these final "resurrection negotiations" (*fukkatsu sesshō*) because the amount is so large that it has implications for the framework of the entire budget. For a dated but still broadly applicable account of such processes in Japanese decision making, see John Creighton Campbell, *Contemporary Japanese Budget Politics* (Berkeley: University of California Press, 1976).

9   Actually, the relationship is not exact because some other small health-care subsidies are also included.

that has to be paid out automatically with medical-care usage.[10] Indeed, some factors in the decision are clearly fictional – the figure for savings incurred by reducing pharmaceutical prices completely ignores spending on newly introduced drugs – and others (the natural increase, premium revenues) are no more than informed guesses that depend on many uncertain assumptions about what will happen in the economy.

It is interesting that no one ever goes back to check all these estimates against the actual results to see how accurate they were.[11] That is probably because all of those concerned know that the process is in a sense symbolic, is more about signifiers of decisions than about decisions themselves. But the signifiers are still significant because they do affect actual behavior. Even if the exact numbers used are known to be fictional, it is understood that the decisions are about the real question of how much more money can be spent and where it will come from. Indeed, in performance terms, we can observe that this Japanese approach to budgeting overall medical-care spending has worked at least as well as in other nations where ceilings are enforced by more rigid mechanisms.

In thinking about why this process works as well as it does, it is noteworthy that of the five choices, two are produced by genuine negotiations. The first is over how much growth in provider income is needed, negotiated mainly with the Japan Medical Association within the Central Council; the fifth is over the amount of the general revenue subsidy, negotiated with the Ministry of Finance during the budget process. Both negotiations are directly affected by the conditions of the moment – the national mood about government spending, the balance of power between the two sides, events in the broader political arena. In fact, high-level politicians are sometimes drawn in, for example, if the JMA feels its demands are not being heard and turns to its friends in the LDP to pressure both the MHW and the MOF.

The process is thus fundamentally quite political, as is perhaps necessary in making a decision that is so expensive. However, it should also be noted that in recent years the politics have become rather placid. Surprises or fireworks displays have been lacking. Although the conflicts of interest are quite real, there has not been too much uncertainty – at the beginning of each biennial cycle, the expectations among the various participants about how

---

10 That is, most subsidies go up with usage and are not constrained by the budget amount. Overruns would lead to adjustments in a later supplementary budget or just be absorbed.

11 But see the study of ''medical inflation'' discussed in the next chapter.

things will turn out probably have not diverged very much. This degree of routinization represents a settlement reached after many years of more extreme conflict, as discussed in the next section, and is a significant accomplishment. The process for deciding how much medical-care spending should go up keeps a good balance between technical and political considerations and is flexible enough to respond to changing conditions without falling into a dangerous boom-or-bust syndrome.

The central role of the Health Insurance Bureau is the key to making the process work. It is there that technical analysis and political judgments are combined to generate the proposals to the JMA and the MOF and other important participants. A single government agency may play a somewhat analogous role in other health-care systems, but the HIB in Japan is quite distinctive in the breadth of its responsibilities. This breadth is due to a unique institutional feature of Japanese health insurance.

The Hybrid Bellwether System

Japan is in effect a cross between a ''single-payer'' and ''all-payers'' system in that there are many insurance carriers, but the national government itself is by far the largest single insurer. The importance of this point can be seen in the process for deciding overall spending already described. The calculations for Government-Managed Health Insurance for the small-business sector are taken much more seriously than those for Society-Managed Health Insurance in large firms or Citizens' Health Insurance for the non-employed, for two reasons.

First, since GMHI is a single national insurance pool with one contribution rate for all, its finances can be seen very clearly. Both SMHI and CHI are made up of thousands of pools, which have varying cost pressures and decide their own contribution rates. Their financial condition can be assessed only in generalities.

Second, ''government'' in the government-managed system is specifically the MHW Health Insurance Bureau. The same officials who estimate overall expenditures and negotiate with providers also are directly responsible for administering the single largest health insurance plan. If HIB officials get their estimates wrong or are too soft on providers, they are stuck with somehow coming up with the money to bail out GMHI. That can be done only by raising the national GMHI premium rate, or appealing to the Ministry of Finance for additional subsidies – neither an attractive prospect.

126

In short, under the current system, the GMHI financial accounts function as the bellwether or regulator for overall health-care spending. The only way that the HIB can adjust GMHI spending to match revenues is by manipulating the fee schedule, which of course applies to *all* the health insurance systems. Because GMHI premiums are largely a percentage of wages, its revenues grow as the economy expands. Moderate revenue growth will allow moderately increased payments to providers. The other health insurance plans fall in line. That means, incidentally, that insurance carriers with weaker finances somehow have to come up with enough money to cover their increased costs without cutting services, while those in a stronger position can put money in the bank – an imbalance that led to the new cross-subsidization mechanisms of the 1980s.

This use of a single relatively simple insurance plan, managed by the government, as the regulator for a pluralistic system appears to be unique to Japan. The idea has a number of advantages that might be worth considering by those interested in health-care reform even in the United States. It is important to note, however, that for such a system to work effectively, several necessary conditions must have been put in place. Our analysis of the Japanese experience suggests the following five conditions:

1. Payment regulations that cover all or nearly all medical care, so that the prices established at the national level will determine expenditures for the entire system.
2. A formula for determining the amount of revenue available, eliminating ad hoc recourse to subsidies and thereby normally linking the amount of possible spending growth to the growth of premium income.
3. Similarly, a way to decide how much money needs to be spent that is simple and essentially "top–down" rather than a "bottom–up" assessment of the specific costs borne by providers.
4. A political power balance that favors the payers' side, so that electoral or interest-group pressures do not overwhelm cost-containment policies.
5. Enough similarity in the financial condition of the various types of insurance carriers to ensure that none will be either impoverished or greatly enriched by overall revenue or expenditure changes.

In a sense, a sixth necessary condition is that the system be managed with enough flexibility to accommodate changing conditions, including shifts in the relative financial strength of the various components of the system.

One might imagine a rational health-care planner deciding that a cross between a single-payer and all-payers system makes the most sense, deducing the necessary conditions just listed, and figuring out how they could be implemented in a systematic way. That is emphatically not what happened in Japan. The conditions came into being one after another, as immediate solutions to a specific set of problems at the time (some of them caused by the previous solution). Most were actually by-products of political struggles over the decision on overall health-care spending, or over how that decision would be made. The protagonists were the Japan Medical Association and the Health Insurance Bureau, and their battle lasted from the late 1950s to the mid-1980s, as we now describe.

THE EVOLUTION OF HEALTH FINANCE POLITICS

For most of the postwar period, decision makers in the Ministry of Health and Welfare, backed up by the majority Liberal Democratic Party, were primarily concerned with bringing the Japanese health-care system up to what they saw as the normal standards of the West. As recounted in the previous chapter, health insurance coverage was expanded to cover the entire population, and benefits were improved by lowering co-payments and other reforms. From the viewpoint of the health bureaucrats, however, holding down spending was always at least an important secondary goal. One reason was their perception that savings were necessary to expand access. Another was their ingrained suspicion of the private-practice physicians represented by the Japan Medical Association, whom they saw as eager to eat up any additional funds that would become available. In fact, battles between the MHW and the JMA, in which the doctors won all the early fights but the Ministry eventually gained the upper hand, dominated the macropolitics of health care for decades. The description of the five stages that follows corresponds to the necessary conditions listed on page 127.

1. Establishing the Universal Fee Schedule. Japanese doctors and the government have long been deeply involved with each other, particularly since the first fee schedule was implemented in 1927. However, a truly national system did not become possible until 1958, when ''health insurance for all'' (*kaihoken*) was enacted. Coincidentally, it was in the previous year that Takemi Tarō, the master strategist, had become president of the JMA. "Health insurance for all," which meant extending mandatory coverage to non-employees such as farmers, was essentially a political initiative, pushed by the newly amalgamated Liberal Democratic Party as a response to electoral gains by socialists in rural areas. However, it was a policy change on which the interests of the JMA and the Health Insurance Bureau largely coincided.[12]

The reason was that since all patients in Japan would now be covered by social insurance, the system as a whole could be rationalized through the fee schedule – the first of the necessary conditions already mentioned. In particular, before "health insurance for all," many local governments had established discrete health insurance programs for non-employee residents, under which they could decide the level of fees for private practitioners, or even supply medical care directly through clinics and hospitals by hiring doctors and public-health nurses themselves. Neither the Health and Welfare Ministry nor the JMA was enthusiastic about this degree of local initiative.

But agreement on the general idea of universal health insurance did not mean that the doctors would fall into the government's plans placidly. For example, the bureaucrats wanted to transform the fee schedule from its traditional fee-for-service basis to a new system based on analysis of actual costs incurred by providers. This formula would favor large hospitals rather than private practitioners and was seen as a move toward "bundling" many charges together rather than charging a separate fee for each service. The JMA vigorously resisted and gained a standoff. Irrational though it seems, the Ministry introduced its new fee schedule but also kept the old one, and providers were allowed to pick between the two schedules freely.[13] The fee-for-service system that was the basis of Japanese medical care would not be transformed to meet bureaucratic convenience.

Yet the Health and Welfare Ministry still hoped to dominate what health providers could do and how much they would be paid for it, and the Japan

---

12 This section is largely drawn from Mikitaka Masuyama and John Creighton Campbell, "The Evolution of Fee-Schedule Politics," in *Containing*, pp. 265–277. Also see Koyama Michio, *Sengo Iryō Hoshō no Shōgen* (Tokyo: Sōgō Rōdō Kenkyūjo, 1985) and, on the politics of the fee schedule, Nishimura Mariko, "Shinryō Hōshū Kaitei no Mekanizumu ni kansuru Rekishiteki Kōsatsu," in Shakai Hoshō Kenkyūjo, ed., *Iryō Hoshō to Iryōhi* (Tokyo: Tokyo Daigaku Shuppankai, 1996), pp. 37–70.
13 To the everlasting confusion of researchers. Both the *Kō* and *Otsu* schedules remained separate although increasingly similar until they were combined in 1994.

Medical Association was determined to resist and indeed to improve the position of private practitioners. The first decade and more from the initiation of universal health insurance thus saw constant skirmishing as both sides jockeyed for advantage.[14] Disputes erupted over such issues as restrictions on what would be covered by health insurance, urban–rural fee differentials, whether and how the Ministry could investigate hospital and physician finances, the size of co-payments, subsidization of financially weak local insurance pools, simplification of reimbursement, and especially treatment guidelines (*chiryō shishin*) that would specify procedures for particular diagnoses – anathema to the doctors.

Alongside these struggles over regulations and the structure of health-care delivery came recurring battles over medical spending, and indeed over how it should be decided. These battles swirled in and around the Central Council. We can infer that Takemi's strategy was (1) to have the JMA dominate the providers' side on the Council, (2) to limit the influence of the payers' side and even the ''public-interest'' members vis à vis the providers, (3) to make the Council's deliberations more autonomous from Health and Welfare Ministry influence, and (4) to make the Ministry go along with Council recommendations (when favorable to the JMA). The JMA repeatedly demonstrated its willingness to disrupt the Central Council process by boycotting meetings, by demanding the resignation of the chairman or the dissolution of the entire Council, and even by having the providers' representatives resign their membership. When such structural tactics failed, Takemi was quite willing to bypass all normal procedures and intervene at the highest levels, as by pushing LDP leaders into forcing a summit meeting with the Health and Welfare Minister to boost fees beyond the level of the Central Council's recommendation. The JMA's ultimate threat was a doctors' strike (formally, refusal to accept health insurance reimbursement), which was often threatened and more than once actually ordered, if largely on a symbolic basis.[15]

Because of the JMA's demonstrated power, for a period of eight years fee-schedule negotiations operated under the ''proposal system,'' quite abnormal in terms of Japanese administrative procedures. This meant that the Central Council itself made the first recommendation for a price increase rather than

14 A good account by a participant in this period is Yoshimura Hitoshi, ''Iryō Hoken no Sanjūnen: Kaikō to Tenbō,'' *Shakai Hoken Junpō* No. 1500-01 (April 1 & 11, 1985), pp. 13–19, 14–17.
15 For a political scientist's account of these conflicts, see William Steslicke, *Doctors in Politics: The Political Life of the Japan Medical Association* (New York: Praeger, 1973).

waiting for the Ministry of Health and Welfare to send over its proposal as a basis for Council discussions. The amount of the increase was supposed to be determined by a complex calculation of the costs and revenues of medical-care providers. However, there was no agreement on how the formula should work – particularly on how much an hour of a physician's time should be valued. The JMA wanted it to be 400 percent of average wages, while the payers' side, particularly Kenporen representing SMHI insurers, argued it should be only 20 percent higher than average wages. The wrangling took a long time but due largely to JMA power and skill ultimately led to a series of large fee-schedule increases.

The new fee-schedule system also accentuated problems on the revenue side. Most of the big-business health insurance societies represented by Kenporen could cover the increased level of spending with small hikes in premium rates – their surpluses declined, but they did not go into red ink in this period. However, the small-business program had more difficulty. In earlier years when Government-Managed Health Insurance had come under pressure, the Health Insurance Bureau had similarly just raised premium rates. For example, rates had been hiked five times, from 3.6 to 6.0 percent of covered wages, from 1947 to 1951. But raising contributions in a national program for a politically pivotal group, small-business employees, was an obvious concern for politicians. An attempt at a further rise to 6.5 percent in 1955 had been killed by the Diet, so that a subsidy out of general revenues had to be provided by the Ministry of Finance. This subsidy had not grown very much for some time, but during the 1960s, due to expanded benefits as well as to the fee-schedule increases forced by the JMA, health-care spending soared, and GMHI began to run big deficits – up to ¥50 billion ($280 million) in 1965. At that point, the Finance Ministry got tough and refused to put up the money.

The Health Insurance Bureau therefore had no choice but to raise GMHI premiums again in 1966 and 1967, to 7.0 percent. Again, the politicians protested. The HIB then tried to find savings on the expenditure side to balance its accounts, including a "temporary" ¥15 co-payment on medications in 1967. That was also an attempt by the Ministry to move toward its old goal of getting doctors to cut down on the amount of drugs they dispense, and it predictably made the JMA furious – the co-payment had to be withdrawn in 1969. Gradually, it was becoming clear to those on both sides that the method for figuring out how much money would be available, and indeed the method for setting fees, were both badly in need of rationalization. Some sort of institutionalized routines were required for both revenue and expenditure decisions.

2. Installing a Logical Methodology for Revenue Decisions. The first step, taken in 1973, was to remove the general revenue subsidy as a subject of the negotiations. On the one hand, the HIB would be assured a regular increase in the subsidy, but on the other, the amount of the increase would be mechanically limited. That is, the budget subsidy to GMHI was set as a fixed proportion of benefit outlays (initially 10 percent) rather than deciding an absolute amount each time. This portion of GMHI revenues would thus rise along with the growth in expenditures. Note that because premiums were a share of covered employees' wages, and wages were expected to go up at roughly the same rate as the indices governing the fee-schedule increases, total revenues and expenditures should now be roughly in balance.

Of course, this neat formula might not work correctly in a given year, and shortfalls were still possible. The Finance Ministry did not want to be liable for all these potential costs; therefore, in 1974 it insisted on a second provision to the deal, that the subsidy rate would be tied to the contribution rate. That is, before taking the easy road of asking for an increase in the budget subsidy rate, the Welfare Ministry would have to get a hike in contributions approved by the legislature. Specifically, in principle, a 0.1 percentage point hike in the premium rate would be required for every 0.8 percentage point hike in the subsidy rate.[16] This change achieved the second condition for effective cost containment noted previously because expenditures were now mechanically linked to revenues in the GMHI system.

3. Simplifying Spending Decisions. However, the MHW did not have the power to decide on its own how much would be spent, whatever decision-making rule it might adopt. As was obvious from a decade of continued skirmishes over various issues, it was necessary – and not easy – to secure agreement from the JMA. Moreover, two recent shifts in the broader political environment would make any effort to control spending particularly difficult. First, the Liberal Democratic Party's political control had been threatened by

---

16 Note that the denominators are different. For example, in 1974, the premium rate was raised from 7.2 to 7.6 percent of covered wages and the subsidy from 10.0 to 13.2 percent of premium income. By 1978, these rates had risen to 8 and 16.4 percent, respectively. See Shakai Hoken Kenkyūjo, ed. and pub., *Shakai Hoken no Ayumi* (Tokyo, 1991), p. 117. This specific ratio was later tacitly abandoned, although the principle of linkage was maintained.

a series of victories by left-wing politicians in many urban prefectures and municipalities, so the politicians were feeling vulnerable to organized constituencies. Second, a new public mood favoring social welfare, particularly for the elderly, had been growing since the late 1960s – the early 1970s have been called the first "old-people boom" in Japan. Such factors made the majority party unusually sensitive to demands for improved social policy.[17]

Several important policy expansions in health care occurred in the early 1970s, including "free" medical care for the elderly (government would cover the co-payments for nearly everyone over 70), substantial reductions in co-payments for non-employees and dependents, and enactment of "catastrophic" coverage to limit out-of-pocket costs to ¥30,000 a month (under $200) in all health insurance plans. And beyond health care, overall public spending rose sharply in this period, and so did inflation – the budget went up by 25 percent, and prices rose over 15 percent in 1973.

This heady atmosphere was the setting for a new deal between the JMA and the government. Doctors were eager to make up for inflation with a large price increase without the delays inherent in the complex cost-based formula and Central Council wrangling. Health Insurance Bureau officials also wanted a quicker process and could see advantages in a simpler way to calculate the fee hike. Perhaps most telling was an administrative imperative: The Ministry of Finance stated that the amount of the subsidy to help finance fee hikes had gotten so large that it could no longer be accommodated in a supplementary budget later in the year, and would have to be included in the regular budget process. Its rather rigid timetable meant that the process could not be allowed to drag out indefinitely until the parties could come to agreement.

The result of these circumstances was that in 1974, when inflation had been pushed up even further after the oil shock, two enormous fee hikes were approved, but on a new basis. The calculation of overall spending was in effect taken away from the Central Council, although it retained its formal role. Spending would be indexed to broad economic trends rather than the estimated costs to providers.[18] Fees for physicians' services would go up with

---

17 John Creighton Campbell, *How Policies Change: The Japanese Government and the Aging Society* (Princeton, NJ: Princeton University Press, 1992), Chapter 5, and for how LDP electoral vulnerability affects public policy in general, Kent Calder, *Crisis and Compensation* (Princeton, NJ: Princeton University Press, 1988).

18 The idea of indexation was in the air in that pension benefit levels had just been tied to price and wage growth. Incidentally, Hiroi argues that indexing was a victory for the JMA

GNP per capita, other personnel costs with average wages, and miscellaneous expenses with the Consumer Price Index (pharmaceuticals would still be tied to market prices as determined by a survey).

In actual practice, the decision on how much overall health spending should go up could not be quite so cut-and-dried because the political forces were much too strong to be contained by a simple formula. The amount was now negotiated between the Finance and Welfare ministries, with cabinet ministers and even the LDP leadership able to play a role; the Central Council just filled in the details. However, the new system was far simpler, and it had the enormous advantage of removing the single most difficult problem, the very subjective and contentious issue of how much physicians should be paid for their time, as a subject of explicit negotiations.

In the short run, moving the decision on total spending away from the Central Council and up to the political level benefited the doctors, since Takemi Tarō could throw his considerable weight into this rather simple decision-making process. Indeed, the "rationalization" of both revenue and spending decisions, as described in these two sections, did not mean economizing at all – although they were necessary conditions for the successful attempts at economizing later.

That is, as noted in the introductory chapter, during the 1970s, even relative to Japan's rapid growth in GNP, national medical expenditure was rising at the same fast clip as in the United States. That was due partly to the "natural increase," which in this period worked to the benefit of providers: There was (1) an enormous increase in usage among people over 65, induced by "free" medical care, and (2) a rise in "intensity" or the average quantity and quality of treatment per case. But the increase was not all "natural" in that the medical fee schedule was also hiked substantially. It went up 19 percent and then by an additional special increase of 16 percent in 1974, 9 percent in 1976, and 11.5 percent in 1978. A key reason was that, until the very end of the 1970s, the political balance of power was still decidedly tipped in favor of the Japan Medical Association.

---

while the end of the "proposal system" that put the decision on fee hikes within the Central Council was a gain for the MHW. Nishimura, on the other hand, argues that the JMA wanted to end the proposal system and was induced to accept the new indexing formula, which could become dangerous to physicians because it did not provide for costs like capital investment, simply by the promise of immediate large fee increases. Hiroi, "Natural Increase"; Nishimura, "Shinryō Hōshū."

4. The Payers' Side Gains the Advantage. It was in the early 1980s that Ministry of Health and Welfare officials were able to take action to constrain the growth of health-care spending. From the 1981 fee-schedule revision, indexation to economic trends was abandoned as the criterion for expenditure growth in favor of the austere decision-making rules, still in effect today, that were described at the beginning of this chapter. It should be emphasized that this was a change of policy, or of informal norms, rather than of formal institutions – no new organizational structures were created, and the fee schedule itself was not appreciably restructured.

In that sense, the main event was a shift in the balance of power from providers to payers. We have seen that in the 1960s the Japan Medical Association had demonstrated its willingness and capacity to disrupt any regular procedures in order to get its own way, and in the 1970s, relative peace was established only by buying off the doctors with generous fee increases. How did the government gain the upper hand in the 1980s, when it had failed so often in the past? Several factors were important.

First, the perception that government spending was getting out of hand had become widespread, and social policy including health-care costs (particularly for "free" medical care for the elderly) was often blamed. The idea of "reconsidering welfare" (*fukushi minaoshiron*) in reaction to the big advances of the early 1970s had gained currency since 1975.[19] More generally, this new national mood was a key factor in the broad "administrative reform campaign" of budget restraints and privatization in 1981–85, which was spearheaded by Prime Minister Nakasone and the Ministry of Finance along with big-business groups.

Second, in the realm of electoral politics, any cutbacks in social policy had been difficult during the 1970s because the ruling party was in a constantly precarious position. However, the era of *hakuchū* or near-parity in the legislature ended when the Liberal Democratic Party finally won a big victory in the summer 1980 general election, and so was no longer as vulnerable to opposition-party attacks.

Third, the Ministry of Health and Welfare had gotten itself together and gained confidence. As often seems to be the case in the Japanese bureaucracy, this shift was associated with strong individual leadership. A creative and aggressive health insurance expert, Yoshimura Hitoshi, who advanced

19 Campbell, *How Policies Change*, chap. 7.

through a series of key positions culminating as Vice-Minister, worked hard for more coherent Ministry strategies.

Fourth, apparently, the opposition weakened. The JMA's long-term strength was vitiated by its aging core membership and its inability to enroll younger physicians, who were mostly working for hospitals. Coincidentally, President Takemi became ill and had to resign in the midst of negotiations.[20] But the doctors did not capitulate so much as they simply adjusted their strategy. By 1980, the old JMA goal of continuously increasing the national resources flowing into health care – enlarging the pie – had become untenable. The JMA therefore took a defensive stance to try to protect the interests of private practitioners by maintaining the relative size of their slice.

A fifth reason is less a structural shift than an immediate practical problem: the increasing burden of old-age medical care on the national treasury. Health-care spending for the elderly from all sources had soared from ¥429 billion in 1973, the first year of "free" medical care for the 70+ population, to ¥857 billion in 1975 and ¥2,127 billion in 1980.[21] This rapid growth put a double-whammy on the budget. First, the government had to spend its own money directly to cover the 30 percent co-payment that applied to the vast majority of the elderly, those enrolled in the Citizens' Health Insurance system. Second, it was also forced to make up the deficits of the CHI system itself – deficits largely caused by the growing numbers of older people and their increased usage of medical care (as noted in the previous chapter, CHI received a subsidy of 50 percent from the national Treasury). Welfare Ministry estimates of these burdens on the national treasury totaled ¥218 billion in 1973, ¥394 billion in 1975, and ¥958 billion in 1980, with only about one-third of these amounts represented by direct subsidies into the free-medical-care program.

20 Note, however, that the Health Care for the Elderly Law and the new fee-schedule methodology – the two biggest changes – were already well underway before Takemi resigned, and indeed it was his agreement to cutbacks in fees that allowed the Central Council to carry out the 1981 reform. Some say that Takemi had, for the first time, personally taken over the negotiations for the JMA and had simply not realized what the Welfare Ministry officials were up to. Others say that Takemi, knowing he had cancer, had decided to worry about the national interest. In any case, there seems to have been dismay in JMA headquarters as the fee-setting process unfolded in 1981, but Takemi's long-established autocratic style made effective protest impossible.
21 The 1980 figure was about $12 billion at our rough PPP figure of $1 = ¥180. For a detailed analysis of the politics of old-age health-care decision making in this period, see Campbell, *How Policies Change*, Chapter 9.

The Finance Ministry had been complaining about this burden since the mid-1970s, and Health Insurance Bureau officials had tried to cooperate – for three years in a row, new co-payments or some other way to limit spending on old-age medical care had been included in early budget drafts, only to be vetoed by LDP politicians. But in the 1980 budget process, a new Finance Ministry strategy against overall governmental spending was introduced. Each ministry had to keep its total budget increase request within 10 percent of its current budget (the ceiling was reduced in subsequent years to minus figures). Ministries were free to decide for themselves how to meet this restriction, but in the Health and Welfare budget, it was obvious that medical-care spending had to be cut.

As a first step in this direction, in the 1981 fee-schedule revision, the formula for figuring the overall fee increase needed was altered by deducting the "natural increase" component of spending growth, as noted earlier. That was the major change from the indexing system used in the 1970s. The next step was a more radical attack on the enormous subsidy to CHI that had become necessary to cover the health-care costs of the elderly. This subsidy was the only budget item where enough savings were possible to meet the new ceiling.

5. *Achieving Fiscal Parity.* It was under this intense pressure that Ministry of Health and Welfare officials came up with a new financial arrangement for health insurance. Each insurer would send a portion of its premium revenues to a "pooling fund" (*kyōshitsukin*), the amount determined by how much in benefits it would have had to pay if it had an average number of the elderly among its enrollees. This new fund in effect took the place of much of the government's direct subsidy from tax revenues, which fell from about 50 percent to just over 20 percent of old-age health-care costs, and also allowed a substantial drop in the subsidy to CHI.[22] The new policy helped solve the Ministry of Health and Welfare's immediate budgetary problems. It had the further effect of making effective macro-level cost containment possible by fulfilling the fifth condition listed previously, financial parity across the health insurance systems.

That is, were it not for these cross-subsidies, a given level of expenditures

---

22   This legislation, the Health Care for the Elderly Law, also introduced a tiny co-payment and started up several educational and preventive programs. It was passed in 1982 despite opposition from both the JMA and the SMHI carriers.

as regulated by the fee schedule would mean that many SMHI carriers would run large surpluses, the national GMHI system would run a small surplus, and a substantial number of the local-government CHI programs would run large deficits.[23] Since the main cause of these differences was variation in the age of the membership, the cross-subsidization mechanism based on the proportion of elderly went a long way toward putting all the systems on an equivalent financial footing. Now, a given increase in the fee schedule would not impoverish some carriers while allowing others to get fat. A fine-tuning of this mechanism, an additional cross-subsidization program to cover retirees aged 60–69, was carried out in 1985.

Allowing for Flexibility

It was the accomplishment of the five basic conditions – universality of rules in the early 1960s, preventing ad hoc access to subsidies and simplifying spending decisions in the early 1970s, and the shift in the political balance of power plus the achievement of fiscal parity in the early 1980s – that allowed the linkage of expenditure-increase decisions to premium-revenue constraints that keeps spending down in Japan. As described earlier, officials in the Health Insurance Bureau have operated for more than a decade within a relatively clear set of rules that tell them how much the fee schedule should be raised.

However, the government gaining the upper hand did not mean that politics had disappeared. Indeed, it was crucial that the cost-containment mechanisms be flexible enough to respond to political pressures. Since the early 1980s, formulas have been adjusted and spending patterns altered slightly to provide the little bit extra that might relieve a problem, either substantive or political. A good illustration of this flexibility was the fee-schedule revisions of 1992, when providers as a whole were granted a raise for the first time since 1981. That is, pharmaceutical prices were cut sharply as in previous years, but this time fees for consultations and other services were raised enough not only to counterbalance the income loss from drug sales but to provide a net esti-

---

23 In fact, the spending constraints implemented in the 1981 fee-schedule revision had given big surpluses to many SMHI pools, a fact that greatly weakened their attempts to fight off this financial restructuring.

mated increase of 2 percent. The odd point is that this increased spending was financed by *lowering* the percentage rates of both health insurance premiums and the Treasury subsidy.

This seemingly perverse process was actually the product of the rules outlined previously. Health Insurance Bureau officials wanted to raise spending a bit for two reasons: Many hospitals were in poor or even dangerous financial condition, as revealed by the survey of institutions, and private-practice doctors in the JMA were clamoring for an increase. The doctors' demands were unusually strident because they had not had a raise in several years, and they knew that the GMHI accounts were running a surplus so the funds would be available.

Still, Health Insurance Bureau officials did not have a free hand in spending these surplus funds. The treasury subsidies to GMHI and CHI were fixed percentages of benefits. If a fee-schedule revision increased benefits, it would also increase the subsidy, and budgeters at the Ministry of Finance would not allow that. The MOF insisted that the subsidy *rate* be reduced, so that the absolute amount of the subsidy would remain roughly constant despite the benefit increase. But then, under the 1973 agreement described earlier, in GMHI the subsidy rate (as a percentage of benefits) and the premium rate (as a percentage of covered wages) are linked, so the premium rate had to be dropped slightly as well.

This outcome demonstrates the utility of linkages in holding down costs. In this and other respects – such as the one-time-only relief granted to SMHI carriers in 1990, as mentioned in the previous chapter – the Japanese system is flexible enough to accommodate new needs, whether of policy (the hospital financial problem) or politics (stepped-up pressure from the JMA). However, the built-in linkages prevent a very large increase in spending. A GMHI surplus cannot all go into benefits; in effect, it is distributed to the workers and firms enrolled through lower contributions and to taxpayers through a lower subsidy, as well as to doctors and hospitals through a benefit increase.[24]

---

24 In the 1994 and 1996 revisions, the strict requirements of linkage were tacitly relaxed, without public mention. Small increases in medical fees were financed somewhat mysteriously, without any hike in either contributions or government subsidies; indeed, in 1996, it was not clear if the fee hike would actually raise spending at all. Such use of "smoke and mirrors," although so far not too large in scope, perhaps was starting to threaten the hard-won credibility of the price-setting mechanism.

Recent Developments

The slight relaxation of spending constraints seen in the 1992 and 1994 fee-schedule revisions had its intended effect. The overall increases, plus some items targeted on inpatient care (surgical fees, nurse staffing), took the hospital sector as a whole out of the red.[25] Pressure from private-practice physicians for higher fees also leveled off for a time, although the JMA was soon reenergized by a new threat from the Health and Welfare Ministry.

In 1996, the GMHI was back into deficit, caused partly by the revisions described earlier but more by wage stagnation in the long recession. At the same time, the Finance Ministry was intent on bringing the overall budget deficit under control through tax hikes and expenditure cuts. The MHW responded with an austerity package that for a time was considered a radical reform in health-care finance. One proposal was a hike in the GMHI contribution rate from 8.2 to 8.6 percent, a new high. Another proposal was increases in patient co-payments: for employees, from 10 to 20 percent; for the elderly, to move from a monthly co-payment of a fixed amount to a regular percentage of 10 or 20 percent; and for everyone, a hike to 40–50 percent of the charge for pharmaceuticals.

The JMA had always opposed increases in co-payments, fearing it would reduce demand for medical care, and any threats to their drug-dispensing profits had particularly raised red flags over the years. It pressured the Liberal Democratic Party to oppose these proposals during the 1997 budget negotiations, and the politicians succeeded in watering down the co-payment increases considerably by the time the budget draft was announced.[26] In the end, the reform was far from radical; it amounted to about the same level of flexibility in responding to political and economic shifts that had characterized decision making since the early 1980s.

---

25 *Iryō Keizai Jittai Chōsa*, 1995. Some individual hospitals had severe financial problems, but most of these were the result of real-estate speculation and the decline of land prices, or sheer bad management.

26 In particular, the proposed co-payment in the old-age health-care program was first converted from a percentage to a fixed fee of ¥500 per outpatient visit, and then at the last stage of negotiations, a cap of four charges per month (per provider) was established; that meant that this co-payment by the elderly could be no more than ¥2,000, or about $11, a month, up from ¥1,200. The additional co-payment for drugs was also progressively cut down and was finally made a maximum of ¥100 per one day's worth of medications, depending on the number of drugs (with children six and under and low-income elderly exempted). *Shakai Hoken Junpō*, Dec. 1, 1996, p. 24; *Asahi Shinbun*, Dec. 22, 1996.

There was a more fundamental problem looming, however: The cross-subsidization system was biting harder and harder as transfers into the Health Care for the Elderly program steadily increased. Growing numbers of large-firm health-insurance societies in the SMHI system were going into the red in the 1990s. The resulting hikes in contribution rates brought an unusual level of complaints from employees, not just because they had to pay more at a time when wages had not been rising much but because their contributions were more and more going to cover other people's medical costs.

To some observers, this growing criticism of SGMI implied a fundamental flaw in Japanese health-care finance, as did the severe financial problems with Citizens' Health Insurance faced by small localities, as described in the previous chapter. It was argued that these flaws could be corrected only by major structural reform, such as a completely separate, tax-financed system of health care for the elderly, amalgamation with the proposed public long-term-care insurance program, or even some form of American-inspired de-regulation and privatization. It remains to be seen whether such calls for large-scale reform will gain momentum in the late 1990s. For what it is worth, our guess is that the 1997 revisions, moderate as they are, will go some distance in mitigating these problems, as would implementation of public Long-Term-Care Insurance, and an upturn in the economy would do even more. The system looks flexible enough to accommodate pressures of this magnitude for some time to come.

CONCLUSION

Despite Japan's reputation for rational planning and consensus decision making, we can see that its approach to determining overall medical expenditures evolved from a series of ad hoc compromises. True, since the early 1980s, it has been the officials in the Health Insurance Bureau who have taken the lead in deciding how much medical spending should rise. But before jumping to a conclusion that bureaucrats naturally run things in Japan, it is important to recognize two points. First, other actors – the Ministry of Finance, the majority party, the Japan Medical Association – hold a near-veto over any particular decision, so the Health Insurance Bureau must keep a close eye on politics while making up its mind. And second, although bureaucratic leadership has prevailed for the last decade or so, in earlier years the JMA and its allies in the LDP consistently won, either in open battles (the 1960s) or through a highly favorable truce (the 1970s).

We may anticipate that the normal ebbs and flows of politics and of national mood will continue to tweak the balance of power back and forth a bit between the Health Insurance Bureau and providers or politicians. Moreover, there is always the possibility of a major shift, akin to what happened in 1973 or 1981. It could be brought about by either a change in the overall system of governance, perhaps as a result of a new party system, or by some crisis within medical care itself.

Possible candidates for the latter cause include intense technology-driven upward pressure on costs or greatly increased demands for higher-quality care (particularly long-term care). Such needs would require increased spending on capital improvements or nursing staff, neither of which can be readily accommodated within the framework of the fee-schedule system. Or perhaps somewhat more likely as sources of change are continuation of the long-term trends of patients receiving outpatient care in hospitals, and the accompanying rapid falloff in the number of private practitioners that seems inevitable given their age profile (see Chapter 3). That would have many implications for how the health-care system operates. Indeed, it might even bring political difficulties from the standpoint of Ministry of Health and Welfare officials because having the JMA as their main antagonist has been extraordinarily convenient.

That is, the legitimacy of the fee-setting process, including the decision on overall spending growth, rests on the consent of the affected parties reached through a negotiation. Since the 1950s, the Central Council was dominated by the JMA; a perception therefore grew that getting the JMA to go along was the key to any deal. This perception has persisted – a typical case of "institutional lag" – even when the JMA lost much of its power and geared down to an unambitious defensive strategy. But the JMA's de facto right to represent providers, even the growing hospital sector, might well be seriously challenged if a sufficient number of hospitals felt sufficiently aggrieved. The Central Council process would then be thrown into confusion, and fee-schedule negotiations would become extremely difficult.

Even if that happens, though, Japan will probably still rely on its basic mechanism for deciding how much overall health-care spending should rise. That mechanism is the use of one portion of the health insurance system as a bellwether, or regulator, for the overall financial balance of medical care. The arrangement is a hybrid, a cross between a single-payer and an all-payers system, sharing virtues (and some defects) of each.

First, compared with a system where the payers' side is made up entirely

142

of independent insurance carriers (called an ''all-payers system,'' as in Germany), it is easier for the insurers' side in the basic negotiations to come up with a coherent position. The financial conditions of individual Health Insurance Societies in the big-business sector, as well as the interests of management and labor representatives, often differ enough to make for difficult decision making within the Federation of Health Insurance Societies (Kenporen). Similar problems plague the National Federation of Citizens' Health Insurance Associations because the financial condition of the local governments (and the few craft-based groups) that are the actual insurance carriers varies considerably. At a broader level, the employment-based schemes and CHI are financed quite differently, and common ground can be hard to find.

Because GMHI is a unified national system, its interests are not so ambiguous. Add in the Health Insurance Bureau's ability to collect, analyze, and withhold data, plus the legitimacy and air of neutrality that goes with being part of the state, and the advantages for relatively effective decision making when the government takes the leading role can be well appreciated.

Second, compared with tax-based single-payer systems, Health Insurance Bureau officials are directly constrained by economic forces. In particular, the financial condition of GMHI is determined by how much medical care is sought by its members and how much they are paying in premiums (which reflects their wages and therefore the overall state of the economy). Less directly but still importantly, the situations of SMHI and CHI cannot be ignored, since their representatives participate in the negotiations and must sign off on any agreement. The Japanese hybrid thus has some of the advantages of an all-payers versus a single-payer system in terms of linking spending to revenues.

Third, it is important to keep in mind that Japan does share an important characteristic with single-payer systems. Since the government rather than private organizations takes the lead in negotiations, policy can be directly influenced by national-level politics. In the Japanese context, it is assumed that legislators and political parties will intervene, either to appeal to voters (by expanding coverage or holding down premiums) or to respond to pressure from provider groups to raise fees. It is also possible that health spending would become the victim of some government-wide crusade against tax-and-spend liberalism – although the fact that underfunding would affect medical care for everyone, not just the poor, should limit such tendencies.

In short, Japan seems to have evolved a reasonably balanced system in which bureaucratic decision makers have enough information and autonomy to make sensible policy choices, but also have to be responsive to economic and political constraints, and how they change from year to year.

Japan's hybrid system, halfway between single-payer and all-payers, and between government management and social bargaining, may thus have lessons for Americans, such as, as noted earlier, a single national insurance system, or multiple but similar systems at the regional or state level, for that difficult category of small-business employees. With appropriate levels of cross-subsidies, financial management of small-business health insurance could be the mechanism for controlling medical spending in the economy as a whole. However, it is not easy to see the political steps that might lead to such a solution in the United States.

6

The Micropolicy of Cost Containment

A procedure for deciding overall health-care expenditures, as described in the previous chapter, is of little use unless the ceiling can be enforced. Fixed prices are the main mechanism for the implementation of government policy – primarily cost containment in recent years, but other goals as well. Of course, the fee schedule directly controls only prices, not volume, but it is supplemented by a variety of devices that effectively constrain the behavior of providers. Most important have been manipulations of relative prices, regulative directives, and a rather ad hoc system of claims review.

American dogma would hold that these methods should not be effective. It is argued that price controls and regulations cannot work because they do not control quantity, they lead to price distortion, and they result in a rebound when repealed. Moreover, many American experts believe that the appropriateness of care must be evaluated based on criteria from well-defined protocols, as defined by professional societies, or evidence from sophisticated databases produced by "outcomes research."

Although these assumptions appear plausible, empirical evidence from the Japanese health-care system indicates that they are more myths based on ideological convictions than universally applicable rules. In Japan, a political mechanism for setting prices, regulative directives by the government, and ad hoc claims reviews have together worked effectively to hold down spending, especially since cost containment became the number-one policy objective in the 1980s. This chapter explores how these techniques have been applied in the micropolicy of cost containment in Japan. The implications for quality are discussed in the next chapter.

HOW THE FEE SCHEDULE WORKS

The fee schedule plays a crucial role in the micropolicy of cost containment. The government uniformly sets fees for all procedures and the price of vir-

145

tually all pharmaceutical and other materials used. It also specifies a variety of conditions for particular treatments. Billing for procedures or material not listed, or charging more than the listed fee, is prohibited. Providers must therefore accept the listed fee as payment in full, or their entire service would be denied payment. With the exception of subsidies to public-sector hospitals, all the money that flows to all providers is controlled by the fee schedule. Consequently, the schedule not only holds down total health expenditures; it also influences what kinds of services will be delivered. It gives incentives to deliver a service if the fee is set at more than the cost to the provider, or disincentives if the fee is set at less than cost.

General Structure of the Fee Schedule

The fee schedule is universal. It does not recognize differences in physicians' qualifications: services provided by a newly licensed resident are paid the same amount as those by a well known specialist. Nor does it recognize any differences among facilities or regions: For a given procedure, the identical fee would be paid whether it were performed in a big university hospital in Tokyo or in a small physician's office in the countryside.[1]

The function of the fee schedule is not necessarily to set a fair price to reflect the cost of each procedure. Such a task would be impossible in any case, given that the fees are uniformly set at the national level. The function is instead to have each broad type of facility's expenditures balanced by its revenue.[2] For example, wages are generally higher in urban compared to rural areas, but the gap is mitigated by the fact that physicians are willing to work for lower salaries in large cities. This approach has had a positive effect in promoting access and ensuring the same level of services to all and, indeed, has made for much better physical facilities in nonmetropolitan areas (since land and construction costs are lower).

Since everything is decided at the national level, there is no scope for

1 Small differences of about $3 now exist in consultation fees (between physicians' offices and hospitals, and among hospitals by their size), and of about $1 a day in room charges (according to geographical area). But all other fees are the same regardless of the facility's characteristics. As noted earlier, the government had attempted to enforce a fee schedule based on actual costs in large hospitals in the early 1950s, but JMA opposition led to keeping the old *Otsu* schedule that benefited private practitioners alongside this new *Kō* schedule.
2 For this purpose, the government conducts the biennial Survey of Medical Institution Finances (Iryō Keizai Jittai Chōsa), which serves as the basis for determining the level and target of increase in the next fee-schedule revision.

146

individual or collective payers and providers to negotiate over fees. Thus, neither side can shift costs or maximize revenue by bargaining over prices or the range of services that should be provided. The billing process itself is very uncomplicated because everyone uses the same fee schedule. These factors have greatly diminished the need for well trained and well paid managers and have helped lower administrative costs in Japan (they are about one-quarter the level of the United States for both payers and providers as a ratio to GDP, or about half as a ratio to total health expenditure).[3]

The present fee schedule ultimately derives from the fee-for-service payments used by office-based physicians when social insurance was first introduced for manual workers in 1927. The fees were set at a low level from the start, 20 percent below the customary charges of that period.[4] Dispensing was the most important component, so much so that the basic unit was based on the fee for a day's dosage of an average drug.[5] These aspects have been retained in the basic structure of the fee structure.

That is, first, fees have been kept at a low level when compared with the United States. In the 1996 fee schedule, the initial consultation fee in Japan is ¥2,300 in hospitals and ¥2,500 in physicians' offices ($13–14 at a PPP rate of $1 = ¥180), which is about a quarter that of the 1992 Medicare Relative Value Scale (RVS) rate.[6] The magnitude of the difference is of about the same order for most other items. For example, the fee for a whole body

---

3   Administrative costs for all payers were 2.3 percent of expenditure in Japan compared with an estimate of 5.8 percent in the United States (including Medicare; rates for private insurance vary between 5.5 percent to 40 percent). A small-scale study using a common accounting method showed that the ratio of administrative costs to expenditure for four Japanese hospitals ranged from 5.1 percent to 7.1 percent, while that for nine American hospitals (in Florida) was between 9.1 percent to 20.0 percent. Naoki Ikegami, Jay Wolfson, and Takanori Ishii, "Comparison of Administrative Costs in Health Care in Japan and the United States," in *Containing*, pp. 80–93.

4   Physicians agreed to reduce their fees because not many patients were initially covered by social insurance, and they thought they could recoup their losses from their private-pay patients. The government justified this reduction by pointing out that with the guaranteed income from insurance, physicians would no longer have to worry about bad debts, so that on balance, it should not lead to a loss of income.

5   There was no fee for a repeat consultation in the original fee schedule. Even after fees for prescribing and dispensing came to be listed in 1958, it was not possible until 1967 to bill for a repeat consultation if medication was dispensed.

6   However, several adjustments are needed in order to make the U.S. RVS rate compatible with that of Japan. For example, we need to add hospital charges for the use of facilities and to subtract the proportion of the RVS rate that pays for the pre- and post-operative visits related to the procedure. These adjustments have been made for the 1992 U.S. RVS by Professor William Hsiao, who kindly made the data available to us.

CAT scan plus diagnosis is only ¥14,200 ($80) compared with $283 in the United States. For a coronary artery bypass surgery for more than two vessels, the fee is ¥605,000 ($3,400) compared with $6,573 in the United States.[7]

Second, 85 percent of the hospitals and 80 percent of the physicians' offices in 1990 were still dispensing medications, an important source of revenue for them. The profits derived from dispensing – that is, the margin (*yakka saeki*) between the fee-schedule price and the amount actually paid to purchase the drug – is estimated to amount to a quarter of the total sum paid by insurance for pharmaceuticals. This amounts to 7 percent of the net revenue for hospitals and 12 percent for physicians' offices. In this and other ways, the fee schedule has continued to favor the office-based physicians.[8]

Third, hospitals continue to be paid in exactly the same way as office-based physicians. Fees for room and board and nursing care have been merely added to the list alongside consultation, diagnostic testing fees, and so forth. There are no explicit mechanisms for reimbursing capital expenditures or administrative costs, which have to be financed from the revenue for providing the listed services after their direct operating costs have been covered.[9] For both individual physicians and hospitals, all payment is made to the facility in which the services have been provided. At the time when the fee schedule was first introduced, paying providers meant paying solo-practitioners, and ever since, hospitals have been treated as aberrations to this general rule despite the fact that their salaried physicians now outnumber the office-based physicians by two to one.

The Fee-schedule Book

The semi-official fee-schedule book, which is extensively used by all providers, is published and distributed by a private company.[10] It is quite mas-

---

7 Of course, comparisons with foreign countries depend crucially on exchange rates. At market rates, Japanese prices in dollars would look much higher in the 1990s, but that figure would not reflect the "real" cost in Japan (e.g., in terms of opportunity costs or hours of work required).

8 Pharmaceuticals comprise a larger portion of physicians' revenues because they have fewer other sources, and because the less-sophisticated drugs that they use are likely to have more substitutes available, which allows for purchasing at greater discounts.

9 As described in Chapter 3, public-sector hospitals do receive subsidies for investment in facility and equipment, determined on a case-by-case basis.

10 This company in fact pays the hotel and other expenses for the fee-schedule negotiations in order to publish the book first and to have two MHW divisions listed as editor.

sive, over two inches thick and weighing three pounds, and lists not only the over 3,000 procedures but also the various conditions and directives that must be fulfilled for the procedure to be reimbursed. There is also a separate pharmaceuticals price-schedule book that lists the price of the more than 13,000 drugs in the Japanese pharmacopoeia by brand name, dosage, and form. Both are given prices in the form of "points" (*tensū*). Each point is equivalent to 10 yen, and this conversion rate has remained constant since 1958.

The fee schedule is divided into a basic section on physicians' consultations and hospitalization, plus specific sections on home-care visits, diagnostic tests, imaging, prescribing and dispensing, injections, rehabilitation, psychotherapy, treatment (*shochi*), surgery, anesthesia, and nuclear therapy. Hospitalization consists of fees for room, board, nursing, and physician's management on a per diem basis. All are generally standard except that nursing fees vary based on the hospital's staffing level (for example, the ratio of qualified nurses and aides to patients). It should be noted that for prescribing and dispensing, and injections, each has an independent section reflecting the continued importance and the historical roots of the fee schedule.

Although the basic format of the fee schedule has remained the same, the content has become more and more complex (thirty years ago, the book weighed less than half a pound). There are several reasons why this has occurred, one being the advance of technology. Every time a new technology has been incorporated into the fee schedule, it has led to an additional code because the preexisting technology has usually been retained. For example, the introduction of microsurgery resulted in doubling the number of codes for the surgical procedures in which this new technology could be applied. Another reason is the introduction in 1983 of a slightly different fee schedule for the elderly covered by the Health Care for the Elderly Law. A third is the continuous addition of more directives that define the conditions under which reimbursement can be made for each procedure.

Each page of the fee-schedule book shows the procedures and their fees on the left-hand side, with the various directives on the right-hand side. The government has considerable discretion in issuing these directives, after consulting about the technical aspects with experts, and past directives can easily be revised. Despite their ad hoc nature, all directives are equally binding, and compliance is checked when claims are reviewed. Examples of the less technical directives include:

149

• The extra charge for an emergency consultation may only be billed if it occurs outside the hours prescribed in the directive, from 8:00 A.M. to 6:00 P.M., not outside the specific regular hours of each physician.
• For multiple operations performed within the same surgical field, only the higher-priced one can be billed.
• To claim fees for some types of rehabilitation, a facility's equipment and staff must be approved by the prefectural governor.

REVISIONS OF THE SCHEDULE

Since the fee schedule has an overwhelming impact on providers' revenue, even the most minor changes are subject to intense scrutiny. Political clout can be an important factor in deciding a dispute. However, the result is not anarchy. Within the constraints imposed by the system, two principles have generally been followed.

The first is to maintain "balance," so that no particular group would be a winner or loser in the long run. The idea is that the share of the pie that each class of providers receives should remain relatively stable. This is one reason why revisions have not been made by simply changing the "conversion factor" of how much money per point, as is done in other countries. That process would lead to those providers who had done better than average since the last fee revision, perhaps due to some technological change, becoming further advantaged by having their healthy revenues increased by the uniform percentage raise. The Japanese principle works against this tendency – when fees are adjusted differentially, a category of providers that had not done so well can get an extra increase by means of a larger point increase for its characteristic services or goods.

The second principle is to maintain a favorable position for office-based physicians, the major constituents of the JMA. It has been estimated that the efforts made by the JMA to increase the fees for the services provided primarily by office-based physicians have added an extra 15 percent to their total revenue.[11]

The first and second objectives are complementary in that maintaining the status quo has been to the advantage of the office-based physicians because

11 Yasuo Takagi, "The Japan Medical Association and Private Practitioners' Income," in *Containing*, pp. 278–285.

their original share was large, and has diminished the spending impact of the increase in the ratio of physicians working in hospital settings. Beyond that, maintaining balance has been a useful strategy in containing conflict among the numerous contenders. It would be difficult to find a different way of revising fees that would not lead to endless battles.

Process

The process of revising the fee schedule starts from the fall of each odd-numbered year (the biennial revisions occur in even-numbered years, with a few exceptions such as an extra revision in 1997). The first stage, which in effect sets the ceiling for projected total health expenditure by deciding on the overall medical-fee hike and drug-price reduction, is completed in December in the process of deciding the framework for the overall budget (see Chapter 5). The next stage is the complicated process of revising the fee of each item.

We can look first at medical procedure fees.[12] As noted previously, because the conversion factor has remained at ¥10 to a point, virtually every item will be changed if only to add a bit to account for inflation; this allows for considerable variation among items without attracting particular notice. Because the principle is one of balancing the remuneration among providers – for example, when pediatricians' relative income began to drop due to the declining birth rate, an extra fee was added for consultations for small children. Similarly, when large hospitals started to increase their share at the expense of office-based physicians because they were being chosen by more patients, the consultation fee for large hospitals was decreased.

Next, the impact of the proposed fee increases on total health expenditure is calculated by multiplying the fee of each item by its past volume. The basis for these estimates is the National Claims Survey, which collects aggregate data on medical-care usage and expenditures by treatment type for each health insurance system.[13] The individual fees are then fine-tuned so

---

12 Medical-procedure fees (*ika shinryō tensu*) exclude the services performed by dentists and prescription pharmacists but include all hospital services. The cost of material (X-ray films, disposables, etc.) are accounted separately in the same way as drugs.

13 Shakai Iryō Shinryō Kōibetsu Chōsa, officially "Survey of Social Medical Care According to Actions Taken," is carried out annually by analyzing a sample of the itemized monthly claims submitted by each provider for each patient. The key indices, broken down for each

that the total will come within the prescribed budget limits. In the final days, the bargaining process is conducted in a sealed room by two people: the front-line official of the Medical Care Division, and the JMA's board member who is in charge of the fee schedule.

Individual pharmaceutical prices, which as noted are nearly always reduced rather than raised, are determined on a somewhat more systematic basis. The biennial Pharmaceutical Price Survey reveals the prices currently being paid to manufacturers or wholesalers by providers for each drug. A formula is then applied, based upon the volume-weighted average market price. Some difference between the schedule price and the market price is allowed, purportedly to cover administrative costs for maintaining stock but actually because it is an accustomed source of income for providers. This difference is called the "reasonable zone" (the English words are used), which started out at 15 percent in 1992 but was decreased to 10 percent in 1997. The schedule price is then reduced by the amount that the market price is below the reasonable zone.[14]

After these prices have been determined, meetings are held with individual manufacturers, and the impact on revenues of the price reductions in all their products are explained. If the companies strongly object, which sometimes happens, they will complain via pharmaceuticals officials and perhaps get a bit of relief.

After all the medical and pharmaceutical fee revisions have been settled, they are printed in the government register in early March and come into effect on April 1. The new fee schedule will be closely scrutinized by all providers because it will have a crucial impact on their financial status for the next two years. However, at this stage, not all the new instructions and

type of health insurance and between inpatient and outpatient care, are number of cases per 100 enrollees, number of days of treatment per case, and cost per day; cost is broken down into treatment categories like examinations, operations, medications, tests, hospitalization, and so forth. A useful annual publication based mainly on this survey, including excellent graphs and examples of the calculations used in analyzing health-care spending, is Ministry of Health and Welfare, Insurance Bureau, Research Division, ed., *Iryōhi Handobukku* (Tokyo: Shakai Hoken Hōki Kenkyūkai).

14 This limitation on price cutting was introduced in 1992 mainly as a result of U.S. government complaints about "unfair" competition, motivated by the undisclosed private deals between Japanese manufacturers and health-care providers. The new system has the effect of keeping prices higher than they would otherwise be by making it difficult for hospitals to negotiate directly with manufacturers.

directives will be ready. In fact, the comprehensive fee-schedule book does not usually come out until late June because of the need to fine-tune the directives. For that reason, the claims reviews for the first three months following the revision (April to June) tend to turn a blind eye to minor mistakes.

Incidentally, even so, the software companies that write and sell programs to process the claims have a very hard time. They have only two weeks from the listing of the new fees in the government register to its execution. This calls for round-the-clock rewriting with further changes needed later to accommodate all the directives. The burden is made worse by the fact that each computer company has completely different software (each marketed as being more efficient), so they each have to do the task individually. It has been estimated that each revision costs a total of ¥30 billion ($170 million) to these companies.[15] This is a rare example in Japan of the common American phenomenon of overcompetition leading to wasteful expenditure in health care.

Introducing New Procedures and Drugs

Changes in the pattern of health-care delivery often require inserting a new item into the fee schedule. Because the effectiveness of the new procedure is somewhat ambiguous, and because it has to be financed from existing funds, a new item is usually hotly contested by established interests. Partly for this reason, its fee usually is set initially at a low level, sometimes having only a symbolic value. The fee is then gradually increased each time there is a fee revision if good medical evidence of efficacy is forthcoming, or perhaps if enough political pressure is maintained. For example, when pharmacists finally succeeded in getting inpatient clinical pharmacy services (such as providing drug information to patients and monitoring side-effects) into the fee schedule in 1988, the initial fee was only ¥1,000 per month per inpatient. However, it has been increased in every fee revision, to ¥6,000 per month in 1994, and then ¥4,500 billable *twice* a month in 1996.

The process is not always so smooth, however. In the case of inpatient psychotherapy, introduced long ago in 1961 at ¥220, the fee had been in-

---

15   See Kazuhiro Araki, "Understanding Japanese Health Care Expenditures: The Medical Fee Schedule," in Daniel I. Okimoto and Aki Yoshikawa, eds., *Japan's Health Care System* (New York: Faulkner & Grey, 1993), pp. 45–62.

creased to only ¥800 by 1996.[16] Moreover, the service can only be billed by physicians, not by psychologists or social workers (who do not have formal licenses). The reason for this poor showing is the political weakness of mental-health professionals, and the result is that little substantial psychotherapy is performed in hospitals. Incidentally, for a new type of diagnostic equipment, such as CAT scan or MRI machines, the process is usually less politicized, and prompt listing is the general rule.

The case of new drugs is more complicated. In principle, the price of an existing drug that has similar pharmacological characteristics is taken as the base line, and if the new drug is judged to be more efficacious its price is normally set at 3 to 15 percent more than the old one (or, in a sense, a bigger differential is created in that the price of the preexisting drug is reduced in the same revision). A few new drugs are supposed to be identified as "innovative" and will be allowed a price 20 to 60 percent higher than the baseline, but this relatively new principle has been applied very sparingly so far.

In the regular process, the pharmaceutical companies have learned to pick the highest-price drug with similar properties as the base for comparison for pricing, even though the existing drug that they pick to demonstrate the effectiveness of the new one may be different. As a result, the Japanese price for many new medications may be considerably higher than in other countries. This price typically is reduced later in successive revisions, but then again it may well be replaced quickly with yet another new drug. It is therefore quite difficult to make definitive statements about how drug prices in Japan compare with those of other nations.[17]

As another cost-constraint measure, in 1984 the government introduced a two-stage process for approving a restricted range of new high-tech procedures in order to slow down the process of diffusion. In the initial stage, provisional approval is given by the Central Social Insurance Medical Care

16 The fee for those hospitalized less than six months is higher, ¥1,500, but 81 percent of psychiatric inpatients have been hospitalized for over six months. Moreover, after the first month of hospitalization, this fee can only be billed once a week. A higher fee of ¥3,500 is set for psychoanalysis but there must be written records that show the content of the free association. The number of psychiatrists is relatively low in Japan, and they do not have much status or political power.

17 For two approaches, see Naoki Ikegami, "Comparison of Pharmaceutical Prices between Japan and the United States," *Containing*, pp. 121–131, and Hama Rokurō, *Yakugai wa Naze Nakunaranaika* (Tokyo: Nihon Hyōronsha, 1996).

Council for the use of the new technology under a tentative fee that can be requested only by a limited number of designated hospitals (mostly university medical centers). At this stage, the procedure itself is not reimbursable under social insurance so is paid out-of-pocket by the patient, but all other services are covered. This is an exception to the general principle that prohibits billing extra for a service not covered by insurance.

The second stage is the formal incorporation into the fee schedule, usually at a price below what had been billed to the patient previously. This stage occurs in theory when scientific efficacy has been established, though in fact other factors also may come into play. In the recent cases of lithotripsy (ESWL) in 1988, and artificial lens insertion for cataracts in 1992, approval was a result of pressure from patients, reflected in questions raised by the opposition parties in the Diet, and in local governments being induced to cover the costs of these procedures from their own budgets. Moderate pressures of this sort quickly lead to inclusion in the fee schedule.

Legitimacy of Prices

An economist trained to assume that there should be "correct" prices for medical goods and services would see this entire Japanese process as arbitrary and irrational. However, without a true market (which probably is impossible in any modern health-care system), there can be no "correct" criterion for setting prices. At a general level, the principle of maintaining balance over time among categories of providers has proven to be a practical guideline and has been effective in avoiding conflict probably because it fits in with broader cultural norms. However, acceptance of that principle does not guarantee that some specific price would not be seen as unfair by some provider, who might well be tempted to obstruct the process (for example, in an American context, by going to court). Lacking the moral authority of the "market," how are Japanese medical prices legitimated?

With respect to fees for medical services, the key is the point long emphasized by William Glaser: agreement between payers and practitioners, achieved through a regular negotiation.[18] This is the most common practice

---

18   William A. Glaser, *Health Insurance Bargaining: Foreign Lessons for Americans* (New York: John Wiley, 1978), and *Health Insurance in Practice* (San Francisco: Jossey-Bass, 1991).

among advanced nations, and Japan's approach is not particularly distinctive. A provider who sees a given fee as too low knows that it is part of some larger bargain, one that is not too different from the deal that had worked without disaster in the previous period, and in any case, the price can always be renegotiated two years later. For that reason, other than carping by a few health economists and others professionally attached to ideals of rationality, the structure of medical fees has not been very controversial in Japan.

The basis of legitimacy is different for pharmaceutical prices in that the most interested providers – the drug manufacturers – are not represented in the negotiations and so do not have the opportunity to agree. For the most part, these prices are still settled without too much conflict thanks to the Pharmaceutical Price Survey. It provides objective evidence of the prices actually charged and allows the use of a systematic formula for downward adjustments in the fee schedule on the basis of experience. Arguments between the Ministry and the industry have usually centered on the terms of the formula rather than on the individual prices it produced.

However, a manufacturer might be particularly unhappy if the impact of price cuts on all its drugs seemed to threaten profits unduly. Holding secret briefings with each manufacturer at the last stages of deciding the fee schedule allows their complaints to be heard, sometimes followed by a few adjustments. The most pointed disputes have not been about the routine price cuts but about an increasingly common practice on the part of the Ministry of making more extreme reductions in the fees for drugs that were enjoying unusually high sales. These inherently arbitrary decisions were strongly resented, and indeed the process broke down in 1994, when word leaked out that an extremely successful anti-cholesterol drug called Provastitin, made by Sankyo, would take an unusually large price cut because the Ministry needed to come up with a little more money for medical fee hikes. The company protested vehemently and got the Ministry to moderate the cut.

The result of this protest, in the next fee-schedule revision, was announcement by the Central Council of an explicit (if extra-legal) rule providing for special treatment of pharmaceuticals with annual sales exceeding ¥15 billion (about $85 million PPP) and with growth about twice expectations. The logic here is that the Pharmaceutical Price Survey cannot be applied to the most popular drugs because they are in high enough demand to make manufacturers' discounts unnecessary, leading to "excessive" profits. The price cut should therefore be determined outside the formula. We would anticipate future protests if this rule is blatantly applied, but Health and Welfare Ministry officials apparently believe that they would prevail because their position would be supported by popular opinion (because pharmaceutical manufacturers are widely believed to overcharge).

The earlier pattern, of private cajoling to get companies to accept essentially arbitrary determinations, is similar to "administrative guidance" in other policy areas in Japan.[19] The Sankyo case reveals the limitations of this practice. For the most part, if participants do not see the decision-making process as legitimate, they will resist, often successfully. The commonest claims to legitimacy are that the decisions were reached by a formula applied to objective data, or were agreed upon through a bargaining process.

CONTROLLING PROVIDER BEHAVIOR

The fee schedule and its accompanying directives have been used to induce changes in the behavior of providers. When Ministry officials observed that volume for some service or product had surged since the last revision, its fee would be lowered, or directives on conditions of use made more restrictive. Such measures have been effective in restricting volume. Less often, fees have been increased in order to encourage provision of certain services. Thus, the government exerts influence on the delivery of services by establishing rules under which all providers must play. This tendency has become more pronounced since the 1981 fee revision, when the principle of indexation was abandoned. From that time, fees began to be set more in line with the government's policy objectives and with less attention to providers' costs.

Specific Targets of Cost Containment

According to health economics reasoning, low fees should be associated with a high volume because of physician-induced demand. This proposition appears to be true for Japan at least in the following three areas:

- *Physician consultation visits:* Japanese physicians typically see an average of 49 patients a day (13 percent see more than a hundred), and the per capita average number of visits per year by patients in Japan is more than double that of the United States.[20]

19 Cf. Stephen R. Reed, *Making Common Sense of Japan* (Pittsburgh: University of Pittsburgh Press, 1993), Chapter 5.
20 These data are from 1983, the most recent available. *Kanja Chōsa*, 1985.

- *Pharmaceuticals:* the per capita level of spending on medication in Japan is about the same as in the United States despite the much lower total health-care expenditures.[21]
- *Laboratory tests:* physicians have incentives to order diagnostic tests, particularly when they can contract out to free-standing for-profit laboratories at relatively low prices, when they receive the full fee-schedule amount.

The last two areas have been the major targets of cost containment; indeed, Japanese health care has long been popularly characterized as "pickled in drugs and tests" (*kusurizuke, kensazuke*). Interestingly, there has been less criticism of the high consultation rate despite its major impact on total health expenditures. One reason is the lower impact of physician-induced demand for consultations, because the decision to first visit a physician usually lies with the patient, and there is some limit to the number of repeat visits that a physician may request.

In the case of pharmaceuticals, two strategies were adopted to decrease spending. One was simply to reduce their reimbursement price. Starting with the 1981 fee-schedule revision, in addition to the national questionnaire survey of the price paid by the providers, on-site inspections of drug wholesalers were carried out to check the actual retail price of popular pharmaceuticals. This resulted in large reductions in their scheduled fees, which in the extreme case of third-generation antibiotics averaged 45.2 percent. This process was continued in later years, so that in 1995 prices for all the drugs that had been on the market since 1981 had been cut by more than 50 percent on average.

Incidentally, although the pharmaceutical makers were initially hit hard by this price-cutting strategy, they were able to cope by rapid introduction of new drugs, for which higher prices could be charged.[22] The share of medications in total national medical spending had dropped sharply from 38 percent to 29 percent from 1980 to 1985 but since then has held steady at about that level. Note also that in recent years neither the profits nor R&D spending of the major pharmaceutical manufacturers has declined.

---

21 Calculated for 1989, at $216 for Japan and $203 for the United States using the OECD PPP rate of ¥199 to $1. Japan's pharmaceutical expenditure amounted to 17.3 percent of the total health expenditure, compared with 8.4 percent for the much higher total in the United States (OECD Health Data File, 1993).

22 Will Mitchell, Thomas Roehl, and John Creighton Campbell, "Sales, R&D, and Profitability in the Japanese Pharmaceutical Industry, 1981–92," in *Containing*, pp. 132–42.

The other strategy was to change the rules of the fee schedule. For example, before the 1981 fee revision, there was a fee of ¥600 for administering every 500-cc bottle of drip infusion. After the revision, the fee could only be billed if the quantity exceeded 550 cc per day, and furthermore, it was fixed at ¥750 per day, regardless of the number of bottles that had been used. As a result of this new regulation, the share of injections and drip infusion in the total medical expenditure decreased dramatically, from 12.9 percent in 1981 to 5.1 percent in the following year.

For diagnostic tests, the other major target of cost containment, ''bundling'' of laboratory test fees was introduced in the 1981 fee revision. That is, while performing twenty-four biochemical tests would formerly have netted twenty-four times the fee for a single test, with bundling the unit fee decreases as the number of tests increases. In 1994, for ten or more tests, the fee became a flat ¥2,150, which is only eight times the average fee for a single test. In addition to bundling, since 1988 the fee has been separated into two parts, one for performing the test and one for interpreting the results. The latter can be billed only once a month irrespective of the number of times the test was actually performed. These measures have at least halted the rapid increase in the share of diagnostic tests. While their ratio to total medical expenditure increased rapidly in the 1970s (from 6.6 to 11.0 percent, 1970 to 1980), this ratio has stabilized since then largely due to the introduction of auto-analyzers and other diagnostic equipment; it was just 10.5 percent in 1993.

Along with pricing measures, directives have also been used to contain the volume of pharmaceuticals and laboratory tests. Since the directives can be issued on an ad hoc and immediate basis without waiting for the next fee revision, they can be effective in counteracting sudden increases in volume.

For example, in 1992 information from the claims review boards (described in the next section) and the pharmaceutical industry's monthly report showed a marked increase in the use of interferons for type-C hepatitis, and an accompanying increase in the number of reported side-effects. The Medical Care Division Director responded by issuing a directive in January 1993, stating that the use of interferon should be restricted to cases in which the diagnosis had been confirmed by biopsy, and that it should be continued only if proved to be effective in the first twelve weeks of its use. Furthermore, the standard period of use should be limited to six months. The physician had to write that he had followed these conditions on the claims form. Similar directives for the use of tumor markers have also been issued, restricting their use to patients who are strongly suspected of having a malignant neoplasm (and then only on one occasion).

The most recent targets for cost containment are "therapeutic medical devices" (*tokutei chiryō zairyō*), disposable material used in surgery and durable equipment such as pacemakers. Although these constitute only 2.5 percent of total medical expenditure, their growth rate has been nearly twice the average. This was partly due to the fact that they were not listed in the fee schedule and were reimbursed according to the actual price paid by the provider, thus allowing manufacturers to set their own prices.

The reform was precipitated by a series of major scandals involving the payment of kickback money to prestigious hospital physicians, including an associate professor at Tokyo University Medical School. Because hospitals were reimbursed fully and had no financial interest in the type of pacemaker to be purchased, the decision had been left entirely to physicians' judgment. However, the problem was that there was very little difference in the quality of pacemakers from a medical point of view. To prevent such incidents occurring in the future, since the 1994 fee revision medical devices such as pacemakers have been listed in the schedule, and their prices will be reduced to reflect market trends.[23]

Policy for Hospitals

Apart from the recent interest in therapeutic medical devices, most cost-containment efforts have been aimed at ambulatory care because it is a larger share of total costs than inpatient care. In fact, despite the expansion of long-term care in hospitals, inpatient care actually decreased from 44.2 percent of total medical expenditures in 1985 to 41.1 percent in 1992, while that of ambulatory care has increased from 43.4 percent to 45.4 percent. This change was not due to an expansion of outpatient surgery or other technological factors. Why has volume expansion not occurred in high-tech inpatient care as has been the case in the United States? There are several reasons.

First, price controls are much more effective when volume cannot be ex-

---

23 This new form of reimbursement was vigorously opposed by the U.S. government because it wanted to maintain high prices for the many therapeutic devices imported from the United States. It is ironic that, as in pharmaceuticals, the U.S. government has opposed price competition in Japan despite the rhetoric heard in the domestic health-care reform debate. The American argument has been that emphasizing price would penalize better-quality equipment.

panded due to time constraints. That is, the difference in fees between Japan and the United States is about the same magnitude for most procedures, but the low fees selectively impose a limit on procedures such as surgical operations, which take up a fixed amount of professional time. Japanese surgical fees are often actually below the average costs for providers, so that a volume increase would result in a net deficit for hospitals. In contrast, the time for prescribing medicine and ordering laboratory tests can easily be compressed to generate more revenue. Although cultural aversion to invasive treatment and differences in physicians' career paths also play a role, this is a key reason why the per capita volume of surgery is only about one-third the level of that in the United States. In that sense, this pattern follows the general rule that low-cost services, such as ordering laboratory tests, are profitable and that expensive services, such as surgery, are unprofitable in Japan.[24]

Second, bed and board fees have been kept at a low level, in comparison with increases in general wages, partly because hospitals have not been able to increase their share of spending due to the conservative principle of "balancing" and partly because the standards of care do not appear to merit high fees. In particular, for nursing services, the highest level of staffing that will be reimbursed is only one nurse per two patients. With such low staffing levels, it is difficult to increase throughput and generate revenue by increasing patient admission through shorter lengths of stay. This is one reason why recovering patients remain hospitalized for longer periods; for example, the average length of stay for a cardiac bypass operation is twenty-five days, compared with nine days in the United States.[25] Also, as has been noted, capital and administrative costs cannot be separately billed.

Given the fact that there appears to be a built-in mechanism for containing costs in inpatient care, the main policy objective pursued through the fee schedule has been to realize greater functional differentiation: between hospitals and office-based physicians, and between acute and long-term care. As noted in Chapter 3, there is a considerable overlap of functions in Japan. The

24 Patient need plus perhaps professional pride are thus the main reasons why surgical operations *are* performed in Japan. As has been noted in Chapter 3, three-quarters of the surgical operations requiring general anesthesia are performed in university and public-sector hospitals, which usually receive subsidies.

25 Naoko Muramatsu and Jersey Liang, "Comparison of Hospital Length of Stay and Charges between Japan and the United States," *Containing*, pp. 155–171. Note that the government would contend that because the intensity of care is not so high, a higher maximum-staffing-level fee is not needed.

former overlap has recently been regarded as the more serious problem due to the ever-increasing popularity of large university and public-sector hospitals with patients, even those who require only primary care. Because patients in these hospitals tend to receive more intensive services, this trend has major cost implications, and it also takes patients away from private practitioners.

As a response, from 1986, consultation fees were differentially increased to provide considerably more to office-based physicians.[26] Moreover, new fees for referrals were introduced in 1988, and academic medical centers were granted an increase in consultation fees in 1993 if more than 30 percent of their new ambulatory-care patients came with a referral. Whether these measures will be sufficient to reverse the trend is quite doubtful, but they do at least convey a message that hospitals should concentrate more on inpatient care and more advanced referred cases in the future.

Concern for the latter overlap derives from the expensive anomaly of so many elderly people receiving custodial care in hospitals rather than in nursing homes or other more appropriate facilities. The government's attack on this problem began in 1981 with a sliding scale for basic hospitalization fees: Fees decreased as the length of stay increased, so that after three months, hospitals now receive only about a third of the initial fee. Such measures have been applied more intensively over the years and have had some effect – the average length of stay decreased from 39.7 days in 1986 to 35.1 days in 1993 (excluding psychiatric and other special hospital beds).

Along with discouraging long stays in ordinary hospitals, the government split off a new institution called a "hospital for the elderly" (*rōjin byōin*), legally a hospital but actually more of a nursing home. All hospitals with at least 60 percent of its inpatients 65 and over, and that did not meet the standards for nurse staffing ratios, automatically are given this designation and become subject to more "bundling" in procedure fees.

Moreover, since excessive use of medication and laboratory tests is seen as driving up costs in long-term care with little medical benefit, a new inclusive per diem payment system was introduced on an optional basis in 1990 for hospitals with a high ratio of elderly patients. As of July 1994, 840

---

26 This was done in part by allowing an extra outpatient fee for the physician's guidance in managing several common illnesses (called Tokutei Shikkan Ryōyō Shidōryō), which in 1996 was ¥2,000 for private practitioners, ¥1,350 for hospitals with less than 100 beds, ¥800 for hospitals with from 100 to 200 beds, and none for larger hospitals.

out of a total of 1,613 hospitals for the elderly had selected this option. Usage of drugs and lab tests in these institutions has been sharply reduced by not allowing separate billing (except for rehabilitation services and imaging) – again, the fee schedule was the mechanism to stimulate change. These reforms met with little effective opposition because restricting spending on inpatient long-term care meant more resources for office-based physicians, who dominate the politics of the fee schedule.

Positive Incentives

Fees in the schedule have also sometimes been used to encourage the provision of certain services. A classic example is renal dialysis. Its fees were initially set at a high level because the government wanted to avoid the ethical problems arising from explicitly rationing its use, and also to respond to pressures from the kidney patients' organization. As a consequence, renal dialysis became widely available in a relatively short time. Today, Japan has the highest per capita number of patients on dialysis. Moreover, extra fees for longer periods on the machine is one reason why the failure rate among dialysis patients is quite low in Japan, even though the proportion of quite ill patients is probably high (there are few transplants and no British-style restrictions on extending this treatment to the elderly).[27]

However, positive incentives in the fee schedule do not always work so well. For example, fees for home visits have been increased as a way to promote community care and decrease the hospitalization of the elderly. This policy goal was shared by the government (as a cost-containment measure) and by the JMA (to increase the revenue of office-based physicians), but the reform did not work. The fee for a home visit was increased from ¥2,000 to ¥5,500 over 13 years, but the average number of home visits actually decreased by more than a third. Apparently, physicians have been unwilling to change their practice pattern despite the generous incentives.

---

27 Once the supply became sufficient, the fees were abruptly cut. Although direct comparisons are difficult due to changes in the directives on what can be separately billed as material costs (initially, distilled water could be billed at a relatively high price), and also due to real decreases in the cost of the material, the initial fee of ¥31,000 was more than halved to ¥13,000 in the 1981 fee revision. However, large-scale providers with economies of scale have managed to maintain their profit margin. Recently, this reduction has threatened quality, according to Niki Ryū, *Nihon no Iryōhi: Kokusai Hikaku no Shikaku Kara* (Tokyo: Igakushoin, 1995), pp. 64–68.

Most often the evidence is inconclusive. The government has long tried to dissuade physicians from dispensing medications in favor of writing prescriptions to be filled by pharmacies. In 1974, the fee for writing a prescription to an outside pharmacy was increased from ¥60 to ¥500. Later, as a result of the 1981 fee revision, the profit margin from dispensing pharmaceuticals was progressively decreased. Both efforts have been stepped up in recent years, with the prescription fee increased to ¥760 in 1994. This reform has had some positive results: The pharmacy share of drug expenditures expanded from 3.6 percent in 1980 to 10.6 percent in 1992. However, the majority of new pharmacies have been established near hospitals and in some cases seem to be engaging in fee-splitting. These problems brought more fine-tuning of policy as the Ministry strived to achieve its long-held vision of each consumer relying on a single "home pharmacy."[28]

Competition Under Regulated Fees

The fee schedule is not the only force that can change provider behavior. Often enough, market competition is still more powerful. Competition for patients among physicians and hospitals is much more widespread in Japan than currently in the United States, where so much of the population is in managed-care systems that restrict access. Since prices are fixed, providers compete mainly on the basis of perceived quality – a safeguard for consumers that must be provided by regulations in a managed-care system.[29] Moreover, competition has often led to technological innovation.

The CAT case provides the classic example of how competition can bring rapid diffusion at low cost. Despite the relatively low fee for each procedure, the per capita number of CAT scan machines installed in Japan is the highest in the world. The first stage was university hospitals installing the equipment regardless of cost for research purposes. Other hospitals realized that a CAT scan machine would help them compete for physicians and patients. The resulting increase in overall revenue compensated for the deficit arising from purchasing and operating the machine itself. Then, innovative manufacturers who wanted to sell the equipment in a highly competitive market began to

28 In the 1996 fee-schedule revision, dispensing service fees were sharply reduced for pharmacies that received a large proportion of their prescriptions from only one hospital.

29 In principle, consumers can switch between managed-care providers when they are dissatisfied; in practice, that option may not be available or can be exercised only in a fixed open-enrollment period.

introduce inexpensive models alongside their state-of-the-art equipment. That made CAT scans affordable even to providers who could not maintain a high volume of patients, including not a few physicians' offices. The government was then able to decrease the fee for head scans, from the original amount of ¥18,000 to ¥16,500, in two parts: taking the picture (¥13,000 with contrast medium) and interpretation (¥3,500, billable only once a month).

Many CAT scan machines installed in Japan may produce marginally less clear pictures than the more expensive types that have become the standard in the United States, but the possibility that this would cause an incorrect diagnosis or a different outcome for the patient is slight. The magnitude of the difference between having a CAT scan or not is much greater than that among the various models. In this case, the combination of regulated fees and market competition appears to have worked better than requiring government approval through a certificate of need (likely to be either rigidly bureaucratic or full of loopholes) or cost-based reimbursement. The course taken by CAT scans is now being followed by MRIs (Magnetic Resonance Imaging), where Japan now also has the highest per capita number of machines in the world.[30]

The effects of competition in the area of pharmaceuticals has been mixed. On the one hand, the fact that providers dispense drugs at fixed prices has led to fierce rivalries among manufacturers and wholesalers to sell to providers at the lowest possible price. These true market prices are picked up by the government in its biennial survey of pharmaceutical costs and are reflected in the next fee-schedule revision. The cycle then repeats as manufacturers again cut prices to give providers some profit. If we compare the 1989 list prices of the top-selling drugs that are common to Japan and the United States, the American prices are two to six times more expensive (calculated in terms of daily dosages using the PPP rate).[31]

On the other hand, competition has done nothing to inhibit the overuse of medications that results from providers dispensing and from fee-for-service

---

30 See Akinori Hisashige, "High-Cost Technology in Health Care: The Adoption and Diffusion of MRI in Japan," *Containing*, pp. 106–120.

31 Although the list price is rarely the price paid by the provider, discounts generally apply in both countries, and even if they were greater in the United States, it is unlikely that this would fully offset the lower Japanese list prices. Note that comparing drug prices is difficult because the drugs that are used are not necessarily the same, daily dosage is not the same, and different assumptions about exchange rates produce quite different results. Ikegami, "Pharmaceutical Expenditure."

financing (except perhaps by ensuring an endless supply of mild drugs such as vitamins, anti-infectives, anti-hypertensive drugs, and cerebral metabolic activators that physicians can dispense without much fear of doing harm). There are no incentives to prescribe a lower-priced drug: The ratio of generics (drugs that are no longer covered by patents) is only 11 percent in Japan compared with 30 percent in the United States.

In fact, the Japanese system encourages manufacturers to keep coming up with ''new'' drugs that are entitled to a higher price, even if in reality they are only marginal adaptations of existing products. Nakagawa has shown that the average time from introduction for the twenty top-selling drugs was 5.7 years in Japan compared with 8.3 years in the United States.[32] The result has been pernicious in the case of antibiotics, where the wide usage of third-generation drugs has led to a high prevalence of MRSA (Methythillin Resistant Staphylococcus Aureus) infection in Japan.

The lesson here is that competition is a potent force in health care, but its effects cannot be evaluated by simplistic analogies with sectors that more closely approximate a true free market. Examples of competition leading to wasteful spending and even unfortunate medical outcomes are rife in the United States but can be found even in Japan's heavily regulated system. On the other hand, in proper context, competitive forces can be the best mechanism for efficiency, again even in Japan.

CLAIMS REVIEW

If Japan is noted for overuse of pharmaceuticals, its fee-for-service financing system would seem to encourage provision of too many goods and services of all kinds. As described earlier, manipulation of prices in the fee schedule has tended to expand provision of inexpensive (and in some cases possibly beneficial) services such as ordinary doctor visits rather than expensive (and in some cases potentially harmful) surgery. However, more direct safeguards against excessive or inappropriate treatment are also required in Japan as elsewhere. Japanese physicians enjoy substantial clinical autonomy and never have to get a preapproval for any procedure or medication, but they are subject to after-the-fact reviews that can result in denial of payment.

Americans tend to believe that the appropriateness of care can only be

---

32 Nakagawa Hiroshi, *Iyakuhin Sangyō no Genjō to Shōrai* (Tokyo: Yakugyō Jihyōsha, 1991), pp. 40–41.

evaluated on an individual basis, with the support of an elaborate database and/or well-defined protocols. The claims review process in Japan does not fulfill these conditions, being ad hoc and impressionistic, but to a surprising extent, it does serve its primary purpose of promoting self-policing by professionals.

Process

Each health-care provider, whether a private practitioner or a hospital, files one claim (called a receipt, *reseputo*) per month for each patient. It lists diagnoses and the content and volume of all the goods and services provided. The claims then undergo a review (*shinsa*) by one of two review boards at the prefectural level, one for the employment-based insurance systems, called the Payment Fund (Shiharai Kikin), and the other for community-based insurance, called the Citizens' Health Insurance Federation (Kokuho Rengōkai). These intermediaries are quasi-public organizations that act as clearinghouses for processing claims and making payments to providers. They then bill each insurance carrier for the total amount of scheduled fees for the services provided to all their enrolled patients, minus the co-payments already paid by the patients. Claims that exceed a certain amount, or that appear to include excessive medications, are sent directly to two central review boards at the national level.

Altogether, about 8,000 members serve on these peer-review boards.[33] All are physicians, and they are nominated in equal proportions by providers, payers, and neutral academics. Because only a few physicians are both willing to serve on a board and have the necessary expertise, however, those appointed tend to share common views regardless of their nominating body. In practice, local medical associations are usually quite influential because they nominate all members from the provider side and, depending on local politics, may even be able to veto other nominations. That does not lead to softer reviews, however, because aggressive revenue maximizers are generally resented by their peers.[34] Thus, self-policing by professionals at the local level works reasonably well.

---

33 *Me de Miru Iryō Hoken Hakusho*, 1994.
34 Such resentment appears to be effective even though the offending behavior would not lead to less revenue for the other providers, as might be the case in an American HMO. In one case, the president of an unusually aggressive hospital chain was actually asked to sit on

In theory, all claims are reviewed, but the actual process is as follows. First, claims are checked by the administrative staff for any errors in formatting or coding of the claims number and so forth. Next, those that appear questionable are sorted out for inspection by the peer-review board. The staff divides providers into three groups based upon impressionistic knowledge of their characteristics: those with an aggressive reputation, those who can be trusted, and those in between. Claims coming from providers in the first category are more likely to be selected for review, especially if they are for large amounts. This sorting process is necessary because of the enormous number of claims (if all were actually examined, they would get only four seconds each). Claims are also grouped by specialty for review by the member who has the necessary expertise. To protect the integrity of the process, the group of providers that each member reviews is changed every three months.

Judging the Appropriateness of Care

The criteria for judging appropriateness are not always clearly defined. Some of the more explicit are that reimbursement should not be made for research purposes, directives must be followed, and drugs may be used only for an approved purpose. However, providers can generally find ways of getting around these restrictions. Since judgment is mainly based on whether the services provided are appropriate for the diagnosis, in many cases, the provider can simply add a diagnosis to justify the treatment. It is not unusual to see five or more diagnoses listed on the claims form.[35] That is another reason why reviewers tend to rely a good deal on their impressionistic knowledge of each provider.

The peer-review boards reject few claims, typically less than 1 percent of the total amount of fees billed. Providers fear rejection nonetheless. Appeals are possible but are time-consuming and uncertain, particularly because records are not kept of how directives have been interpreted in the past. Worse still, getting too many rejections could lead to a bad reputation and more trouble in the future.

the peer-review board, on the assumption that greater peer pressure for moderation would result.

35   That might be appropriate behavior in medical terms because using an approved drug for a nonapproved use may be clinically justified. There is always a time lag in obtaining approval for broadening usage.

Incidentally, paradoxically enough, this approach may well be more effective than employing clear and straightforward criteria, since those could be more easily predicted and then gamed by savvy providers. Physicians are willing to go along with all this threatening ambiguity because they fear any sort of statistical analysis of claims, which could lead to more government control in the long run. For that reason, they have successfully resisted electronic filing – even though most claims are prepared on a computer, they are printed out and submitted as hard copy.[36]

The effect of this review process is to penalize providers that stand out from local community standards. That could well be unfair to anyone with entrepreneurial tendencies and, indeed, might be seen as another example of collaboration between government and an industry to maintain the status quo, as often criticized within and outside Japan. The system also tolerates regional variation. For example, Kyoto and Osaka are prefectures that historically have had more permissive norms (their claims average about one-sixth higher than the national level). On the other hand, local professionals are likely to understand how the health facilities in their community really behave. In fact, the reviews done at the national level for high-cost claims are not necessarily more effective than the local reviews, even though that process is formally more rigorous.

Review by the Payers

There is also a second-stage review (called *tenken*) conducted by each insurance carrier. The extent to which the review is done carefully varies greatly. All insurers routinely check whether the patient is enrolled in their plan and if duplicate claims have been filed by mistake. Most insurers also send members notices of the costs that each had incurred during the past month, for checking. Should the patient report a discrepancy, the carrier will demand a review by the review board. However, fewer than half of the carriers actually examine the contents of claims for appropriateness of care. Carriers that are in the red are encouraged by the government to be more rigorous in their reviews.

If the carriers choose to do so, they do have a major advantage over the

---

36 Review-board staff reenter the data manually into computers, though they are experimenting with optical readers to do the job. Because providers use different commercial software, introduction of direct electronic filing is said to be impossible.

peer-review boards in making more rigorous examinations. The latter can review only the cross-sectional claims data for each calendar month, whereas the carriers can follow the entire sequence of medical services to a patient delivered by a given provider over a long period (because they keep the claim forms). Since carriers rarely have the professional staff to do real reviews, many contract with a specialized company, which works for a percentage of the amount saved to the payers. Needless to say, providers strongly object to such arrangements, ostensibly on grounds of privacy.

In recent years, it is Citizens' Health Insurance managers who have tried to be the most stringent in their *tenken* claims review because they have been under the most financial pressure. They also have an interest in demonstrating zeal in holding down costs to their mayors and to higher levels of government. Stories are told of local officials visiting a hospital for the elderly to ask the director to discharge some of the patients whose long-term care was inflating expenditures, although such instances are no doubt quite rare. However, particularly in more rural communities, it is likely that providers would feel some informal pressure to avoid pushing costs up too much.

Unfortunately, there has been little research on the impact of *tenken* reviews by insurance carriers. Too much rigor might become counterproductive from the point of view of total cost containment because it would place a burden on the initial *shinsa* peer-review boards, which must individually inspect each objection from a payer.[37] The rule of thumb for carriers is that the savings from denying payment for inappropriate care should at least exceed their own administrative costs. In a more general sense, whether payers that have established a reputation for being tough in their reviews have a sentinel effect on providers is not known.

On-site Inspections

Besides these review processes, there are two heavier measures to check provider behavior. The first is called "guidance" (*shidō*). This is an on-site inspection conducted by the prefectural government in conjunction with the local medical association and consists of cross-checking medical records for a random sample of claims. Any divergences from the directives are pointed out, and the amount that has been improperly billed is calculated. Based on

---

37   These objections are handled in the same way as the objections from the providers. Payers cannot unilaterally deny any payment based just on their own judgment.

this sample, the inspectors then estimate the amount that should be refunded for all patients. The provider is then asked to go through its records for the past year to determine the amount that should be paid back to each payer. The process by which providers are chosen for *shidō* is not clear, but revenue maximizers appear to be selected disproportionally.

The second such measure is an audit (*kansa*), undertaken when a blatant infringement of the regulations is suspected, such as billing for services not provided. Temporary or permanent cancellation of the facility's designation as a social insurance carrier may follow. In 1992, 45 facilities and 75 physicians were subjected to an audit, of which 20 facilities and 21 physicians had their carrier status canceled.

Financial scandals in health care are a staple item for the newspapers and magazines, and no doubt considerable shady behavior or outright cheating goes on without being detected in Japan as elsewhere. Certainly, there is "waste" in medical spending. In comparison with the United States, however, the simplicity of the financing system and the explicit and implicit controls on aggressive revenue maximization – including claims review – have been effective mechanisms for efficiency.

CONCLUSION

Empirical evidence from Japan shows that the combination of regulated fees, government directives, and ad hoc claims review has been successful in containing costs. As reported in Chapter 1, health-care spending has been kept nearly level as a share of GDP since the early 1980s. The key has been control over prices: "Medical inflation" (price increases for medical services and products, exclusive of volume) is not usually calculated in Japan, but a recent study indicates that health-care prices as a whole went up only 0.4 percent a year from 1979 to 1993. That extraordinarily low rate resulted from the regular reductions of pharmaceutical prices, but even if that category is left out, the inflation rate for all other medical services and products was just 2.8 percent a year, which was a little over the Consumer Price Index for this period (2.33%) but below the average increase in wages (3.34%) – a sharp contrast to the double-digit medical inflation in the United States in this era.[38]

38 The small price increases that did occur were for inpatient care (0.8% per year); prices in outpatient care were virtually flat for the entire period (0.08% per year). That result was not a goal; it was because the cost cutting came in pharmaceuticals, which are a higher

171

It is also worth noting again that pricing was used effectively to control volume, contrary to the conventional wisdom. Prices have been most constrained, and in some cases even reduced, for those procedures and products that had seen a surge in usage in the period prior to a fee-schedule revision. In that sense, the Japanese approach of revising every fee separately in each revision has advantages over the more common practice (in U.S. Medicare and many European systems) of adjusting a "conversion factor" that applies to all fees to control prices.

It is clearly the fee schedule that has played the key role. Indeed, it has not only set the price; it has also defined how and which services can be billed. The American practice of unbundling and charging $10 for an aspirin or $15 for "thermal therapy kits" (ice bags) becomes impossible under this system. Administrative costs are low because all negotiations are done at the national level, and a uniform format is used for billing purposes. We note as well that fixed prices do not necessarily inhibit competition – they can make for real competition, not just cream-skimming, by putting pressure on providers and manufacturers to decrease costs. However, as the case of pharmaceuticals well illustrates, competition cannot be the main principle for cost control in health care.

Contrary to the usual American assumptions, we have seen that volume can be constrained in a fee-for-service system, or at least that overusage can be channeled into relatively inexpensive and harmless areas. Japan's success in limiting the amount of surgery largely by means of low prices is particularly noteworthy. Moreover, a fee schedule that is revised regularly can provide a quick response to cost surges caused by technological change, as was true with lab tests.

As for other common American assumptions, we find that rebounds become a nonissue if fees are permanently regulated.[39] And price "distortions" are not a real problem at all: Whether fees are appropriate or not is a meta-

<hr>

proportion of outpatient expenditure. This study was based on analyzing claim forms in GMHI. See Ikegami Naoki, Ikeda Shunya, and Suzuki Reiko, "Iryōhi no Suii: Kakaku Shisū kara no Bunseki," *Byōin Kanri* 34:2 (1997), 53–62. For the concept of medical inflation and American data, see Paul J. Feldstein, *Health Care Economics*, 4th ed. (New York: Delmar Publishers, 1993), pp. 53–73.

39 They were a problem during the Carter administration because price controls for hospitals were removed as a result of pressure from the providers. Parenthetically, note that the view that regulations cannot work in the United States is partly due to their having been inadequately applied (e.g., physicians' fees and hospital ambulatory care were left untouched by Diagnostic-Related Group prospective payment reform in the Medicare system).

physical argument, and the quest for "correct" prices is often counterproductive. One reason why the Japanese government never again attempted a large-scale cost analysis after the one conducted in 1954 was because the variability across facilities and physicians was so great that averages had no meaning and, worse still, turned out not to settle anything. That is, the process did not contribute to reaching agreement on "fair" compensation for physicians and other health professionals. Quite the opposite – having all the detailed data actually led to more arguments. Subsequent revisions have been left largely to political negotiations, which promoted compromise on prices.

Finally, American experts often argue that across-the-board directives cannot work because they do not take into account the unique characteristics of each case. Big databases and detailed, professionally defined protocols are seen as necessary. However, Japan's rather ad hoc approach to directives and claims review, relying more on general professional judgments than scientific procedures, turns out to work fairly well – of course, a crucial point is that they are linked to the payment system. It is, after all, quite difficult to design an internally consistent and scientific review process when health care itself is so idiosyncratic and so much is left to the physician's discretion.

The more general problem in health care is that it is difficult to judge what is appropriate if expenditure limits are not clearly specified and the word "rationing" continues to be avoided. The Japanese approach is clearly primitive compared to the sophisticated techniques found in the better managed-care organizations of the United States, but it may be better. Rationing occurs, but it is not very prohibitive and indeed is not at all explicit in the complicated structure of the fee schedule. The claims review process based on the provider's past record is subjective, but remember that any consistent and rationally designed system could readily be gamed and so would soon become ineffective. And in terms of outcomes, being "pickled in medication and lab tests" in Japan might be better than being "pickled in surgery" in the United States. What is excessive or not can be judged only on a relative scale based on values and resource limits, not in absolute terms, and the Japanese approach is more realistic on that score.

As we have repeatedly observed, the Japanese health-care system was not rationally designed. Its characteristics evolved piecemeal over time in response to specific problems. The balance of political forces at each juncture has generally dictated incremental rather than radical change, and maintenance of the status quo has come to be a strategy in itself.

Nowhere is that point more evident than in the structure of the fee schedule, a relic of the era when ambulatory care by office-based physicians was still the norm. Continued domination by the JMA left hospital services, especially high-tech medicine and nursing, poorly reimbursed, with no provision for capital investment or administrative overhead. Similarly, the key role of local medical associations in the claims review process has discouraged providers from becoming aggressive revenue maximizers. Thus, it could be said that office-based physicians and the government have become de facto allies in maintaining the status quo by preventing the encroachment of hospitals and the expensive high-tech medicine that they promote.[40]

Obviously, the reliance on maintaining the status quo in Japan has come at a price. Besides the issue of quality (discussed in the next chapter), the major problem is rigidity. Incremental adjustments are fine if health-care needs remain essentially the same. Unfortunately, as has been described in Chapter 3, the relative importance of both long-term care and high-tech care have increased but have not easily been accommodated in the fee schedule. We suggest some alternative payment mechanisms in the final chapter. We retain our belief, however, that Japan's basic approach to the problems of modern health care is more realistic than American dreams of a ''rational'' and ''competitive'' system.

---

40 Interestingly, a similar alliance could have developed in the United States if President Truman had been successful in introducing national health insurance after World War II, when the majority of physicians were still general practitioners.

7

The Quality Problem

IS Japanese health care inexpensive because it is cheap? Are the savings primarily due to low quality?

The most basic measure of the quality of a national health-care system must be how well it keeps its people healthy. By that standard, Japan does at least as well as any other nation. As observed at the outset, in average life expectancy at birth or infant mortality rate, Japan is number one. Although the main reasons no doubt lie outside the formal health-care system, it is certainly difficult to claim that Japanese quality is inferior in this macro sense.

But the discussion cannot end here. We should also consider criteria that may not be quite so fundamental but yet are important in their own right. Will a patient with a given problem receive as accurate a diagnosis and as appropriate a treatment in Japan as in the United States? And will the patient feel satisfied with how he or she has been "treated" in a broader sense? On the latter point, it seems that Japanese are not very satisfied. According to an international public-opinion survey conducted by Louis Harris and Associates in 1990 (referred to in Chapter 2), Japan had the lowest overall satisfaction rating among six countries: Just 16 percent said that they were "very satisfied" with the quality compared to 55 percent in the United States and Canada.

Of course, since few of the respondents have any direct experience or knowledge of health care in other countries, these results cannot translate directly into comparative judgments about quality. Nor is it necessarily true that most Japanese are not satisfied. Given a simple choice between satisfied or not satisfied, only about one-quarter of Japanese say they are dissatisfied, and this proportion has been stable for about a decade.[1] On the other hand, Japanese (as well as foreigners visiting Japan) frequently point out one prob-

---

1 *"Kenkōzukui to Iryō" ni kansuru Chōsa Kekka Hōkokusho* (Tokyo: Kenporen, 1995).

lem area or another that they see as indicative of a generally low-quality system.

The common complaints about bad quality cited by both Japanese and foreigners provide a good starting point for our discussion. We examine each problem area to see how justified the complaints are, and then we ask the extent to which the problems are due to insufficient funding, to how the health-care system is organized, or to Japanese sociocultural factors. We also look briefly at attempts to correct the problem. Next, we look at the other side of the coin, a few areas where Japan arguably has better quality than the United States. Lastly, we take a brief look at an area where both Japan and the United States have done poorly: long-term care. We conclude with a few suggestions toward a new perspective for thinking about the quality issue, in both Japan and the United States.

FIVE PROBLEM AREAS

Five quality problems in the Japanese health-care system have frequently been pointed out:

- Long waiting time and short consultation time, as summed up by the catch-phrase "wait for three hours, be seen for three minutes."
- Lack of information and accountability by physicians and within the health-care system generally.
- Run-down and understaffed hospitals that may not provide an adequate level of services and comfort for the patient.
- Low quantity and quality of medical research, particularly basic research.
- Poor quality of professional judgment in diagnosis and treatment.

The last is an aspect not as often explicitly criticized as the other problems, but in our view, it is actually the most significant weak point in an evaluation of the overall quality of the Japanese health-care system.

Long Waiting Time, Short Consultation Time

Over the years, long waiting times have been identified by more Japanese than any other problem when they are asked about dissatisfaction with health

176

care.[2] Waits indeed can be long in Japan, and people usually expect a visit to a hospital to take an entire morning (the usual joke is that a patient has to be in good health to have the necessary stamina).

Several mitigating points are usually overlooked. First, long waits are usually limited to large hospitals. In physicians' offices and smaller hospitals, the waiting time is usually less than half an hour or about the same as in the United States with an appointment (where in fact the wait may be much longer without an appointment, in emergency rooms or walk-in clinics). Second, when Japanese complain about waiting, they usually include the time waiting for their bill and prescribed medications (see Chapter 3). In the United States, patients have to wait again in pharmacies and may have to spend considerable time filling in reimbursement forms (not to mention dealing with billing errors later). Third, patients are always seen on the same day, usually by the physician of their choice, unlike the waiting lists for an appointment that may stretch up to three months for a popular physician or hospital outpatient clinic in the United States.

The reason why waiting time is so long in Japanese large hospitals is deceptively simple. Since patients are free to choose the facility they want, presumably the one they see as having the best quality, those few hospitals are necessarily crowded. To avoid the nuisance of maintaining bookings long in advance and satisfy patients used to same-day treatment, most hospitals do not have regular appointment systems and so cannot limit the number of patients coming on a given day. An unavoidable consequence is that the consultation time is short. Time needs to be rationed as efficiently as possible if a physician is to see over eighty patients during a morning session (that could drag on until 2 P.M.). Outpatient departments resemble a factory assembly line in some hospitals – for example, with patients in stirrups lined up in partitioned rows as the gynecologist goes through the internal examinations. Other factors that encourage short consultations are the fee schedule, which pays little per visit but does not regulate their length or frequency, and a two-week limitation on the quantity of medication that can be prescribed and dispensed at one time for most drugs. Consultation times are therefore also short in physicians' offices and small hospitals where the number of patients is not excessive.

Note incidentally that the shortness of consultation time may be compensated to some extent by the greater frequency of visits. That is to say, if a

2   E.g., about half of those dissatisfied, according to the Harris poll noted earlier.

patient comes often, there is less need to undergo an extensive examination every time, and indeed the physician may be better able to observe changes in medical or even psychosocial conditions. That style of treatment might be advantageous for the growing number of elderly patients with chronic conditions.[3] Since the per capita number of outpatient visits to physicians and hospitals in Japan is more than twice that in the United States, the total time spent with a physician per year may not be as different in the two countries as it appears.

Several measures have been introduced to try to relieve congestion, but they all have run into contradictory objectives and thus have not been wholeheartedly carried through. The first is an attempt to limit the outpatients coming to large hospitals to only those who have been referred by office-based physicians. This policy has been effective in a few specialized hospitals such as the National Cancer Center, but it has not worked in many public hospitals because of the popular view that every citizen has a right to unrestricted access, especially to a hospital owned by the local government.

The second tentative step is rationing by price: If the difference in out-of-pocket cost between physicians' offices and large hospitals were large enough, then more patients would select the former. A surcharge was therefore introduced for the initial consultation to patients who come to university hospitals without a referral. However, because it was argued that the surcharge should not be too much of a burden for those with low income, the fee was set at only about $8, which largely defeated its purpose.[4] The third effort is to allow longer prescriptions for certain chronic illnesses such as epilepsy. However, the prevailing view that too much medicine is being handed out discourages a large-scale move in this direction.[5]

Since these measures have been largely unsuccessful, it has been left to the patient to decide whether to get quick service by going to a physician's office, or to wait much longer to go to a large hospital with perceived higher quality. The trouble is that more and more patients are choosing the latter. Since effective rationing by a pricing mechanism is ruled out for egalitarian

---

3 Ruth Campbell, "The Three-Minute Cure: Doctors and Elderly Patients in Japan," in *Containing*, pp. 226–233.

4 This surcharge was extended to all hospitals with 200 beds or more from 1996 on. Note that another contradiction is with the policy objective noted in Chapter 6 to discourage hospitals from focusing on ambulatory care (e.g., by *lowering* their fees for repeat visits).

5 The Harris poll mentioned previously has 19 percent of those dissatisfied mentioning over-medication. The previous chapter takes up this problem.

reasons, the only alternative would appear to be to strengthen the referral system between physicians' offices and the large hospitals. That would further resemble the systems found in Europe, which as noted in Chapter 3 is the direction in which Japan appears to be heading.

In any event, this particular problem area appears to be somewhat overblown in the public mind. It is interesting that waits to get admitted for inpatient care have not become a major social issue, despite the fact that they have potentially graver consequences (all ambulatory patients are at least seen, albeit briefly, on the same day). The reason is probably that only the most prestigious hospitals have appreciable waiting lists, and even there, patients who are unable or unwilling to wait are usually referred to an affiliated hospital without causing too much ill feeling. In any case, neither type of waiting is really the product of underspending and would not be corrected by increasing resources.

Lack of Information and Accountability

Many complaints have to do with physicians not providing enough information, not listening to patients, and generally taking an attitude seen at best as paternalistic and at worst as arrogant. In some respects, these attitudes and a general disregard for responsibility can be seen not only at the level of the individual provider, but throughout the health-care system.

In a recent national survey, 42 percent of those expressing dissatisfaction with medical care mentioned lack of information from providers, the second most popular complaint. In particular, patients complain about drugs dispensed without any explanation of intended effects, let alone side-effects (a book that gives information about many drugs by their identifying lot numbers actually became a best-seller). Also, patients are usually not allowed to look at their own medical records unless a court order is secured. In general, patients are rarely brought into the medical decision-making process. Although the term "informed consent" has become familiar to many Japanese through the mass media, it remains an uncommon practice in everyday clinical settings.[6] Considerable attention both in Japan and

6 The term *infōmudo konsento* was mentioned 194 times in Japan's three largest newspapers in 1994, up from just 10 in 1989. It is usually translated as *setsumei to dōi*, or "explanation and consent," and in general the practice in Japan does not include alternative treatments and risks versus benefits. See Robert B. LeFlar, "Informed Consent and Patients' Rights in

abroad has focused on the still widespread practice of not telling patients that they have cancer.[7]

At the policy level, resentment and mistrust of physicians has crystallized in attitudes about heart transplants, stemming from public criticism following the first and only such operation in 1968. Questions were raised about the brain death of the donor and even whether the recipient had any real need of the transplant. Although criminal proceedings were dropped due to lack of evidence, the surgeon in charge never responded to demands for more information or admitted any wrongdoing. This case has come to symbolize Japanese doubts about the integrity of physicians in general – many profess to believe that physicians would prematurely declare donors as brain dead and that families would be intensely pressured to donate organs. One result has been that no heart transplants (and relatively few transplants of other organs) are carried out in Japan. Another is an impasse over a legal definition of death.[8]

A classic case of lack of accountability is lax supervision and inspection of hospitals. Regulations about staffing ratios and so forth are not very demanding in Japan, but even those regulations are often not enforced very stringently. In a 1997 scandal that drew criticism from the Governor of Osaka Prefecture, it was revealed that a group of three hospitals had listed fictitious doctors and nurses on its employment rolls for several years. The deception was possible because hospital inspections were announced a week or two in advance, rather than coming by surprise, so the hospitals had time to prepare. Complaints about substandard care from a citizens' activist group went long ignored, perhaps because the chairman of the group's board was friendly with MHW officials and he had invited a good many local and national notables to be advisors to the hospital group – apparently even well-known physicians had allowed their names to be used with no attention to hospital practices.[9]

High-level cronyism was also a major factor in the HIV-contaminated blood-products scandal that occurred in 1983, although full details were revealed and the issue of compensation resolved only in 1996, in a blaze of

Japan," *Houston Law Review* 33:1 (1996), pp. 1–113, which is an excellent review of these problems from a legal viewpoint

7 Ibid.
8 Eric A. Feldman, "Over My Dead Body: The Enigma and Economics of Death in Japan," in *Containing*, pp. 234–247. Note that a bill allowing "brain death" (albeit with qualifications) and perhaps paving the way for more transplants was passed by the Diet in 1997.
9 *Asahi Shinbun*, May 23, 1997.

publicity and criticism. Hemophilia patients in Japan were dependent on imported blood coagulants, a product handled by a small number of domestic and foreign pharmaceutical houses. Well after the time that it had become widely known in the West that HIV-infected blood was coming from commercial donors in dangerous amounts, the Ministry of Health and Welfare rejected advice to accept foreign test data or speed testing of treatment methods in Japan. Even after mandating that blood be heated to destroy the HIV organism, the Ministry somehow allowed one company to continue selling off its own supply, resulting in the infection of many additional patients. Even the usually rather cynical Japanese were shocked by this disregard of professional accountability in favor of protecting cozy relationships at the highest levels.

The various criticisms about lack of accountability and information brought a variety of responses from physicians and the government. They observe that excessive numbers of patients necessitate short consultation times that allow little time for giving much explanation, and that it is not possible to keep records in good order because they do not have the support of medical record librarians and so cannot dictate their notes.[10] They also claim that there is still no consensus about disclosing the diagnosis of cancer, and indeed that the contents of prescriptions cannot be explained because there is always a possibility that they may include anti-cancer drugs. This point has some merit: The ambivalent attitude toward being told a grave prognosis, which many Japanese still harbor, is at least one valid reason why it is difficult to disclose accurate information.[11]

Several reasons can be postulated why a general lack of information and lack of empathy from physicians should have become a major problem in Japan. The first is the shortage of physicians and hospitals – not an absolute

---

10 Record keeping is indeed very poor. Indeed, many hospitals destroy their records after the legal minimum of five years – a serious problem in the tainted-blood debacle, because these hospitals were unable to determine who had actually received the untreated blood coagulants and were thus at risk for HIV infection. The profession of medical-record librarian is still not established in Japan, and less than one-sixth of hospitals have a full-time staff member working in this field.

11 E.g., in a recent survey, 64 percent of Japanese said that if they had cancer, then they would like to be told so, but at the same time, 58 percent said that they would not disclose the diagnosis to their immediate families. *Yomiuri Shinbun*, Oct. 28, 1994. Since physicians usually consult with the family first before telling the patient, it is not clear what action the physician should take. One view is that it is better to leave the decision about whether to tell or not up to the family rather than to the physician.

shortage for the last decade or so, but a relative shortage of large hospitals with perceived high quality. There is no pressure for physicians to become more attentive in such hospitals, especially as most of them are in the public sector.

A second reason is the legal system. Along with other types of tort litigation, medical malpractice suits are still rare in Japan; only about 440 new cases were brought to court in 1993.[12] Consequently, there is less pressure for physicians to practice informed consent and to worry about accountability. However, this difference between the United States and Japan may be somewhat overblown. Although the number of formally contested suits in Japan may be low, those that do occur have considerable sentinel effect, and a growing number of cases are settled before coming to court.

A third reason is culture. It would be surprising if something so human as the doctor–patient relationship would not reflect broader cultural patterns. For example, Japanese as individuals tend to be reluctant to give out much information to outsiders. Effective communication in Japan requires a long-term relationship established through frequent contacts, and then it does not require too many words because both parties know each other well. Relationships tend to be social rather than formal and contracted. Moreover, individual responsibility for particular actions tends to be diffused.[13]

This cultural pattern has had a particularly pernicious effect in health care. That is, an intimate social relationship might be possible with office-based physicians living in the same community with their patients, but it is much less likely in a hospital setting where a physician may see a given patient only once or twice. Thus, with the increasing importance of hospital care, there is more need of a formal contractual relationship between the two parties. This disjuncture has also occurred in the United States, but the problem is much worse in Japan simply because such formal contractual relationships are generally seen as unnatural.

All three of these factors are structural and difficult to improve. Investing more resources is not likely to lead directly to better quality, except perhaps in improving the state of medical records. However, what is at stake is not so much the administrative problem of keeping well-organized records as the

12 Ibid.
13 Lack of responsibility has been attributed to the lack of clear sense of cause and effect in Japanese thinking: See, e.g., Harumi Befu, *Japan: An Anthropological Introduction* (San Francisco: Chandler, 1971), pp. 95–119.

whole attitude toward professional accountability, which is further examined in the last problem area.

Run-down and Understaffed Hospitals

Japanese hospitals are quite poor in physical and human resources compared to American hospitals. Apart from the crowding in the outpatient department mentioned earlier, the average amount of total floor space per bed is well under one-third the amount in the United States (35 compared with 126 square meters). Some of this difference should be discounted because so many Japanese hospitals have functions similar to U.S. nursing homes.[14] Still, less than 10 percent of hospital rooms are private or semi-private in Japan, while the vast majority are such in the United States. Investment in general hospitals, as calculated by tangible fixed assets per bed, is also just under half that of the United States (when converted by the PPP rate).[15] There is a similar big difference in human resources. Even at best, Japanese university hospitals are at about a third of the U.S.'s average staff level: Total staff per patient is 1.85 compared with 5.54 for the United States (for licensed nurses, 0.67 versus 1.58).[16]

These differences are still greater when we look only at private-sector hospitals in Japan, because they do not get government subsidies. Both floor space and tangible fixed assets per bed are half that of the public sector, and the staffing level is 20 percent less. Of course, the higher standards in the public sector contribute to their attractiveness to patients, exacerbating the two problems just described.

However, it should be pointed out that no matter how run-down Japanese hospitals may look, their level has improved considerably in the last thirty years, and the common image of reliance on families for care is much less applicable today. All hospitals now satisfy the basic sanitary and fire-hazard requirements. Also, although private-duty nurse's aides (*tsukisoi*) are still

---

14 Note also the general scarcity and high price of land in Japan. However, in housing the difference is only between 83 and 135 square meters per inhabitant in Japan and in the United States.

15 Figures for 1989, using ¥199 = $1. Kōichi Kawabuchi, "Comparison of Capital Costs in Health Care Between Japan and the United States," in *Containing*, pp. 73–79.

16 MHW, Iryō Shisetsu Chōsa, 1992. The figures for the United States are for the nonfederal community hospitals that constitute over 90 percent of total acute-care beds. If compared to U.S. university hospitals, the differences would be about fivefold (see Chapter 3).

used for heavy-care patients, the cost has mostly been covered by health insurance and the government is currently phasing out *tsukisoi* by paying more to hospitals so that more regularly employed aides can be hired. Today, the main area where the family is likely to shoulder a greater burden than Americans in most hospitals is laundry, still regarded as a personal responsibility. In particular, meals have improved, as a target of the government's efforts to improve quality, and now are mostly served at normal meal times (formerly, evening meals were often served at 4:30 to save on labor costs).

Moreover, lower staffing levels in Japan must be considered in relation to intensity of care. Even in university hospitals, the average length of stay is nearly a month. This means that nurses care for less sick patients on average; because the intensity of hospital activities is much lower, there is less need of staff.[17] It is not clear whether short stays are more efficient or not, because an increase in throughput may be offset by an increase in labor and other costs. Nor is it certain that a short stay is always beneficial for the patient. We also note that in the United States the staffing level more than tripled from 0.96 in 1960 to 3.35 in 1990, an increase not completely explained by expansions in ambulatory care or drops in average length of stay in that period (only from 21.6 to 12.4 days for all hospitals).[18]

Further improvements in Japanese hospitals would require investing substantially more resources. Unlike some of the other problem areas, more spending would definitely improve quality, especially in the private sector. We ask, however, how much *should* hospital quality be improved? Standards are much higher in the United States because charges are much higher (bed and board rates in U.S. hospitals are about five times Japanese rates, PPP). Recall that in health-care costs and standards, it is the United States that is the deviant while Europe and Japan cluster around the norm. Private rooms are quite unusual in Europe, too (indeed, Japanese public hospitals are probably at about European standards).[19]

In Japan, hospitals are not terrific, but they are plentiful, inexpensive, and

17 The staffing level per bed improved from 0.54 in 1960 to 0.79 in 1985. The average length of stay increased from 28 days to 39 days during this period, but that is a function of the increase in long-term care in hospitals.
18 OECD 1993 data; see Naoki Ikegami and Yoshinori Hiroi, "Factors in Health Care Spending: An Eight-Nation Comparison," in *Containing*, pp. 33–44.
19 Interestingly, there is not much demand for private or semi-private rooms in Japanese hospitals even though the extra charges are modest – for that reason, their proportion has not increased in the last decade.

egalitarian. The clear contrast is with the United States, where quality was given priority over access. At the end of World War II, instead of making universal coverage a national goal, public money was devoted to improving hospitals through the Hill-Burton Act. Subsequently, cost-based reimbursement under Medicare and other insurance plans, which prevailed until the mid-1980s, assured the hospitals of a return on their capital investment. Investment was high because hospitals had to meet the demands of high-status physicians and to attract those patients who could afford to pay the full charge. In other words, U.S. hospitals were geared to the upper segment of the market, while Japanese hospitals have neither been faced with these competitive pressures nor given the funds to pursue such goals.

This discussion has mostly concentrated on the patient-comfort side of hospital services. If we look at physical facilities for the actual provision of medical care, it becomes much harder to argue that standards are appreciably lower in Japan. For high-tech diagnostic equipment, the per capita number of CAT scans and MRIs in Japan is the highest in the world.[20] Intensive Care Units, surgical theaters, and other facilities directly related to medical treatments are substantially fewer in number than in the United States because the demand is so much less, but the quantity seems to be comparable to the other OECD nations, and the quality is about as good as anywhere. After all, the available medical statistics do not reveal particular quality problems in Japanese hospitals.[21]

Mediocre Medical Research

Despite the fact that the university clinical departments focus more on research than clinical practice, their efforts are not reflected in the number of publications in high-quality academic journals. This tendency is not limited to research in the medical field: Citation rates for Japanese papers are roughly half that of the United States in basic science. Using a more familiar index, the number of Nobel prizes won by Japanese in science is five, with only one in the biomedical science field.

20 As noted in Chapter 6, Japanese machines tend to be less expensive because of the fee schedule, but the difference in patient outcomes due to slightly less clear pictures, for example, is negligible.
21 In particular, there is no evidence that the incidence of iatrogenic diseases is high in Japan, with the exception of MRSA infections (due to overuse of antibiotics).

The obvious reason for this poor record is the lack of research funds.[22] Neither the Education nor the Health and Welfare Ministry has been generous in funding research. Furthermore, the Education Ministry tends to distribute small amounts to well-established figures in each discipline without much regard to quality. The MHW is somewhat more flexible, but its total grants amount to less than one-tenth of the National Institute of Health research budget in the United States. Moreover, there are not many research grants from the private sector in Japan partly because tax deductions are minimal.

Setting money aside, the hierarchical structure of university departments in medicine as elsewhere is hardly a nurturing environment for creative ideas. The traditional method of intimate apprenticeship described earlier emphasizes continuity with the past. Very often, a retiring professor would personally select the most promising (if not the most ingratiating) of his disciples as his successor. In prestigious universities, over 90 percent of the faculty are alumni, and in many other universities, most faculty graduated from a single prestigious university. Such a system makes it difficult to conduct rigorous internal or external evaluations. One factor here is that Japanese universities were originally established less for conducting original research than for efficiently disseminating the science that had been developed in the West.

But, again, we must ask what is the cost to the quality of medical care? Granted that the search for new frontiers carries an intrinsic value, the assumption that in all cases it does actually lead to practical societal benefits should not be accepted without skepticism. Whether the massive American investment in cancer research has paid off or not is controversial: The death rate from cancer did not change from 1950 to 1990.[23] Recent developments in genetic engineering may lead to an ultimate cure for some diseases, but

---

22   For publications, see Alun Anderson, "Japanese Academics Bemoan the Cost of Years of Neglect," *Science* 258 (1992), 564–569. According to the National Science Board, total nondefense R & D spending in Japan was half that of the United States, and the government R & D support for health constitutes a much smaller ratio: 4.8 percent in Japan compared with 12.9 percent in the United States in 1989 (the denominator includes defense, which amounted to 9.0 percent and 65.5 percent of the total, respectively). However, note that Japanese public spending for health-care research was higher than in France and only slightly lower than in Germany and the United Kingdom – in this as so many other areas, it is the United States that is the outlier. See U.S. National Science Board, *Social and Engineering Indicators*, 1993 edition.

23   Tim Beardsley, "A War Not Won: Trends in Cancer Epidemiology," *Science* 270 (1994), pp. 120–26.

most are likely to remain as intractable as ever. We certainly do not condone the Japanese government's reluctance to support basic research in health care, but we suggest that Americans might think about the opportunity costs of its current massive investment and whether it is more likely to increase or decrease the total cost of health care in the future.

Weak Professional Standards

The foregoing criticisms are the main ones usually brought up in discussions of the quality of the Japanese health-care system. Less often directly addressed, but actually the most important problem area, is "quality" in the sense of technical proficiency in the actual process of care delivery, as defined by professional standards.

One reason that this problem draws less attention is that it is difficult to analyze. In particular, intense efforts in the United States so far have fallen well short of developing a systematic and reliable method for measuring the quality of performance in terms of patient outcomes. Our criteria must therefore be based on inputs, or what is often called "structure and process": whether services are delivered by those with appropriate training, whether clinical "best practice" is effectively pursued and disseminated, and whether adequate safeguards are built into the process of providing care. We find that Japan falls somewhat short on all three counts.

First, we must look at training: The Japanese pattern of medical education – six undergraduate years plus two recommended years of residency – is somewhat shorter and less thorough than the pattern in the United States. More importantly, it tends to be quite idiosyncratic from one medical school (or even department) to another, and advanced instruction owes more to the apprenticeship or even disciple model than to science. The fact that the large number of doctors who go on to the Doctor of Medical Science degree do so within the same department, and then will probably go on to practice within a network of affiliated hospitals, intensifies the fragmented, inward-looking character of the Japanese medical world and inhibits top-quality training.

Still, we would assess the average level of skill and knowledge achieved by Japanese physicians as reasonably good by world standards. The gap with other advanced nations is probably greater in the areas of standardization and diffusion of "best practice." Fragmentation has hindered the development of

187

specialty boards.[24] The Japan Medical Association has successfully maintained the principles that physicians are free to proclaim any specialty they wish, and that accreditation will not lead to any differences in reimbursement by the point-fee system (as is common in Europe).

Finally, with regard to safeguards, we observe that few hospitals have quality assurance programs and that there are no mandatory reviews of process. The only formal reviews are by the government on whether the hospital meets established structural standards such as minimum floor space per bed and physician- and nurse-to-patient staffing ratios. Conducting peer reviews is usually technically not possible because the state of medical records is so poor that they may be incomprehensible even to the writer. In reality, quality control usually does not go beyond supervision of younger physicians by older ones in university and other large hospitals. A new quasi-public foundation for evaluating the quality of care is scheduled to begin operation in 1997, but the training of surveyors has just begun, and it remains to be seen what impact this new institution will have on quality.

The problems of professional standards that we observe in Japan are partly due to resource constraints – as noted previously, more money could bring better record keeping – but often seem to be part and parcel of fundamental attributes of Japanese social organization. Some indeed are the same attributes that are often touted as key strengths of Japanese-style management: For example, the pattern of physicians working within a closed network of affiliated hospitals for their entire professional lives is similar to "lifetime employment" in the corporate world, and each university clinical department develops its intensive competitive spirit by concentrating on "market share" in terms of supplying doctors to posts in prestigious hospitals.

Why should a system that works to produce high-quality products in the corporate world lead to bad results in health care? One reason is that physicians identify with the department where they did their graduate work rather than with either the hospital where they are employed or their specialized colleagues throughout Japan. One could argue that either a "corporate" or a professional orientation would be more positive for quality than this "ver-

24 Formal certification as a specialist was initiated only in 1963 (by anesthesiologists); twenty-two professional societies had been organized by 1980, when they got together to establish a Council on Certification. However, only 10 percent of these specialists have been certified through a formal examination process (the rest were grandfathered in); moreover, nurses and other health professionals have far less recognition of specialized qualifications than in the United States.

tical clique'' attachment. Another reason is that university clinical departments compete for posts and research funds but not for customers, because prestigious hospitals are always overflowing with patients. In that sense, they lack work accountability. Finally, rather than the intensive efforts at training and diffusing ''best practice'' found in leading manufacturing companies in Japan, health care is characterized by personal, master–disciple training based on inductive apprenticeship, or internalizing the method used by the master.[25]

Having said all that, we should also look at the other side of the coin. Our definition of quality here has been the professional's normative definition of good clinical practice. However, three additional issues can be raised. First, with respect to a given medical intervention, should it have been made at all? For example, a surgical operation may have been expertly performed in an ideal environment, but was it really needed? The possible harm coming from the fact that the per capita number of surgical operations is three times greater in the United States compared with Japan needs to be taken into account.

Second, professionals rarely address the cost issue, nor the related question of the optimal degree of specialization. In the United States, there has been a strong internal pressure for physicians – and then allied health personnel as well – to specialize and to establish organizations based on common professional skills. The result is a proliferation of accredited qualifications, all claiming an indispensable role in the delivery of health care. Such specialization no doubt improves quality to some degree, but perhaps not to the extent needed to justify such higher costs.[26]

The third issue often ignored in discussions of professional quality is the impact of the vested interests of professional organizations even beyond those of physicians themselves. Like craft unions, such associations are primarily concerned with improving the status, earnings, and working conditions of their members. Because prestige and income tend to be correlated with the length of the training period, there has been a constant push for more training

25 That is, as in traditional ''schools'' of flower arrangement (*kadō*) and tea ceremony (*chadō*), there is a clear rank order from the head of the school (*iemoto*) down to the most recently enrolled student.
26 Professional specialization is not always positive even for quality – e.g., phlebotomists may be skilled in drawing blood, but the fact that they are not allowed to do any other tasks can be a critical limitation in an emergency, and also sap their morale. Note also that although phlebotomists' hourly wages may be lower than those of nurses, total labor costs may be higher – it is hard to make full use of their work hours due to the limitations of the license and the need to employ enough to cover peak hours.

to bring standards closer to those of physicians. The implications for costs are obvious, but beyond that, such competitive professionalization can actually have a negative impact on quality. Because even the United States cannot afford to have all its health services delivered by such high-level professionals, actual hands-on care may be delivered by an unskilled and underpaid aide – an especially serious problem in long-term care but becoming common more generally as managed-care intensifies pressures on costs.

It is clear, in short, that the professional level of quality is lower in Japan. However, that does not necessarily mean that American practices are ideal and should be adopted as the goal for Japan. It might be more productive to strive for a higher degree of professionalism by setting organizational goals for quality within each hospital, and to evaluate performance closely.

AREAS WHERE JAPAN MAY HAVE BETTER QUALITY

In truth, any definition of quality should include access, because a health-care system must always address the issue of social justice. The Japanese system is clearly superior to the American system in that regard. Indeed, expanding access was the number-one priority in Japanese health policy, until that objective had been substantially achieved and the cost-containment goal came to the fore in the 1980s. And even beyond better access, in a few areas Japan may have better quality in classic terms than the United States. An excellent example is renal dialysis, where, as noted in Chapter 6, Japanese outcomes are better. Several other such areas can be described briefly.

Prenatal and Child Care

Outcome measures for infant mortality and children's health are impressive in Japan. Infant mortality at 4.2 per one thousand live births (1994) is the lowest in the world, much better than the United States' 8.4 (1993).[27] Clearly, much of this difference is due to reasons outside of the health-care system: For example, only 1.5 percent of live births are by teen-age mothers in Japan compared with 12.8 percent in the United States (and note the absolute number of live births by mothers under fifteen – 22 in Japan, 11,486 in the United

---

27 Data from *Kokumin Eisei no Dōkō*, 1996, p. 443, and *Health United States*, 1995, p. 102.

States.)[28] But such social differences cannot explain the sharp *decline* in the infant mortality rate in Japan: It had been extremely high in 1950 (60.1 per thousand).

The cause, clearly, was public policy: an intense campaign to improve maternal and infant health in the early 1950s. The public-health measures that are still applied today include a "mother and infant handbook" (*boshi techō*) issued to each expectant mother that records all the important health data in pregnancy, and then up to the child's sixth birthday (an extensive screening program in the school health system takes over at that point). Home visits are made by a public-health nurse before and after birth, and regular health check-ups are provided either in public-health centers or by a family doctor (paid directly by the local government, not via health insurance). These programs are almost universally utilized.

Screening

Japan seems to have the most elaborate health screening program in the world. Hisamichi has calculated that on average everyone gets one screening per year, mostly done en masse rather than individually in a clinician's office.[29] Screening is popular for several reasons. First, the successful eradication of tuberculosis after World War II engendered an optimistic view of the effectiveness of screening, among both the general public and professionals. Second, once a national network of public-health centers (*hokenjo*) had been established for this purpose, new missions had to be found once tuberculosis ceased to be a major hazard. Third, preventive care is one of the few services where payers are given a free hand in Japan. Those with ample funds, such as SMHI societies in young and rapidly growing companies, offered elaborate screening programs that then had a demonstration or leveling-up effect on other payers.

Considerable doubt can be raised about this indiscriminate screening. It developed from the notion that "the more screening, the better," with little in the way of cost-effectiveness analysis. Research in the United States implies that most screening is not worth its cost, and there is no reason to expect

28 All Japanese data are 1992; U.S.A., 1989. *Jinkō no Dōkō: Nihon to Sekai*, 1996, p. 56. More poverty, AIDS, drug addiction, and so on, in the United States should also be taken into account.
29 Hisamichi Shigeru, "Tenki ni tatsu Gan Taisaku," Chairman's address to the *Dai 27kai Nihon Hōkaki Shūdankenshū Gakkai Sōkai* in 1988.

markedly different results in Japan.[30] However, we suggest that screening may have an indirect benefit in making people more aware of their health, and the direct costs are not very high. Here, too, there may be a middle ground between the alternatives of too much screening in Japan and too little in the United States.

Organizational Identity

It was argued previously that professional quality standards were impaired in Japan by overidentification with the "vertical cliques" based on medical-school departments, to the detriment of attachments either to specialized organizations or to the hospitals where the physician works. Nonetheless, compared with the United States, Japanese hospitals do have some of the positive aspects of Japanese corporate organization, and these can contribute to good performance. Japanese hospitals have higher retention rates, wider job spans, and organization-based labor unions. First, the turnover rate for nurses is generally less than 10 percent a year.[31] Second, physicians and other professionals readily work outside of their specialized areas, especially in smaller private hospitals, because of the limited availability of other staff. Also, licenses for allied health personnel are broadly defined. For example, the "clinical test technician" (*rinshō kensa gishi*) license allows both laboratory and physiological testing. Lastly, where there are unions, they are always single-hospital based with all workers (sometimes even including physicians) as members.

Beyond these structural aspects, many hospitals have adopted practices similar to those that have succeeded in building employee loyalty and commitment in Japanese corporations. These include orientation seminars to introduce new employees to the hospital's mission, morning briefings (*chōrei*) with the entire staff attending, overnight visits to hot-spring resorts to encourage informal bonding among the staff (physicians do participate), and subsidies for sports and other recreation. Such practices bring higher staff morale and better communication, ultimately resulting in better patient care.

Such organizational factors have generally been neglected in American

---

30 For such American research, see Louise Russell, *Is Prevention Better than Cure?* (Washington, DC: Brookings, 1986).

31 That rate is about the same as for female workers in general: Ikegami Naoki, "Naasu no Teichakuritsu," *Byōin* 47 (1988), pp. 427–430.

hospitals, which tend to focus more on the expertise of each individual. Probably there is a trade-off between the quality that can be achieved by each person concentrating on a narrowly defined specialty, and the quality that can be achieved through better group cohesion. Perhaps the former is more important in acute-care settings and the latter in long-term-care settings. Both deserve attention, though we must also guard against the danger of pursuing either goal more for the benefit of hospital staff than of patients.

LONG-TERM CARE: EVERYBODY'S PROBLEM

We noted in Chapter 4 that population aging, particularly for the old-old, is very rapid in Japan. However, worries about how to provide adequate long-term care are hardly unique, and the dilemma has certainly not been "solved" by the United States or any other country. One key barrier is simply resources: Even countries that have done a decent job in providing adequate pensions and acute medical care for their growing numbers of older people have not really faced up to the vast human and financial resources needed to look after the sizable minority of the aged who cannot care for themselves. The issue of public versus private responsibility is also quite perplexing.

A further difficulty is that the needs of the frail, disabled, or chronically ill elderly do not sort themselves out easily into the conventional discrete categories of social policy: income maintenance, medical treatment, personal care, social support, and the intangibles expressed by the Japanese term *ikigai*, or a sense of "life worth." All these needs are often mixed and interact. As a matter of public policy and administration, long-term care often falls awkwardly between bureaucratic responsibilities for medical care on the one hand and social welfare on the other, or at a more detailed level among such policy areas as public health, health insurance, medical service delivery, institutional care, community services, housing, and encouragement of family and volunteer assistance.

This aspect of the long-term-care problem is particularly troublesome in Japan because it is unusually prone to the affliction of "vertical administration" (*tatewari gyōsei*), or fragmentation of governmental structures and processes.[32] Despite many calls for a more rational and comprehensive long-term-care policy, reform efforts have gotten bogged down in battles

---

32 See Chapter 2, and for many examples from the development of postwar policies for the elderly, see Campbell, *How Policies Change.*

between ministries, between bureaus with different jurisdictions within the Ministry of Health and Welfare, between "generalist" and "expert" (physician) officials, and of course between organized constituency groups.

To look first at institutional long-term care, it is easy to see over-medicalization in the straightforward sense that most of the institutionalized elderly are in hospitals. This unusual situation is a product of the initiation of "free medical care" for the elderly in 1973, which brought a surge of long-term admissions of elderly people with or without severe medical problems. The number of elderly hospital inpatients grew from 157,000 in 1970 to 402,000 in 1980 and up to 688,000 in 1993 – nearly half of everyone in hospitals at any one time.[33] The great majority of these patients are in private-sector hospitals, many of which in effect became nursing homes without the name. True nursing homes, called "Special Homes for the Aged" (*tokubetsu yōgo rōjin homu*) and included within social-welfare administration with no connection to medical care, grew incrementally through this period to some 224,000 beds (nearly all full) in 1995. Incidentally, the proportion of those 65 and over that is institutionalized is 5.7 percent (of which 4.4 percent are in hospitals, 1.0 percent in nursing homes, and 0.2 percent in other institutions), a figure very close to that of the United States despite the conventional wisdom of family care being so important in Japan.[34]

Although hard data are difficult to find, it appears that the quality of nursing-home care in Japan is on average somewhat better than in the United States in that the staff is better trained, better paid, and stays on the job much longer. However, there is a severe shortage of nursing homes in urban areas, with waiting times in Tokyo of two or three years unless the older person is willing to be moved far from home. Long-term care in hospitals is more available (if sometimes at a price), but the quality is often poor – very little space, few opportunities for recreation or "human" services, too many drugs and tests. Conditions in the worst of them have often been sensationalized in the press.

The other point worth mentioning is that Japan is very short of public or private facilities to provide care at a level of intensity below that of a nursing

33   48.2 percent; see the MHW's *Kanja Chōsa*, 1993.
34   The American figures are for 1985 and include 4.6 percent in nursing homes, 0.7 percent in regular hospitals, and 0.4 percent in psychiatric hospitals. *Health United States*, 1991, Tables 81 and 93, and Esther Hing, "Use of Nursing Homes by the Elderly: Preliminary Data from the 1985 National Nursing Home Survey," NCHS Advance Data 135, Table 1 (May 14, 1987). Japanese data from *Kanja Chōsa*, 1992.

home or hospital, such as boarding care and especially various types of congregate housing, where so many somewhat frail American older people live.

The government has been trying to fix the institutional-care problem for twenty years, mainly to control costs but also to improve quality standards. One effort has been to institutionalize the conversion of many hospitals into de facto nursing homes by moving from fee-for-service to capitated payments and altering staffing requirements. Another effort was the creation of a new type of institution called Health Facilities for the Elderly (*rōjin hoken shisetsu*), which were supposed to fill a niche halfway between a hospital and nursing home and to focus on relatively short-term rehabilitation. In practice, although their 100,000 new beds have somewhat alleviated the chronic shortage of long-term care, these facilities have not been operated too differently from other institutions – in particular, they have found it difficult to return patients to their families, so average length of stay has been longer than planned, and many of those discharged go to hospitals or nursing homes.

The government's long-run plan is to unite the administration of all three types of long-term-care institutions into a common framework, through the proposed new public Long-Term-Care Insurance (LTCI) system described in Chapter 4. That is supposed to lead to a more rational allocation of patients, so that those needing heavier care will be in hospitals and so forth – today, many hospital patients are not particularly frail. For many years, government plans have also called for more congregate housing (often called "care housing" in Japan), which presumably could also be paid for in part by LTCI. However, the bureaucratic obstacles to these plans are formidable, and although it is clear that the amount of resources devoted to institutional long-term care will continue to expand, no doubt at an accelerated rate if LTCI is passed, it is doubtful that the system itself will be transformed any time soon.

Actually, the LTCI proposal is aimed more at improving community or in-home long-term-care services rather than institutions, and indeed it is this sector that has already been expanding at a very rapid pace (albeit from a small base). A major step forward was the 1989 Gold Plan, or "Ten-Year Strategy on Health and Welfare for the Aged," an election campaign promise by the majority Liberal Democratic Party that called for a doubling or tripling of various home-care services – home helpers, day-care, respite care, and so on – as well as institutional beds. The 1989 Gold Plan was generously supported even through a period of austerity budgets, and in 1994 most of its goals were revised upward (the New Gold Plan). These services generally fall within the field of social welfare and are delivered by local governments (directly or on a contract basis), with a bias toward lower-income people. LTCI would cover everyone and provide much greater financing, no doubt increasing demand enormously.

As with institutions, the expansion of community-based long-term care is being hampered by problems of fragmented jurisdiction and conflicts between, in particular, social-welfare, public-health, and private medical-practitioner interests. One current focal point is how eligibility or the content of care plans will be decided under LTCI, but struggles have been going on for years in many other areas as well. The chief contenders are office-based physicians, public-health centers (*hokenjo*) and the public-health nurses who dominate their staff, and local-government officials working at the welfare office (*fukushi jimusho*). The latter two groups are backed up at the national level by, respectively, the physician "experts" (*gikan*) and the generalist (*jimukan*) officials in the Ministry of Health and Welfare. The government has recently been attempting to amalgamate management of health and welfare services at the municipal level, but this administrative reform by itself is unlikely to end the bickering.[35]

Financing and bureaucratic fragmentation aside, the big problem for community services (and institutional care as well) is manpower, or more realistically womanpower. The combination of growing numbers of frail elderly and greatly expanded services will require more and more labor, no doubt more than will be made available by freeing up housewives from some responsibility of caring for their own elderly relatives, or for that matter by further relaxation of restrictions on foreign workers. The solution to this labor shortage may lie more in such macro trends as improved productivity in Japan's bloated retail and wholesale sales sector or long-term stagnation in economic growth than in any specific measures. In any case, the high-profile commitment to long-term care for the elderly, which so far has been shared by the government, the media, and the general public (and for that matter by all political parties and interest groups), indicates that the quantity and to a lesser extent the quality of care will continue to expand rapidly in Japan.

We do think that two additional fundamental problems will prove hard to manage. One is the threat to the egalitarian basis of Japanese health care presented by LTCI, where in both institutional and community settings, better-off recipients will be able to supplement their insurance benefits out-of-

35 Called for by the Regional Health Act (Chiiki Hoken Hō) of 1994. Early experiments in combining municipal health centers with welfare offices have had mixed success.

pocket to obtain higher-quality care. Both practical and political problems can be anticipated. The other is the lack of anything like professional social work in planning and managing long-term care at both the macro and micro levels. Among the three contenders for authority noted previously, social welfare is represented by government officials who have no professional training and no institutionalized regard for the interests of individual clients.[36] We may well doubt whether nonmedical needs will be adequately considered.

CONCLUSION

To what extent are the quality problems in Japanese health care attributable simply to not spending enough money? Of the five problem areas we identified, the first – long waits and short consultations – would not be resolved with more funds because the fault lies in unrestricted access. Patients gravitate to large hospitals with the best perceived quality. The second problem, lack of information provided by physicians, is also not much related to money. It stems from ambivalent attitudes toward hearing a bad prognosis on the part of patients, and a general unwillingness to share information or to enter into formal contractual relationships found in many aspects of Japanese society.

Both the third and fourth problems, run-down and understaffed hospitals and the lack of quality research, could certainly be improved with more money. However, with regard to hospital care, we do not see much merit in the American pattern of luxurious private rooms on the one hand and very short stays (and the necessary high staffing ratios) on the other. Moreover, Japanese shortcomings in physical resources mostly pertain more to patient comfort rather than medical care – recall the generous provision of CAT and MRI equipment. As for research, a combination of insufficient funds and the stifling effects of academic hierarchy have indeed produced mediocrity, but here again we should take into account the opportunity costs of generously funding professionals to pursue their own projects, and ask to what extent actual medical care would be improved by more and better research.

---

36 In 1987, the MHW generalists introduced two new licenses in the human service field that has been directly under their control. One is the certified social worker (*shakai fukushishi*) mainly to work in welfare offices, and the other is the certified care worker (*kaigo fukush-ishi*) mainly to work in Special Homes for the Aged. Graduation from an accredited school is not mandatory for either, but passing the examination has been particularly difficult for the former so that there were only 7,784 who had this license in 1995. *Kōsei Hakusho*, 1996, p. 412.

The problem that we consider most serious is the fifth, weak professional standards. Lack of resources is one but not the only factor here. Professionals in Japan are not systematically trained to acquire standardized skills, specialty boards for physicians remain undeveloped, and there are no programs leading to specialized certification for nurses and other professionals. Formal peer review is virtually nonexistent, partly because the state of medical records is so poor. As a result, patients have evaluated quality by the outward physical resources of the facility, which has led to exacerbation of the first two problem areas. In looking at the United States, it is no doubt true that the emphasis on developing the individualized skills of professionals has led to such problematical areas as excessive number of surgical operations or general disregard of costs. Nonetheless, it is this area that demands the most additional attention, money, and creative thinking in Japan.

At the same time, in attempting to improve on all these quality problems, every effort should be made to maintain the egalitarian access and the low costs of the Japanese health-care system. This brings us to the last point. Americans may be able to blame their poor record in macro-health indicators on social factors outside of the health-care system. They can also feel pride in the excellence of their professionals and the impressive number of Nobel prizes that have been won by American researchers. However, they should also be more aware of the opportunity costs that are incurred in order to achieve these successes, even beyond the most obvious problem of restricted access.

In particular, the problem of population aging will be affecting the United States only slightly less rapidly than in Japan. This implies that the major focus of the medical-care system needs to shift in the direction of long-term care. In this environment, the dividends from investing in the individual expertise of professionals are likely to be less, while those from attention to on-the-job training and group cohesion may turn out to be more.[37] The most noteworthy comparison here, though, is between an American government doing its best to shed responsibility for all aspects of the aging society, at a time when the Japanese government is doing its best to direct new resources into long-term care.

---

37 It is possible that the American penchant for management fads could help – the "total quality improvement" movement has been far more influential in hospitals in the United States than in Japan, despite having been invented by Japanese corporations.

8

Lessons?

VIEWED from the United States, our account of Japanese health policy must seem strange indeed. The most general differences can be seen, allowing some oversimplification, at the level of values. The three standard criteria for assessing health policy are access, quality, and cost. These are usually seen as trade-offs: It is assumed that maximizing any one criterion means that one cannot do very well with the other two. The Japanese have put the emphasis on access, and *equal* access at that, while the American system highly values quality.

Cost has been a big concern in both countries. American experience until the mid-1990s indicated that an emphasis on quality made it difficult to control costs and inhibited progress on access. The more recent success in holding down costs seems to be at some expense of both access and quality. However, we would argue, the Japanese case demonstrates that universal egalitarian access is compatible with cost control – in fact, it may well be *necessary* for effective cost control.[1] Japan's current challenge is to improve quality.

In this concluding chapter, we review the key mechanisms that link egalitarian access with cost control in Japan, noting as well the economic, political, and cultural factors that have allowed this successful linkage to persist. We then look again at the downside of Japanese success and offer a few suggestions for improvement. Finally, we speculate a bit about possible "lessons for America" in the Japanese experience.

1 Cf. Mark A. Goldberg, Theodore R. Marmor, and Joseph White, "The Relation between Universal Health Insurance and Cost Control," *New England Journal of Medicine* 332:11 (March 16, 1995), pp. 742–744.

EGALITARIAN COST CONTROL IN JAPAN

To start, we should emphasize once again two points made in Chapter 1. First, health-care costs in Japan are genuinely low. The OECD official statistics that are commonly used for international comparisons do leave out some items that are included in health-care costs in the United States and elsewhere, but adding all of them in, even with quite generous estimates of "gifts" and other items that are difficult to measure, results in an increase of less than one percentage point of GDP. Health-care spending per capita is about half the level of that in the United States and is lower than in any other large industrialized nation save the United Kingdom.

Second, although social differences (e.g., the relative frequency of anti-social behavior, poor eating habits, litigiousness, etc.) no doubt account for some of the gap in health spending between the United States and Japan, they cannot explain everything. In the 1970s, the share of GDP devoted to medical care was rising at about the same rapid pace in Japan and the United States, but in Japan it leveled off in the early 1980s. The reason was a change in health policy, not a change in social customs.

Indeed, it should be clear from our analysis throughout the book that low spending in Japan is largely a matter of institutional mechanisms and how they are operated. Moreover, in our view, the four most important mechanisms are profoundly egalitarian, which is why they work as well as they do.

The first mechanism is the existence of a fee schedule, and the fact that, with only a few exceptions, it is mandatory for all goods and services, to all patients, and to all providers. Its total coverage was what made it possible for the government to level off medical costs in 1981, by in effect imposing a ceiling on overall spending, and even to constrain volume increases by "bundling" and selective fee decreases. The structure of the fee schedule itself holds down costs by making expensive, high-tech medical care relatively unprofitable and cheap outpatient primary care relatively profitable, because inflating volume in the latter does not push total spending up much. Moreover, a uniform fee schedule requires much less administrative spending on billing and accounting, and it inhibits entrepreneurial behavior on the part of providers.

The second mechanism is the universal health insurance system. Because virtually everyone is assigned to a given carrier automatically, the administrative costs and adverse selection problems of competitive enrollment are avoided. But rather than a "single-payer" tax-based system with the government as the provider, where politicians have been known to bid up benefit levels, health insurance in Japan is mostly fragmented into relatively small insurance carriers at the level of the firm or the municipality. Their ability to pay benefits is directly linked to revenues from premiums. This means that insurance managers in company-level societies and local governments have an incentive to watch costs carefully, such as scrutinizing invoices, in order to avoid raising premiums on their immediate constituents. The Health Insurance Bureau of Welfare Ministry has similar concerns with regard to Government-Managed Health Insurance, which serves as the "bellwether" that provides signals for regulating the entire system.

The third mechanism is the substantial subsidy from taxes. The key is that the proportion of total medical spending directly paid from general revenues (today about one-quarter) is fixed in the short run. That means that the Ministry of Health and Welfare is under constant pressure for austerity from the Ministry of Finance. The motivation for cost control in Japan thus comes from two sources, the direct connection with premiums and the direct connection with public spending (and so ultimately the level of taxation). Note also that the Japanese tax system, which relies mainly on a sharply progressive income tax plus taxes on corporate profits, is one of the most egalitarian in the world, and that health insurance contributions are also based on the ability to pay.

The fourth mechanism is cross-subsidization. Differential subsidies to the insurance carriers, and actual transfers of funds among them, ensure that similar burdens are borne by the various groups within the population regardless of their income or health. Egalitarian norms, which have become deeply ingrained in Japanese thinking about medical care, bring automatic suspicion of anything that looks like a special advantage to any group (for example, the "free" treatment granted to people over 70 in 1973 was widely resented, bringing the co-payment, albeit a small symbolic one, that was restored in 1983). When no group gets very much ahead, there is little chance of demonstration effects or "leveling up" of health insurance coverage.

The key is that these mechanisms are mandatory. When it comes to financing health care, neither consumers nor providers have much room to choose, and everyone is treated in similar fashion – what Americans might call "cookie-cutter" health policy. Why, we might ask, do the more affluent consumers and the more powerful providers not rebel in the name of freedom and demand more for themselves? And how can so rigid a system avoid being eaten away, if not overthrown, by social, economic, and technological change?

Several conditions have made it possible for the Japanese health-care system to go on operating effectively over the years.

First, although both consumers and providers are very constrained with regard to health-care financing, they have a lot of choice where it matters most. Physicians can choose whatever treatment they think is most appropriate with little worry about outside interference, and patients are free to go to any provider they wish for their outpatient and inpatient care. In fact, Japanese consumers shop around quite a bit, and at least in the private sector, physicians and hospitals must strive to keep their patients satisfied because provider income depends on volume.

Second, the rigidity of the system is offset by a certain amount of leakage. One type is the tolerance of "gifts" that give well-off patients at least the illusion that they are getting better treatment, and provide some extra income to high-status physicians. Allowing old-age hospitals to levy "extra" monthly charges for long-term care is another example of practices that are at best doubtfully legitimate but are winked at by regulators, thereby providing a way for the affluent to buy better-than-average care without forcing a major reform in the system.

Third, somewhat similarly, the health insurance system is set up so that the better-off and healthier groups in the population, who pay a lot in premiums and taxes and use relatively little health care, get some extra benefits like coverage of co-payments and preventive care that are not too important medically or economically but are quite visible. That makes it appear that they have the advantage in the system compared to the less healthy and wealthy whose health care is actually heavily subsidized. Again, resentments are minimized.

Fourth, largely for historical reasons, the providers who benefit most from the system have been able to monopolize political power, to the extent that others who might be less satisfied have not been able to gain much influence. Happily for cost containment, the power-holders are private-practice physicians, who do not have as much capacity to drive up spending as specialists and hospitals do. On the other hand, note that hospital-based specialists, with

202

their lower power and income, do have the compensation of higher status and a more interesting practice.

Fifth, the politics of system maintenance has generally been handled so as to allow incremental changes without too much disturbance to the expectations and relationships that have built up over time. The fee schedule is revised every two years, allowing adjustments in the incomes of the various providers to preserve their relative positions. Similarly, contribution and subsidy rates across the various health insurance systems have also been modified from time to time. The fact that the roster of participants in the negotiations has been so stable for so long helps this process work relatively smoothly.[2]

All that might be seen as fine-tuning, but even when more radical change has occurred, to a remarkable extent much has been held constant. "Health insurance for all" in 1961 maintained the existing fragmented system rather than bringing everyone into a single system. "Free medical care" for the elderly in 1972 eliminated the co-payment in existing insurance systems with no attempts to change the delivery system. Leveling off spending in the early 1980s was accomplished without much change in the relative positions of various providers. Converting many of Japan's hospitals from medical to long-term-care institutions is certainly a large-scale change, but it is being carried out step by step over more than a decade, not all at once.

That is, in health care as in other organizational settings in Japan, the underlying operating principle is a sense of "balance" – among consumers, among providers, even between consumers and providers. It is assumed that violating balance is dangerous and can lead to trouble. At root, of course, balance is defined by the status quo. It is a conservative principle. However, because the environment is always changing, and demands are constantly renewed for more cost control on the one hand and quality improvement on the other, preserving the balance of interests and power and thereby avoiding trouble often requires significant policy change.

PROBLEMS AND SOLUTIONS

We suggest that more policy change is needed today particularly in two areas, where the cookie-cutter uniformity and resistance to change of the Japanese

---

2 For a strong argument for the importance of collaboration and stability, see William A. Glaser, "Doctors and Public Authorities: The Trend toward Collaboration," *Journal of Health Policy, Politics and Law* 19:4 (Winter, 1994), 705–727.

system, along with a sheer lack of enough money due to constant cost cutting, have led to deepening problems in health-care finance and service delivery. One problem is high-tech acute care, and the other is long-term care for the elderly.

Improving the Big Hospitals

As we have argued, the constraints built into the fee schedule have succeeded in blunting the impact of technological change on health-care spending in Japan. However, doctors and patients in Japan as elsewhere demand the most up-to-date treatments. Because the prices set in the fee schedule are usually insufficient to cover the capital cost of buying expensive machinery or upgrading facilities, improvements have mainly been limited to hospitals that have access to subsidies from a university or government. The result is something of an informal functional differentiation, with university and public hospitals increasingly handling most tertiary care.

That would be fine, except that the impact goes much further. The availability of high-tech procedures and well-trained specialists, plus relatively attractive facilities compared with those of the financially squeezed private hospitals, have made the public and university hospitals more and more attractive even to ordinary patients seeking routine outpatient care. The most advanced hospitals have every incentive to deliver such primary care because it is the most profitable type of treatment. The result is a misallocation of medical resources and higher spending than necessary (if only because more services are typically provided to patients at advanced hospitals, even when they just come for a routine visit).

We believe that this problem could be corrected by a partial relaxation of the principle that all providers are paid the same fee for a given treatment. After all, it is only in Japan that physicians and hospitals are paid under the same framework. A separate payment system could provide a new and better set of incentives for hospitals.

Specifically, hospitals that provide high-tech care, including private-sector hospitals that see themselves as strong enough to compete in this sector, should be paid on an inclusive fee system: a per diem basis for inpatient care, and a per visit basis for outpatient care. The level of these charges would be individually determined for each hospital, based initially on its previous revenue and thereafter on a formula made up of specific performance indicators. These might include productivity measures, such as average length of stay and bed occupancy rate; indicators for the provision of tertiary care, such as number of operations; indicators evaluating the establishment of networks with private practitioners, such as the ratio of referrals; and indicators of satisfaction among patients and local practitioners. If direct measures of quality of care can be developed, those would be added as well. Which indicators should be included in the formula, and their weights, would be negotiated periodically at the prefectural level between insurance carriers (including local and national government) and the individual hospitals.

The new payment system would be budget neutral, in that the hospital sectors' total revenue from health insurance or public subsidy would stay the same, at least in the short run. However, the system would lead to efficiency savings because the high-tech hospitals would no longer have to dispense medication and order laboratory tests in order to generate revenue. They could increase their revenue only by meeting performance targets. Although meeting such targets would mean higher costs, efficiently managed hospitals would then improve nurse staffing ratios, expand facilities, buy more equipment, and so forth, leading to higher quality.

Another benefit is that hospitals would become more accountable to their communities. First, local governments would have the key role in setting the performance criteria and evaluating the results and could concentrate resources where most needed.[3] Second, current government subsidies could be opened to bidding by both public and large private hospitals, giving the locality a direct way to improve hospital services. Indeed, the ability of local governments to spend more money to improve their hospitals would be enhanced. This reform would bring the acute-care sector in Japan much closer to the planned, regulated hospital systems found in most of Europe, and it would put real teeth into the regional health-care planning process that so far has been used only for limiting the number of beds.[4]

The first and second benefits will also have a synergic effect. By encouraging specialization and so concentrating resources for ICUs or complex sur-

---

3   That should lead to more specialization. Compare, e.g., Ken Aoki et al., "Functional Differentiation and Competition," in Aki Yoshikawa, Jayanga Bhattacharya, and William B. Vogt, eds., *Health Economics of Japan: Patients, Doctors, and Hospitals under a Universal Health Insurance System* (Tokyo: University of Tokyo Press, 1996), pp. 203–219. More specialization should lead to improved outcomes.
4   For details, see Naoki Ikegami, "Kinō Bunka no Tame no Shinshiharai Hōshiki Shian," *Shakai Hoken Junpō* 1800, 1801 (1993), 6–9, 10–13. For Europe, see William A. Glaser, *Paying The Hospital* (San Francisco: Jossey-Bass, 1987).

gical procedures in particular hospitals, according to the regional health plan, the new system would lead not only to more efficient use of resources but also much better care (because "practice makes perfect" – high volume is a prerequisite for quality).

This reform, we believe, will help channel existing trends in Japanese health care into an effective "trifurcation." At one extreme, university and public hospitals, plus the best large private hospitals, would be induced to specialize in high-quality acute inpatient care. At the other extreme, many private hospitals would complete their current journey to becoming nursing homes. In between, the smaller "community" hospitals (public or private), particularly in less urban areas, would continue to provide regular inpatient and outpatient care to local residents, and some would take an active part in community care for the elderly as well.

Improving Long-term Care

The other major problem is long-term care. It became over-medicalized in Japan mainly because, back in 1972, the initiation of "free medical care" allowed the infirm (or not so infirm) elderly to enter hospitals at little cost, at a time when few nursing-home beds or community-care facilities were available. Most institutional care was thus provided in hospital settings, which gave too little attention to the human side of care in favor of excess medication and testing. Rationalization and improvement of long-term care has been a major priority for the government since the early 1980s. It has pushed many hospitals that mostly serve old people, plus the new "health facilities for the elderly," more toward per diem payments, and it has sharply increased the provision of nursing homes and community-care services (particularly with the 1989 Gold Plan).

The idea of public Long-Term-Care Insurance (LTCI) first proposed in 1994 is the logical next step. Its key provisions are: (1) tapping a new source of financing through a new form of social insurance, matched by increased subsidies from general revenues; (2) formally converting many hospitals into long-term-care facilities, eventually grouping all such facilities (including nursing homes) into a single category; and (3) continuing to expand community care, including stimulation of private-sector agencies, and balancing the incentives for community versus institutional care.

The introduction of public LTCI would be a major advance for Japan and could become an important model for other countries. It does not solve all the problems in this area, however, and it inevitably will create some new ones. We see three main difficulties. One is the problem of assessing eligibility for various levels of care. If this were strictly a medical matter, it could be left to the physician's professional judgment. However, the need for long-term care involves many psychological and social factors as well. Moreover it is an area in which consumers feel more knowledgeable and so are likely to be more outspoken and demanding, even in Japan.

A possible solution is a standardized, comprehensive assessment instrument to determine eligibility. It would serve as a means for communication among the various professionals providing care and would also be part of a manual that provides guidelines for how to write up a care plan. Such a pedagogic approach is necessary in Japan because neither health-care nor social-service administrators have much experience or training in long-term care. An instrument called "Minimum Data Set – Home Care," devised by clinicians and researchers from several countries primarily for care-planning purposes, has now been successfully tested in Japan. It could become the basis for deciding eligibility for LTCI and could also be used for "case-weighted" reimbursement for institutional care.[5]

Whether or not this particular instrument comes to be adopted, we feel strongly that a rigorous procedure for determining eligibility and deciding the appropriate level of benefits is essential. Making local government responsible both for eligibility determination and for financial management of the program is a sensible first step toward preventing overly generous benefits, but it is not enough. Unless the decisions are in the hands of professionals who are competent to assess need – and, realistically speaking, are not in a position to profit by providing the care themselves – long-term-care insurance could easily drift into being seen as an entitlement for everybody who gets old. The result would be a bankrupt program and a severe threat to all plans for dealing with Japan's aging society.

A second problem brought to the fore by the prospect of LTCI amounts to a fundamental challenge to Japanese egalitarian principles in medical care. The new plan is to pay a basic allowance based on the degree of infirmity, but it is assumed that consumers who are better off will be able to purchase

---

5   Such reimbursement systems and the assessment instruments that they require have recently
    been introduced in American nursing homes. Without such a system, it is to the advantage
    of institutions to cherry-pick patients needing the lightest care and to leave the most frail
    and sickly to someone else. See Naoki Ikegami et al., "Applying RUG-III in Japanese Long-
    Term-Care Facilities," *Gerontologist* 34 (1994), 628–39.

additional services with their own money at least with regard to community care, and perhaps to institutional care as well. Such differential treatment based on income would seem to violate the norm of equal treatment for all in both the medical-care and social-welfare systems, and to raise difficult ethical and perhaps political questions.

In our view, this problem is serious but not fatal. Long-term care is different from acute care and need not be as egalitarian, for both ethical and practical reasons. After all, in many respects long-term care is similar to ordinary life, where in Japan as elsewhere income largely determines one's degree of comfort (size of house, quality of food, assistance from household help or appliances). The key is that the level of the basic support supplied by Long-Term-Care Insurance should be high enough so that even those without additional resources will have a decent standard of living. Finding that balance will be a difficult task for Japanese policy makers, but it should not be impossible.

A third problem is how the rise of long-term care will fit into current trends in health-care delivery in Japan. In particular, the trend toward increased reliance on public and university hospitals even for routine outpatient care runs counter to the needs of frail elderly people living in the community. Neighborhood office-based physicians are in the best position to participate in deciding eligibility, writing up care plans, and ensuring that each patient gets the services he or she needs. Unfortunately, it is in this era when they are most needed that so many private practitioners are getting old themselves and retiring.

We would note, however, that the necessary conditions for a real rejuvenation of office-based physicians are currently emerging. On the one hand, medical-school enrollments have doubled since the 1970s; on the other, regional limitations on the number of hospital beds means that the growth rate of salaried positions will be much lower than in the past. The relative incentives for physicians to go into private practice are increasing. It would make sense for the government to encourage this development, as by relaxing regulations that currently inhibit group practice, and by providing more training for primary care and the management of chronic illness in medical schools.

Just as important is reform aimed at functional differentiation, as suggested previously. If new payment incentives move public and university hospitals toward high-tech tertiary care, more routine outpatient services will be left for office-based physicians and small community hospitals. They should be able to prosper under the current payment system, even given its tight cost controls, plus some additional revenues through public LTCI.

Future Prospects

At the time this book was being finished, with rampant worry about a stagnant economy and spiraling deficits, Japan was in the midst of one of its periodic enthusiasms for "structural reform" (*kōzō kaikaku*). As in the early 1980s, the main themes were deregulation, privatization, and small government, and groups of experts were painting Japan's future in alarmist terms. As a typical example, one blue-ribbon commission forecast in 1995 that unless drastic steps were taken, the combined tax and social-security burden would rise to 60 percent of national income by the year 2025.[6] This commission and other groups set a goal of keeping this figure below 50 percent by cutting government spending.

Social policy was getting particular attention in the hubbub about reform, with the phrase "Japan has the most rapidly aging society in the world" ceaselessly repeated. Along with changes in pensions and social-welfare programs, health care was to get a start on reform with a fee-schedule revision and passage of public long-term-care insurance in 1997, to be followed by a more "radical reform" (*bappon kaikaku*) in the medical-care delivery and insurance systems in the medium term.[7] The planned fee-schedule revisions were rather modest in conception (larger co-payments for employees and the elderly, small premium increases, a minor surcharge on prescriptions), and were pared down further when politicians reviewed them – they were not really even a first step toward a response to what was called in an official report the "crisis situation" of "structural deficit" in health insurance that, if left unresolved, would inevitably lead to "the disintegration of the health-insurance-for-all system."[8]

What of the "radical reform" to follow? In the same report, we find phrases about efficiency, balance of burdens and benefits, individual respon-

6 They totaled 37 percent in 1995; the panel said that if its suggested reforms were adopted, the burden in 2025 could be held to 46 percent of national income. *Nikkei Weekly*, Dec. 2, 1995.
7 E.g., see the report on the conference of chairs of seven MHW councils (*shingikai*) on Nov. 29, 1996, in *Shakai Hoken Junpō* 1931 (Dec. 1, 1996), pp. 20–23.
8 From the Nov. 27, 1996, report of the Health Care Council (Iryō Hoken Shingikai), *Kongo no Iryō Hoken Seido no arikata to Heisei 9 nen Kaikaku ni tuite (Kengisho)*.

sibility for health, consumer choice, competition, functional differentiation, shortening hospitalization and eliminating "social hospitalization," cuts in drug usage, constraints on the supply of physicians and hospital beds, movement away from fee-for-service payment, tighter reviews of medical treatments, better information systems, rationalization of the fragmented health insurance system, and higher quality. Actually, all these phrases had been invoked frequently since the late 1970s. The question was whether the reform fever that was promising to engulf the Japanese economy and polity in the late 1990s would in fact lead to dramatic restructuring of the health-care system.

We doubt it and instead expect continued tinkering at the margins as has been the case for years. Such incremental measures have been quite successful, as we have seen, in holding down health-care expenditures as a share of the total economy. The "crisis," if it should be called that, is more about how health-care spending flows through various government and social insurance accounts. That problem would be substantially alleviated by enacting public long-term-care insurance, which along with improving quality of care for infirm older people, promises to move a substantial chunk of spending for hospitalization out of the medical insurance system. Of course, this program would mean a substantial increase in overall social spending, but in our view, that is inevitable as a cost of the aging society.

It is striking that in all the anti-government rhetoric and talk of crisis, few voices have been claiming that long-term-care insurance is too bureaucratic and expensive and should not be passed. This is an indication that responsible reformers are willing to focus on social problems and see that in some cases governmental solutions are the best available. We hope it also indicates an ability to discriminate between areas that really do need radical solutions (for example, a good case can be made for the public pension system) and areas that instead call for constant watching, plus quick responses when some element of expenditure starts to get out of hand.

The latter, we have argued, is the story of the Japanese health-care system. It clearly faces some challenges, but over the years, it has demonstrated the capacity to deal with tough problems and achieve some remarkable successes. Americans in particular need to be reminded that the Japanese population is quite healthy by world standards despite its low spending levels.

Moreover, Japan's health-care system includes some features that many Americans see as very attractive. It gives considerable freedom to consumers to pick the providers they want, and to providers to offer the treatments they think are most appropriate. In structural terms, Japan's pluralistic, employment-based health insurance system is not as radically different from the American pattern as are single-payer systems. Such factors offer the potential for cross-cultural learning.

LESSONS FOR AMERICANS?

In the late 1990s, chances that the United States will quickly move toward what we would consider a reasonable health-care system do not appear great. However, it is not too improbable that the political mood will eventually change so that concern for access will again become a priority for public policy. We also think it is likely that current mechanisms for cost control will not work very well in the long run. If so, we hope that the foregoing chapters have provided some points for consideration. We would like to highlight three sets of suggestions.

First, some of the most important lessons should be drawn not just from the Japanese experience but from nearly all the industrialized nations. Almost everyone has found that a fee schedule and universal coverage are the basic components of a reasonable health-care system. Both have to be mandatory in principle and allow only a few exceptions in practice. The advantages of all these "normal" systems over how health care works in the United States (either the old ways, or newer ideas about managed care) have been well argued by William Glaser, Ted Marmor, Joseph White, and others, and they need not further occupy our attention here.[9]

Second, within the overall normal pattern of health care, Japan has some distinctive institutions that are worth attention. One is Government-Managed Health Insurance (GMHI). One of the most difficult problems for health insurance reform in the United States is how to cover small-business employees. The Japanese solution is to enroll all of them in a single system, with equal employer and employee wage-proportional contributions and a moderate subsidy from the general budget. The system is managed by the

---

9 E.g., William A. Glaser, "The United States Needs a Health System Like Other Countries," *Journal of the American Medical Association* 270 (August 25, 1993), pp. 980–984; Theodore H. Marmor, *Understanding Health Care Reform* (New Haven, CT: Yale University Press, 1994); Joseph White, *Competing Solutions: American Health Care Proposals and International Experience* (Washington, DC: Brookings, 1995); Health Care Study Group, "Understanding the Choices in Health Care Reform," *Journal of Health Politics, Policy, and Law* 19 (1994), pp. 499–541.

same government agency that handles the fee schedule, giving it a strong incentive to hold down costs for its own enrollees and, by extension, everyone else. GMHI for small-business employees could work in the United States, perhaps on a shared federal–state basis.[10]

Another Japanese institution worth a look is the mechanism for equalization of burdens, applied across broad categories defined by employment (the main mechanism for equalization across individuals, assessing health insurance premiums as a percentage of wages, is used nearly everywhere except the United States). On the one hand, these broad divisions should allow interest-group politics to maintain a rough balance among the categories. On the other, the rather intricate pattern of subsidization and of marginally differentiated benefits means that precise calculations of relative advantage and disadvantage are difficult enough to inhibit conflict.

Finally, among Japan's distinctive institutions, we point to the incentive structure that rewards relatively inexpensive primary-care services and makes high-cost procedures not very profitable. The effect, of course, is that highly trained specialists do not do as well financially as physicians who are working essentially as general practitioners. This approach may run counter to the typically American sense of fairness – that the person who has invested more in education and is more skilled should be paid more – but perhaps a marginal shift in this direction would be tolerated. It could both save money and cut down on the current oversupply of specialists without quotas or rationing.

The third set of potential lessons has less to do with the substance of health policy than with process, with the approach to carrying out reform. If we look at attempts to change health policy in Japan and the United States in the postwar period, particularly in recent years, two differences stand out. The American cases show strong programmatic leadership, usually from the

---

10 We offer here a brief sketch of how the overall system might work, generally along the lines of several European systems. Large corporations would be required to self-insure their employees or to contract for private insurance coverage, providing at least the GMHI benefit package. The self- or non-employed could be covered by an expansion of the existing Medicaid system, but with premiums proportional to income up to a ceiling; a substantial subsidy would be provided. Relative values (points per procedure) would be negotiated at the national level between insurers and providers, and the conversion factor (dollars per point) would be set by the states. Note that, unlike Japan and more like Germany, it might make sense to cover only physician fees under the universal fee schedule. Inpatient charges could be determined separately for each hospital, either through a formula established at the federal or state level, or through negotiations between the hospital and insurance carriers.

212

President, and heavy applications of scientific expertise. The Japanese cases show neither. Lack of leadership and of real policy analysis are often cited as key weaknesses of decision making in Japan, and yet its record of effective health policy is considerably better than that of the United States. Why?

We suggest that the American health-care policy area has been plagued by too much of an emphasis on top–down leadership, and also on expertise. Strong leaders are tempted to try to make big changes by proposing comprehensive policies; such attempts immediately generate opposition from both entrenched interests and the opposing political party. Moreover, when there are lots of experts around – people whose livelihoods and reputations depend on their producing attention-grabbing policy studies – a political fight about health-care reform will quickly be turned into an academic debate about theories, models, and data. Such arcane debates confuse the general public as well as decision makers themselves; the effect may be to obscure important choices more than to advance understanding about how proposed policy changes would work in the real world.

This scenario in the 1990s resulted in failure, not only of the Clinton plan itself but of the very idea of purposeful reform of health care in the public interest. Big provider and insurance complexes were left to make deals with big employers, using theories about managed care to drive down costs. Government was left on the sidelines, fretting about paying for its own gigantic Medicare and Medicaid systems, and toying with ineffectual access and quality remedies that seemed likely to multiply in numbers and complexity in the future with little impact on the overall system.[11]

The Japanese (and indeed the European) case demonstrates that government can accomplish substantial change in the health-care system in the public interest. Needed first is acknowledgment that the health-care policy area, relative to other policy areas, has two distinctive characteristics. In the realm of power, it is and forever will be dominated by interest-group politics, and in the realm of knowledge, real-world experience is considerably more valuable than theories and models. Policy areas with these characteristics are likely to be run better under Japanese-style politics than under American-style politics.

---

11 For example, in 1996, Congress helped a few Americans keep the right to have health insurance (at whatever cost) when they changed jobs, even as the number of people with no insurance and decreasing access to public hospitals soared, and it protected mothers delivering babies from premature discharge from the hospital, while physicians and patients increasingly ran into barriers for all sorts of medical care.

That is, when strong programmatic leadership is not a possibility, policy change becomes a matter of carrying out shifts in the balance of well-established interests. When little scientific expertise is available, policy ideas tend to be gleaned from the operation of existing programs at home or in foreign countries, and instead of theories about good policy, we find rules-of-thumb. These two propositions hold for most policy making in Japan, not infrequently to its detriment – for example, a big reason why the deregulation movement has been far less successful in Japan than in the United States is because it depends on strong programmatic leadership and a belief that academic theories matter.[12]

The differences in decision-making styles between the two countries show up clearly in their approaches to determining fee schedules – a one-shot scientific research project followed by a big open fight over the Medicare Relative Value Scale in the United States, and biennial political negotiations conducted privately among a small and stable group of participants in Japan. In fact, the institution that handles the fee schedule (the Central Social Insurance Medical Care Council, or Chūikyō) has also provided the structure for negotiating substantial reforms, such as the cost-control measures of the early 1980s. Such reforms do require leadership in the sense of a strong commitment to move policy in a particular direction – in this case, cost control. However, the Ministry of Health and Welfare's behind-the-scenes pulling and hauling is quite different from the American ideal of sweeping top–down reform.

We think the United States also needs a more structured process in which the powerful interested parties in medical care – providers, insurers, and the government – can reach acceptable accommodations. Of course, even in Japan the Central Council was not simply invented out of whole cloth and imposed on the participants. It evolved out of severe conflicts over the scope of participation and the rules of the game; indeed, it continues to evolve as the environment of health policy shifts. So we make no claim that establishing an American Central Council would be a quick and easy solution to all the problems of health-care reform, but we do believe that focusing more on developing a workable political process and less on grand economic

---

12 For the American case, see Martha Derthick and Paul Quirk, *The Politics of Deregulation* (Washington, DC: Brookings, 1985). For Japan (compared with Great Britain), see Steven K. Vogel, *Freer Markets, More Rules: Regulatory Reform in Advanced Industrial Countries* (Ithaca, NY: Cornell University Press, 1996).

models would be a better route to a decent health-care system in the United States.

When we compare the American and Japanese health-care systems in terms of the three classic criteria, it is clear that Japan has done far better with respect to access and cost. All Japanese citizens are entitled to heath care, and on a very egalitarian basis in terms of both services received and burdens borne. Indeed, Japan shows up very well compared to all the industrialized nations of the world on these two measures, while the United States is clearly the worst – truly excessive costs, and far too many people with limited access.

The trickier question is quality. There is no question that in some respects Americans do buy higher quality with all the money that they spend on health care (as noted in Chapter 1, more than $2,000 extra every year for every man, woman, and child compared to Japan). The majority of Americans can stay in a much more comfortable hospital, with the most modern equipment, and the physicians they see are well trained and are motivated to maintain high standards in their practice. Americans also get first crack at the fruits of the gigantic medical research establishment. The ideology of science among practitioners in this sense serves Americans well.

Moreover, the ideology of consumerism among the general public has also been embodied in health care to a substantial degree in the United States. Certainly when compared to Japanese, Americans are likelier to have their diagnosis adequately explained by their doctor and to be consulted about the treatment that they will receive. Many argue that an expansion of the individual's responsibility for his or her own health care should be the direction of future reforms. This view of course dovetails neatly with the dominance of the ideology of health economics in health policy circles.

That is, many American experts believe that the best way to control costs while maintaining quality is for consumers to choose among competing providers. That choice might be on a case-by-case basis among individual doctors and hospitals, as urged by proponents of "medical savings plans" and the like, but the dominant view is that the consumer's choice would be made on a yearly basis by choosing among organizations of providers like Health Maintenance Organizations. In either case, the governing assumption is that the consumer will make a rational decision by balancing cost against the extent of need and the quality of service offered.

We believe that although such assumptions work well enough for ordinary consumption, they are unrealistic for health care. First, consumers usually must rely on the provider to determine how much medical care they need. That advice is likely to be biased in one direction in a fee-for-service system and in the other direction in a capitated system like an HMO, but in either case, it severely vitiates the assumption that consumers can rationally pursue their own interests. Second, the consumer really has no reliable way to measure quality at present, and so far the results of experimentation with "outcomes research," either among alternative treatments or among providers, have only limited value even for relatively well-defined surgical procedures. Decisions are therefore likely to be made on the basis of surrogate indicators for true quality, such as friendliness of staff or marginal differences in services provided, if not simply as a result of more effective marketing. Moreover, it is not necessarily the consumer as an individual who is allowed to make decisions – increasingly, employers make the key choices, often choosing lower premiums over higher quality.

These considerations plus the obvious point that HMOs, like any capitated system, profit by providing as little medical care as possible, mean that an elaborate set of regulations will be needed for a managed-care system to work in the real world. In turn, officials with authority have to write and rewrite the regulations, monitor compliance, and take action against violators – in short, bureaucracy. In fact, under managed care, the combination of a big internal bureaucracy to regulate treatment and a big external bureaucracy to oversee performance will inevitably incur high costs in terms of both money and aggravation.

The irony is that "normal" systems as in Japan are much simpler and less bureaucratic and actually give the consumer the most important choice, which is not to make a difficult decision based on matching up imagined future needs with various assortments of benefits and costs. A Japanese who doesn't like the treatment goes to find another provider.

It is for these reasons that Japan and most of the other industrialized nations of the world have found that systems with universal mandatory coverage, fixed fee schedules, provisions for financial equalization, and policy making by negotiation between payers and providers are the best way to deal with the fundamental problems of health care. We hope that the United States will eventually come to that conclusion as well, and although it certainly would and should not adopt the Japanese model wholesale, we have suggested a few points that are worth a look. More fundamentally, we propose that Ja-

216

pan's rather old-fashioned assumptions about health care actually provide a better basis for a decent system than the American approach.

First, consider the general public: The ideal of ''selfless service'' that many Japanese still see as desirable for their physicians is of course largely mythical, but surely it is more conducive to system performance than is an image of doctors as revenue maximizers, as would inevitably be assumed in market-model health care. Despite considerable suspicion among Japanese about how well doctors actually live up to the ideal, their respect for the authority of physicians remains widespread. This contributes to patients having confidence in the treatments they receive, and to doctors feeling a bit more responsibility to meet such high expectations.

Second, on the part of providers, the ideology of professional autonomy that has long been stressed by the Japan Medical Association (along with its concern for income) is a better basis for a decent health-care system than is the American glorification of science. Much medical care is determined less by objective indicators than by judgment based on experience; at the extreme, it approaches an art. Japanese physicians have been zealous about protecting their individual right to make judgments against interference by bureaucrats or the dictates of a protocol or ''treatment guideline.'' Such bureaucratic interference in medical decisions, and imposition of protocols that purport to be based on scientific research, are the hallmarks of HMO-style health care.

It is ironic that the glorification of science that justified higher and higher spending on health care has now left American physicians without an effective ideological defense against the use of science for cost cutting. Japanese insurers have pushed for guidelines and protocols, too, but lacking the aura of scientific legitimacy, these efforts have been easier to be brushed off by doctors as cost-control gimmicks. American physicians might be better off today if they had downplayed science and instead emphasized the virtues of professional judgment and medicine as art.[13]

Third, on the part of government, the ideology of a public responsibility for assuring the population of good care on an equal basis is essential. In a formal sense, only a democratically elected government can provide true accountability to citizens. In a practical sense, the national government has to be involved because substantial public expenditures will always be needed

---

13   For similar observations, see Gary S. Belkin, ''The Technocratic Wish: Making Sense and Finding Power in the 'Managed' Medical Markerplace,'' *Journal of Health Policy, Politics and Law* 22:2 (April 1997), 509–532.

for decent health care. Rather than just being one among many interested parties, moreover, the national government is in the best position to take a broader view and work for coherence. We argue that this coherence is best achieved by government pursuing the basic value of equality, because other participants in a pluralistic system can be counted on to argue for one special advantage or another.

Expectations of selfless service versus consumer rights, judgment and art in medicine versus science, government pursuit of egalitarian goals versus keeping hands off private market competition – to American health policy experts, Japan seems mired in old-fashioned ideology. And, indeed, as we have argued at several junctures, Japan could certainly use some small doses of American-style health care. Japanese patients might well act more like consumers who have a right to information and consultation. Japanese doctors' performance would improve if they paid more attention to scientific "best-practice" and professional standards. The Japanese government probably could make better health policy if it adopted a bit more of the analytical rigor of health economics. In fact, all these lessons are being learned in Japan, though certainly not as rapidly as everyone would wish.

But it is the Japanese system that is working better and that should be providing more lessons. Unfortunately, the Pacific somehow seems to be much wider when looking from the United States to Japan. If Japanese are unusually good at learning lessons from abroad, then Americans are unusually bad – most often they see the experience of others as irrelevant to their special situations and unique national character. We are convinced that these ways of thinking must change if the United States is to build a decent health-care system for its citizens.

Index

Index

contribution rates, 1, 101–2, 114, 132, 141, 203
co-payments, 15–16, 43, 82, 108
  changes in, 109, 114, 128, 133, 140
  as cost control, 44
  differentials in, 93, 94
  for elderly, 16, 49, 110–11, 140n.26
cosmetic surgery, 95n.10
cost containment, 4, 49, 110, 116–44
  budget formulation and, 117–24
  conditions essential for, 85, 127, 138, 139, 171
  directives as measure of, 149–50, 159–60, 173
  drug expenditures, 119, 122–23, 125
  egalitarian, 200–2
  factors motivating, 201
  fee schedule and, 17–18, 38, 64, 84, 116–17, 119–22, 149–50, 171–4
  GMHI as regulator of, 126–8
  and health economics, 48–9, 50, 108
  HIB role in, 118, 120–1, 126, 131
  high-tech procedures approvals and, 154–5
  pooling fund effects, 137
  rationing, 173, 178
  and revenues, 117–18, 123–4, 125
  specific targets of, 157–60
  see also cross-subsidization; fee schedule
Council on Certification, 188n.24
cross-subsidization
  as egalitarian measure, 1, 114, 201
  fiscal parity from, 137–8
  to old-age health coverage, 34, 49, 110, 137–8, 141
  spending and, 44
  summary of Japanese approach, 114–15
  two forms of, 90–3, 109, 127

day-care services, 65
Democratic Socialist Party, 34
dentists, 31
diagnosis disclosure, 180
Diagnostic-Related Groups (DRGs), 22, 172n.39
diagnostic testing, 159
Diet (Japanese legislature), 32, 33n.12, 41, 49, 113, 118, 131, 155
diet (nutrition), 11
directives, 149–50, 159–60, 173
direct transfer payments, 90–2
doctors. *See* physicians
Doctors in Politics (Steslicke), 43
Doctors' League, 32

"dread-disease" coverage, 98–9
drug addiction, 11
drugs
  dispensing of, 2, 58n.12, 60, 61, 82, 164–6
  and fee schedule, 119, 120, 122–3, 124, 152, 154, 155–7, 159
  fee-schedule regulations, 82n.39
  introduction of new, 154
  Japanese vs. U.S spending levels, 158
  over-the-counter spending, 5
  overusage of, 2, 53, 159, 162, 165–6, 178
  prescription coverage, 16
  price determination, 119, 152, 154
  price reduction, 125, 138, 149, 156–9, 171
  as revenue for physicians, 148

education, 49, 187
egalitarian policies, 87–115
  burden of payment and, 90, 212
  cost control and, 200–2
  cross-subsidization as, 1, 114, 201
  equality of care, 18, 47, 51, 88–93, 104, 113, 196–7, 198, 200, 210–11
  gifts and, 94–8
  mechanisms of, 89–93
  professional standards and, 51, 198
  as underlying Japanese health-care principle, 51
elderly. *See* geriatric care
England. *See* Great Britain
epilepsy, 178
equality of health care. *See* egalitarian policies
evolution of health care
  early, 43, 45–8, 51, 53–68, 104–7
  as piecemeal process, 173
  postwar reform, 59–63, 85–6, 127, 209–10
  recent, 63–8, 140–1
experts
  American vs. Japanese, 35–6
  gikan, 26, 196

Factory Law of 1911, 104
fairness. *See* egalitarian policies
family care, 55, 58, 59, 61, 64, 183, 194
"family Dietmen" (*zoku giin*), 41, 42
farmers, 105–6
Federation of Health Insurance Societies. *See* Kenporen
fee-for-service, 17, 49, 107, 119, 129, 147, 165–6, 172

220

Index

227